# all about
## machine arts

## Decorative Techniques from A to Z

from *Sew News*, *Creative Machine Embroidery*, and C&T Publishing

C&T PUBLISHING

Text and artwork © 2004 C&T Publishing, *Sew News*, *Creative Machine Embroidery*

Publisher: Amy Marson

Editorial Director: Gailen Runge

Editors: Lynn Koolish, Linda Turner Griepentrog, Annette Gentry Bailey

Copyeditor/Proofreader: Sarah Dunn/Stacy Chamness

Cover Designer: Kristen Yenche

Design Director/Book Designer: Kristen Yenche

Production Assistants: Luke Mulks, Shawn Garcia

Published by C&T Publishing, Inc., P.O. Box 1456, Lafayette, California, 94549

Front cover photo by Garry Gay, styling by Garry Gay and Diane Pedersen

Back cover: Pillow by Wendy Hill, *Reach Out* by Hari Walner, *Out-of-Sight Circles* by Mary Mashuta, Decorative bindings by Lynn Koolish, Dimensional Embroidery by Linda McGehee, Decorative stitching by Kristen Dibbs

Attention Teachers: C&T Publishing, Inc. encourages you to use this book as a text for teaching. Contact us at 800-284-1114 or www.ctpub.com for more information about the C&T Teachers Program.

We take great care to ensure that the information included in this book is accurate and presented in good faith, but no warranty is provided nor results guaranteed. Having no control over the choices of materials or procedures used, neither the author nor C&T Publishing, Inc. shall have any liability to any person or entity with respect to any loss or damage caused directly or indirectly by the information contained in this book. For your convenience, we post an up-to-date listing of corrections on our web page (www.ctpub.com). If a correction is not already noted, please contact our customer service department at ctinfo@ctpub.com or at P.O. Box 1456, Lafayette, California, 94549.

Trademarked (™) and Registered Trademark (®) names are used throughout this book. Rather than use the symbols with every occurrence of a trademark and registered trademark name, we are using the names only in the editorial fashion and to the benefit of the owner, with no intention of infringement.

Library of Congress Cataloging-in-Publication Data

All about machine arts : decorative techniques from A to Z.
     p. cm.
  ISBN 1-57120-227-7 (paper trade)
  1. Machine sewing. 2. Fancy work. I. Title.
TT713.A45 2004
646.2'044—dc22
                              2003022777

Printed in China
10 9 8 7 6 5 4 3 2 1

# Sew News

Creating for You and Your Home

Editor: Linda Turner Griepentrog

Senior Editor: Marla Stefanelli

Associate Editor: Laura Rintala

Assistant Editor: Elizabeth Tisinger

Contributing Editors: Janet Klaer, Susan Voigt-Reising

Art Director: Mary Shaub

Senior Designer: Ann Inez Hardell

Designer: Jane Henderson

Photographers: Melissa Karlin Mahoney and Joe Hancock Studio

*Sew News* (ISSN 1541-5414) is published monthly by Primedia Consumer Magazine and Internet Group, a division of Primedia, Inc., 741 Corporate Circle, Suite A, Golden, CO 80401.

*Sew News* can be reached at www.sewnews.com

# Creative Machine Embroidery

Editor: Annette Gentry Bailey

Contributing Editor: Jeanine Twigg

Senior Designer: Dena Jenkins

Photographer: Kevin May

*Creative Machine Embroidery* (ISSN 1541-5414) is published bi-monthly in February, April, June, August, October, and December by Primedia Consumer Magazine and Internet Group, a division of Primedia, Inc., 741 Corporate Circle, Suite A, Golden, CO 80401.

*Creative Machine Embroidery* can be reached at www.cmemag.com

# PRIMEDIA

# INTRODUCTION

Welcome to the world of machine arts where machine stitching meets decorative thread and possibilities abound for garments, quilts, and home décor.

No matter what type of machine you use, you'll find ideas and inspiration, tips and techniques in this book. It doesn't matter if you are a beginning quilter, an avid garment sewer, or an old hand at home décor, you'll find new and interesting ways to use your machine.

Get new ideas for using your favorite techniques, or better yet, try something new—just be sure to "follow this thread" in each section for more information on related topics and techniques.

# ON THE COVER

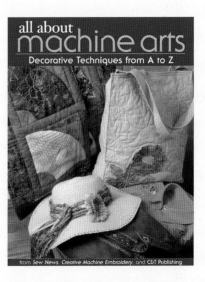

### Fantasy A Machine Arts Sampler
See pages 106–110 for satin stitch appliqué, pages 113–115 for bobbinwork, page 126 for couching, page 127 for crazy quilt stitching, pages 185–186 for pintucks, and pages 235–236 for tucks.

### Tote Bag
See page 126 for couching, pages 156–158 for free-motion quilting, pages 170–171 for spun lace, and page 202 for satin-stitched edges.

### Hat Band
See page 172 for thread and ribbon scarves.

### Cutwork Blouse
See pages 128–129 for cutwork embroidery.

### Denim Shirt
See pages 116–118 for built-in stitches and page 120 for decorative buttonholes.

# Contents

# User's Guide to

The *Glorious Gallery* offers an overview brimming with ideas for machine artistry. Find the inspiration to try something new, and make your next project a real work of art.

Every great artist needs a great studio. Explore the *Successful Studios* and discover ideas for your own sewing space, large or small.

To become a master artist, first you must master your machine. Find the fundamentals in *Mastering Machines*.

# all about machine arts

Don't get started without *Everything Essential*. Here are the essential elements of machine arts, including thread, color, fabric, and more.

As every artist and craftsperson knows, the right equipment is indispensable. *Terrific Tools* features the tools and supplies you need for successful machine artistry.

For even more information, check out Suggested Reading and Resources on pages 249–251.

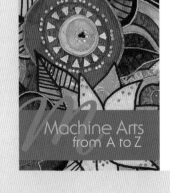

Looking for tips and techniques? *Machine Arts from A to Z* shows you how to do it all, so you can become a real machine artist.

# Glorious Gallery

**Kindred Creatures** quilt by Nancy Odom, based on original design by Laurel Burch

How better to capture Laurel Burch's bold graphic lines than satin stitch appliqué? Built-in stitches and machine embroidery add embellished detail to Laurel's assembled kindred creatures.

*See pages 106–110 for satin stitch appliqué,*
*pages 116-118 for built-in stitches,*
*and page 134 for references to embroidery basics.*

 **Red and Navy Block** by Kristen Dibbs

It's hard to believe that a simple square of fabric can be so transformed by stitching and embroidery. On its own or as part of a quilt, it is simply magical.

*See page 119 for Kristen's approach to decorative machine stitching and page 13 for another example of Kristen's stitching and embroidery.*

 **Reach Out** by Hari Walner

The celebration of a new adventure in quilting is gloriously captured in fabric and thread. Trapunto raises the waves of light above the quilted background, adding depth and dimension.

*See pages 156–158 for free-motion quilting, and*
*pages 234–235 for Hari's trapunto technique.*

**Cutwork Blouse**
by Marlis Bennett

*Embroidery design: Marlis Bennett*

Lacy and elegant or bold and graphic, cutwork adds charming detail to all types of garments.

*See pages 128–129 for Marlis's cutwork techniques, and pages 129–130 for Nancy's cutwork on fleece.*

**Cutwork Blouse**
by Elizabeth Tisinger
*Embroidery design: Michelle Pullen*
*Husqvarna Viking #26*

**Cutwork Fleece**
by Nancy Cornwell

**Investments** by Cindy Cummins

This vest proves that sergers are not just for finishing seam allowances. Creative serger stitching is an integral element of an intriguing design.

*See pages 220–221 for serger textures and embellishments.*

**Vest** by Kristen Dibbs

This vest is another example of just how well quilting goes with decorative stitching and embellishing.

*See page 119 for Kristen's approach to decorative machine stitching and quilting.*

***Time Warp*** by Ricky Tims

Multicolored hand-dyed fabric provides the setting for masterful machine stitching. From the radiant center out to the free-form feather-quilted borders, trapunto and bobbinwork make this quilt sing with movement and energy.

*See pages 113–115 for bobbinwork, pages 156–158 for free-motion quilting, pages 234–235 for trapunto, and page 155 for another example of Ricky's quilting.*

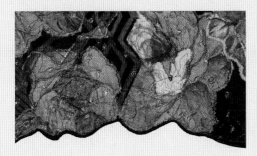 **Vest** by Rosemary Eichorn

A quilted fantasy of decorative stitching, this vest is the perfect attire for the well-dressed machine artist.

*See page 77 for Rosemary's tips for troubleshooting decorative threads, pages 113–115 for bobbinwork, pages 156–158 for free-motion quilting, and page 202 for satin stitch edge finishes.*

 **Lily** by Jane Sassaman

Colorful graphic shapes are defined by bold lines of satin stitching that add highlights and contrasting shadows.

*See pages 106–110 for satin stitch appliqué, and page 189 for Jane's technique for using quilting templates.*

**Smocked Dress**
by Deborah Yedziniak

Smocking is easier than ever with machine stitching and embellishing.

*See pages 116–118 for built-in decorative stitching and pages 226–228 for Deborah's machine smocking techniques.*

**Beaded Evening Purse** by Pauline Richards

Machine-stitched beading makes this evening purse an elegant and unique accessory.

*See page 112 for Pauline's machine beading techniques.*

### *Candle Holder*

by Linda Griepentrog

Embroidery meets metal. Use this machine embroidery technique to get the look of folk art tin punching.

*See pages 175–176 for Linda's techniques for embroidery on metal.*

*Embroidery design:* Creative Machine Embroidery *magazine original*

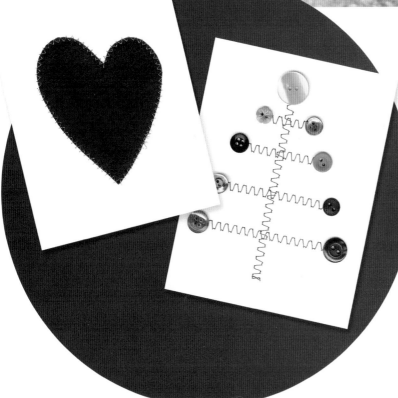

### *Holiday Cards* by Marla Stefanelli

Stitching on paper is fun for kids and grown-ups alike. Make your own greeting cards and other paper projects.

*See pages 184–185 for Marla's tips for stitching on paper.*

**Drift** by Libby Lehman
Threadplay at its best. From delicate to bold, expressive threadwork provides vibrant color and texture.

*See pages 106–110 for satin stitch appliqué, pages 156–158 for free-motion quilting, and pages 201–202 for satin stitching.*

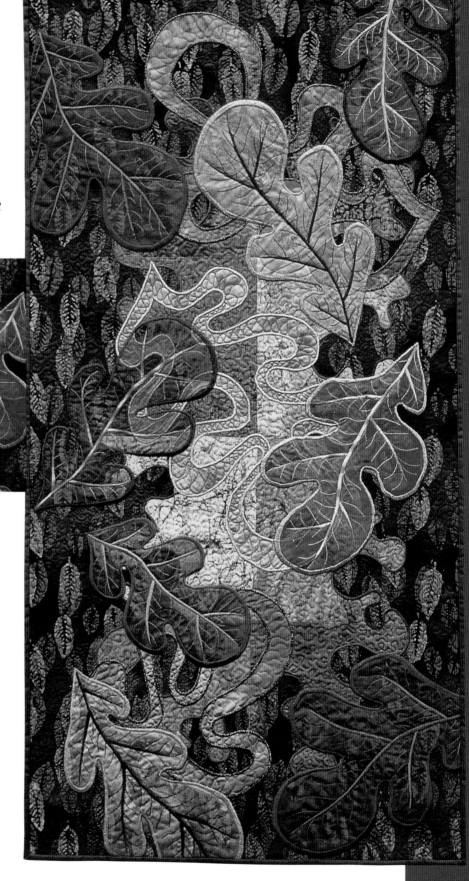

 ***The Grandfather*** by Hollis Chatelaine

The dramatic use of quilting the contours makes this dye-painted quilt an awe-inspiring masterpiece.

*See pages 156–157 for free-motion quilting and page 158 for Hollis's approach to quilting.*

### *Machine Embroidered Fleece Pillow*

by Nancy Cornwell

Fleece never looked so inviting. Enhance fleece's natural texture with machine embroidery.

*See pages 142–143 for Nancy's fleece embroidery techniques and pages 151–152 for more ideas using fleece.*

*Embroidery designs: Husqvarna Viking disk #101*

 *Chenille jacket* by Katrina Lamken

Chevron designs enhance this warm and cozy chenille jacket.

*See pages 122–124 for chenille techniques.*

*Quilted Garden* by Jewel Hewlett
and Marla Stefanelli
Embroidered panels are stitched to print fabric
for a unique garden quilt.

*See pages 193–195 for for combining quilting
and embroidery.*

*Embroidery designs: Jewel Hewlett.*

***Fantasy*** A Machine Arts Sampler by Lynn Koolish

What a fun way to try out all the machine arts techniques. This contemporary sampler displays the diversity of decorative stitching and embroidery.

*See pages 106–110 for satin stitch appliqué, pages 113–115 for bobbin-work, page 126 for couching, page 127 for crazy quilt stitching, pages 185–186 for pintucks, and, pages 235–237 for tucks.*

***Pieced Delight Vest*** by Rebecca Kemp Brent

Update an old-fashioned favorite with contemporary stitching techniques and style. Crazy quilting is the perfect partner for decorative machine stitching and embroidery.

*See page 127 for Rebecca's crazy quilt stitching technique.*

*Embroidery Designs: Brother cards # 29 and #45, Artistic Design Lace & Romantic Designs by Sue Box*

**Paris** by Hari Walner (quilt top) and Linda V. Taylor (quilting)

Classic quilting takes on a new dimension with trapunto and exquisitely detailed longarm quilting.

*See page 174 for Linda's tips on threads for longarm quilting, and pages 234–235 for Hari's trapunto technique.*

**_Big Thread_** by Laura Wasilowski

Big thread (hand-dyed size 12 perle cotton) amplifies the quilting in *Big Thread*. Colorful thread is the perfect counterpoint to the colorful fabric in this whimsical quilt.

*See pages 156–158 for free-motion quilting.*

**_Vest_** by Annrae Roberts

Silk flowers take on new life in this elegant shadow appliqué vest.

*See page 110 for shadow appliqué.*

**Tote Bag** by Lynn Koolish and Lyda McAuliff

Large-scale machine stitched floral motif adds color and dimension to a quilted tote bag.

*See page 126 for couching, pages 156–158 for free-motion quilting, pages 170–171 for spun lace, and page 202 for satin stitched edges.*

**Embroidered Dress** by Christy Burcham

What little girl wouldn't love wearing this sunny embroidered dress? This easy technique is perfect for all types of kids' clothing.

*See page 134 for references to embroidery basics, and page 177 for Christy's mirror-image embroidery techniques.*

*Embroidery design: Oklahoma Embroidery Supply & Design #CR119*

***Elegant Dining*** by Sara Meyer-Snuggerud

Add an elegant touch to any room setting with the creative use of embroidery.

*See pages 138–139 for Sara's tips on embroidery for the dining room.*

*Embroidery design: Oklahoma Embroidery Supply & Design #CR054*

### *Spun-lace Vest*

by Sharee Dawn Roberts

With machine stitching and beautiful thread, machine-spun lace adds a romantic and elegant touch to any outfit.

*See pages 170–171 for Sharee's spun lace technique, and pages 169–170 for more machine lace.*

*Garment modeled by Patti Lee.*

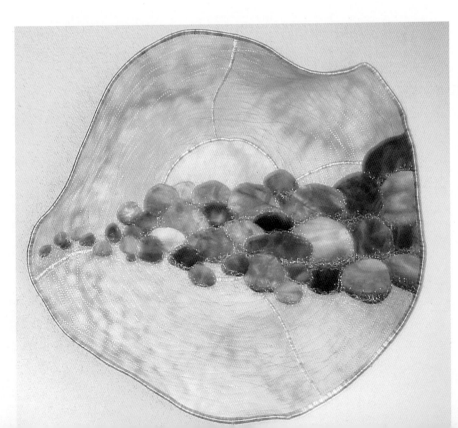

### *Stones Bowl* by Linda Johansen

Fabric bowls are a unique showcase for decorative threads and free-motion stitching.

*See pages 152–153 for free-motion stitching and page 202 for satin stitched edges.*

 **Serger-trimmed Pillow**

by Naomi Baker

Now you can always have perfectly matched trim—use your serger to create unique braids and cording for all types of embellishing.

*See pages 208–209 for Naomi's techniques for creating serger trims.*

**Surface-stitched Pillows**

by Wendy Hill

Surface stitching adds sophisticated color and texture to any fabric. Use this versatile technique to create unique fabric for garments, quilting, and home décor.

*See pages 229–232 for Wendy's surface stitching techniques.*

**_Embroidered and Appliquéd Pillows_** by Barbara Weiland

These sunny pillows are appliquéd and embroidered in one easy step.

*See page 138 for Barbara's embroidered appliqué technique.*

*Embroidery designs:* Creative Machine Embroidery *magazine originals*

**_Chenille Scarf_** by Nancy Restuccia

Double your wardrobe with one scarf. This two-sided chenille scarf provides two color variations in one stylish accessory.

*See pages 122–123 for Nancy's chenille techniques.*

# Successful Studios

From picture perfect to creative chaos, spacious to cozy; whether you're a seasoned professional or a beginning sewer, you need a sewing space to call your own. Here is a look at some studios to give you ideas of what you can do with your sewing space.

Host of "America Sews", Sue Hausmann made the large family area on the lower level of her home into a hobby/sewing/computing center. She stores her fabric and projects in drawers and cabinets while she keeps her thread on several types of racks. She uses the bar area of the room for a pressing station.

Sue displays her collection of toy sewing machines, antique sewing notions, pincushions, sewing pictures, memorabilia, vintage garments, and quilts around the room. She says she

doesn't mind the clutter because it brings her so much pleasure. Many of the items were gifts from friends through the years and she thinks of those friends as she works.

Quilter and author Joyce Becker has a studio that is perfect for her style of quilting.

The numerous threads used in her heavily-stitched quilts are stored in modular wooden drawer units while fabric and batting are stored in a tall, skinny bookcase. Notions are stored in an assortment of tins, plastic see-through boxes, and baskets.

Her design wall, ironing board, and sewing machine are all within reach, making it easy to work on those luscious landscape quilts.

Hollis Chatelaine is known for her spectacular quilts that incorporate dye painting and contour quilting using many colors of thread.

Threads are sorted by color and stored in a rolling cart that can be moved to the sewing machine when she is quilting. Hollis changes thread colors often, so the spools selected for a project are placed in the basket on top to be within easy reach.

She calls it her dungeon, but Laura Wasilowski's studio is more like a magician's workroom from which emerge luscious threads and fanciful fused quilts. Laura's studio used to be the family room, so when she took it over for sewing she had brighter lighting installed.

Plastic bins hold the thread that Laura dyes. The bins are on wheels so she can move them to the sewing machine when she needs them. Bigger cones of purchased threads are stored on shelves when not being used.

The sewing table has an additional table behind it to support quilts while Laura is quilting them on the machine.

F ounder of Oklahoma Embroidery Supply & Design, Mary Newton notes that her sewing room was a result of a major home remodel two years ago. The room "appeared" when the contractor was working out the logisitics of the downstairs kitchen remodel. Perched in the treetops, and surrounded by natural light from the windows, the sewing machine and serger are on opposite sides of the U-shaped work area, with additional work and storage space available.

P ati Palmer, the founder of Palmer/Pletsch, had her sewing room designed by Lynette Black, author of *Dream Sewing Spaces*. The space was designed to accommodate video production so the machines are on islands. Storage cabinets with shelves abound, and Pati loves the fact that she can open one door and see everything. The table doubles for planning and teacher training sessions.

The cutting table is on wheels and is covered with two padded boards that are great for fusing, cutting, and steaming fabric. The light fixtures are "kitchen" fixtures to produce abundant light. In addition, the walls, blinds, et cetera are white to reflect the most light. Bright colors are used to accent the room.

When author and lecturer Mary Roehr moved to Arizona 12 years ago she had to combine everything from a sewing room and study into one room. Some clever organization details include a wall quilt that doubles as a bulletin board; a large sewing basket to store quilting, top-stitching, and serger thread; and two large glass brandy snifters—one for dark colors, and one for white and pastels. Mary contends that this is the simplest, most organized, and pleasant room she's ever sewn in.

Author and designer Stephanie Corina Goddard converted a room in her home into a place where she can research techniques and stitch projects. Storage abounds under the daybed, in the closet, and on the back of the door. Large racks keep thread organized and available. Filing cabinets are tucked under the cutting table, and when needed, a laptop can be moved on top. Large plastic tubs which Stephanie never stacks higher than she can lift, hold a bounty of fabric.

Known for her Threadplay quilts, quilter, teacher, and author Libby Lehman is surrounded by fabric and thread in her studio. She uses a variety of storage options for threads including miniature display drawers, wire drawers with plastic inserts so the thread can be sorted by color, and thread racks for larger spools and cones. Regardless of the type of storage, Libby is careful to keep all her thread out of direct sunlight.

Quilting hoops are hung under wall-mounted thread storage and there are plenty of shelves and racks for books, fabric, and binders of quilt photographs.

# Mastering Machines

Sewing machines and sergers have long been used for their functionality, but they can also be tools for creative expression. Marry a machine with beautiful fabrics, lustrous threads, and imagination, and you have the tools to reach a new level of sewing expression. Whether stitching quilts, home décor items, garments, or gifts, you'll want to know and understand all you can about your machines.

# SEWING MACHINES

**Ann Price Gosch**

*Basic machine-stitch formation hasn't changed in the 150 years since Elias Howe patented the sewing machine. The upper thread, carried by the needle, meets the lower thread, carried by the bobbin, to form a lockstitch. Today's machines include these parts, plus additional features that make them versatile and easy to operate.*

*You should always refer to the manual for your specific machine as your explore new directions in machine arts, but here's a quick guide to some of the common terms, functions, and features of today's machines.*

**Balance:** A computer function that enables you to fine-tune reverse and multi-directional stitches to suit any fabric and thread. The balance adjustment allows you to stretch out or close up the stitches to make sure they are positioned correctly when the fabric is moving in reverse or sideways.

**Bobbin:** Thread wound onto a small, specially shaped spool or bobbin provides the bottom thread for machine sewing. A *front-loading* bobbin is inserted into a separate bobbin case, then placed vertically into the shuttle from the front. A *top-loading* bobbin is placed horizontally into the shuttle's built-in bobbin case via a sliding needle plate; it's also called a *drop-in* bobbin.

**Built-in needle threader:** A built-in feature on some machines that makes threading the needle easier and faster.

**Dual feed:** A built-in feature on some machines that works with the feed dogs to promote even feeding of multiple fabric layers; similar to a walking foot.

**Elongation:** A computer function that directs the machine to lengthen a motif or sequence while maintaining the stitch density.

**Feed dogs:** "Teeth" under the presser foot move the fabric through the machine during stitching. On most machines, the feed dogs can be lowered ("dropped") to eliminate the feeding action for free-motion work. On older machines, there may be a metal plate that can be snapped in place to cover the feed dogs.

**Hook race cover:** A plate holds the shuttle in the race (see "Race"). On many machines, it can be opened and the shuttle removed for oiling the race.

**Hook—Oscillating or Rotary:** The shuttle movement determines how the machine forms a stitch. The *oscillator* hooks the needle thread as it swings back and forth in a semicircle; the *rotary* hook travels in a continuous circle, hooking the needle thread on each rotation.

**Knee lift:** An L-shape extension lever, operated by the knee, which raises and lowers the presser foot. This accessory is available on some machines and enables you to keep both hands on the fabric.

**Lateral feed:** Fabric feeding from side to side, not just from front to back, provides directional stitching capabilities—for embroidery or mending and patching—without turning the fabric.

**Lockstitch:** The stitch used by sewing machines is formed by the looping of two threads, one on each side of the fabric being sewn. It differs from the serger's 2-thread overedge stitch, which locks at the fabric edge, not at the seamline.

**Memory cards, cartridges, or cassettes:** Computer disks or cards store stitches or patterns and enable you to expand the capabilities of your machine.

**Mirror imaging:** A computer function that enables the machine to stitch the reverse image of a motif or sequence without turning the fabric around. Some machines have end-to-end as well as side-to-side mirror-image capabilities.

**Multi-directional stitches:** Large-scale decorative stitches are created by moving the fabric in many directions; also called omni-directional stitches.

**Needle position:** A function that allows you to move the needle position away from center; helpful when edge stitching, inserting zippers, sewing piping, or whenever stitch placement requires "fine-tuning."

**Needle stop:** An electronic feature that raises the needle to the highest position when the machine stops, completing the last stitch. This saves turning the handwheel to raise the needle. Most machines also offer the option of automatic needle stop down, so you can keep your hands on the work when the needle must remain in the fabric for frequent pivoting or repositioning.

**Pattern start:** A function that allows you to start a decorative stitch or motif at the beginning of the stitch sequence.

**Programming:** An electronic feature that allows you to create personalized stitch designs by combining built-in motifs, customizing built-in stitches, or using computer technology to convert designs from other media into stitching designs.

**Race:** The circular track in which the shuttle operates.

**Reverse:** Stitching backward; this can be *continuous* so it is locked into the backward mode until it's deliberately canceled; or *instant*, so the machine stitches backward only while the button or lever is held in position.

**Shuttle:** The moving holder that carries the bobbin thread as it "hooks" the needle thread to form a lockstitch (see "Hook").

**Single pattern selection:** A computer function that directs the machine to stitch one complete motif or sequence, then stop automatically.

**Thread cutter:** Some machines will clip the top and bobbin threads at the touch of a button.

## Tip

### Master Your Machine

A great way to master your machine is to take advantage of classes and clubs offered by your machine dealer. Clubs vary by dealer and machine, but membership often includes a subscription to the club magazine and monthly classes. Classes and clubs provide a supportive environment for learning both basic machine operation and maintenance as well as a wide variety of machine techniques.

If you have access to the Internet, machine manufacturer's websites offer a wealth of information, projects, lessons, design downloads, and more. See Resources on page 250 for website addresses.

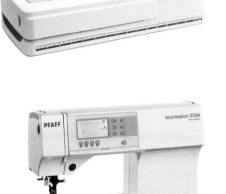

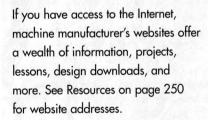

## Electronic or Computerized?

*Ann Price Gosch*

If you plan to buy a sewing machine or serger, your first option is whether to choose a computerized or an electronic model. Though it's still possible to purchase an all-mechanical machine, electronics have been added to most models to increase operating ease and speed. Electronic merely means electrical signals replace some mechanical switches, levers, and gears.

A sewing machine or serger, for example, may have an electronic needle stop. That means an electrical signal "tells" the needle to stop in the highest position, instead of you turning the handwheel to bring the needle up mechanically. Many machines now have an electronic foot control that maintains the machine's full needle-penetration power even at the slowest speed. A mechanical foot control, by contrast, loses power as it loses speed so it can be difficult to pierce heavy fabrics without "flooring" the foot pedal.

Computerized means the machine also has a memory. As you select the sewing machine's zigzag stitch or the serger's 3-thread overlock, for example, the machine automatically adjusts for the ideal settings, which are in the memory (though you generally can override the preprogramming for special circumstances). Memory also allows you to string stitches into a sequence to, for example, write words, names, and dates with the machine's built-in alphabet and numerals.

In short, computerization greatly expands a sewing machine's capabilities and versatility because so much stitch-formation data can be stored on a computer microchip. With the latest computer links to sewing, you can even convert designs from other media into stitchery or create original stitch designs.

## Don't Overlook an Older Machine

*Lynn Koolish*

Having the latest, greatest sewing machine can be fun, but don't forget that many older, mechanical sewing machines have decorative stitching capabilities. In addition to a zigzag stitch, this machine (purchased in the early 1970s) uses plastic discs or cams to create decorative stitches.

*Interchangable cams on an older Elna sewing machine create decorative stitches.*

## Better Straight Stitching

*Lynn Koolish*

Sewing machines that have zigzag or decorative stitching capabilities come with a throat plate that is designed to accommodate the widest stitch available on the machine.

*Zigzag throat plate*

However, for straight stitching, a throat plate with a round hole that is just big enough to accommodate the needle, sometimes referred to as a straight stitch throat plate, will often facilitate better straight stitches. It will also make it more difficult for the starting edge of fabric to get pulled down when you start stitching.

Straight stitch throat plates are available from your sewing machine dealer.

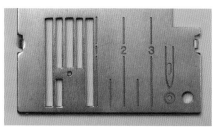

*Straight stitch throat plate*

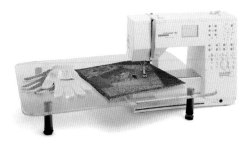

# STITCH DICTIONARY

Whether your sewing machine has a few stitches, or a few hundred—using the built-in stitches can open a new world of decorative stitching.

Different machine manufacturers group and name their built-in stitches differently, but what you do with the stitches is more important than what the stitches are named or even what they were originally designed for. Be creative, if a stitch reminds you of grass growing in a field, use it that way, it doesn't matter if it was originally designed for sewing elastic or finishing hems.

The length, width, and density of most stitches can be adjusted. When you add the ability to flip stitches right-to-left or upside-down, the variety is almost endless. The easiest way to become familiar with your stitches, is to stitch out your own stitch dictionary so you can experiment with your available stitches to find the ones you like the best.

In addition to learning how to flip stitches right-to-left and upside-down, get to know the following functions if they are available on your machine. All machines work a bit differently, so you'll need to consult your manual.

**Pattern start:** Start a stitch pattern or motif at the beginning of the sequence.

**Single pattern:** Limit the stitching to one repeat of the pattern. On most machines this will cause the machine to automatically tie off the stitching at the end of the sequence.

**Balance:** Fine-tune reverse and multi-directional stitches to make sure the stitches are positioned correctly when the fabric is moving in reverse or sideways.

**Memory or pattern saving:** Build and save sequences of stitches for lettering and for stitch combinations.

Stitches are listed in alphabetical order and page references are provided for more information and ideas for using specific stitches. See pages 116–119 for more ideas on using built-in stitches in general.

*(Continued on next page)*

## Bartack Stitches

Bartacks are designed to reinforce stress points such as pockets, vents, and belt loops in garments. But, bartacks offer many decorative opportunities. For unique uses, see pages 111 and 228.

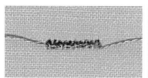

## Blanket Stitches

A true blanket stitch is one stitch forward, one stitch left, and one stitch back to the right. Some machines offer stitches that use several stitches forward and/or to the side. For appliqué, a true blanket stitch is easiest to use, but the other variations offer many decorative possibilities. See pages 103–106 for blanket stitch appliqué.

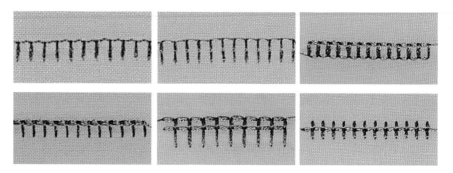

## Bridge and Fagoting Stitches

Bridge or fagoting stitches are used to "bridge the gap" between two pieces of fabric, lace, or trim. Your machine may have a stitch specifically called a fagoting stitch, but many stitches that go back-and-forth, including zigzag stitches and crazy quilting stitches, can be used for fagoting or bridging. See pages 115–116 for bridge stitching.

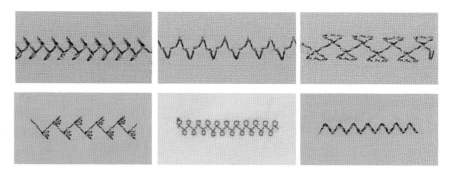

## Buttonhole Stitches

There are many styles of buttonholes and buttonhole stitches that can serve as the basis of decorative buttonholes. Consult your manual for the buttonhole stitch available on your machine. See page 120 for decorative additions to buttonholes.

## Cable Stitches

Stitches that look like knitted cables can be used in long rows, borders, and as individual stitches.

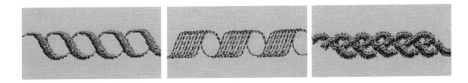

## Circular Stitches

Many machines offer built-in eyelet stitches in a few sizes, but there are other decorative stitches in circular designs. See pages 147–148 for eyelets.

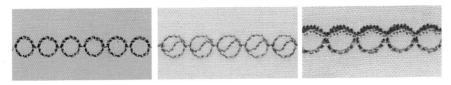

## Cross-stitch Stitches

Cross-stitch patterns and combinations are often available in one or two sizes. The stitches may include scrollwork or other decorative elements. See page 128 for cross-stitch.

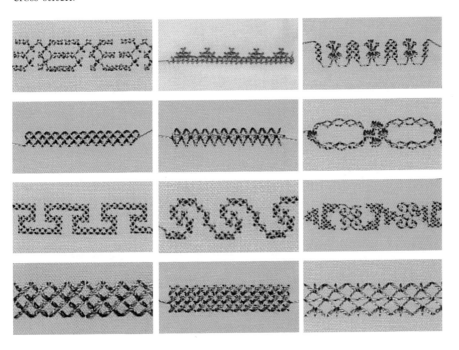

*(Continued on next page)*

## Floral Stitches

Many decorative stitches are floral and foliage designs. Both outline and filled designs are usually available. They can be used alone or combined into sequences.

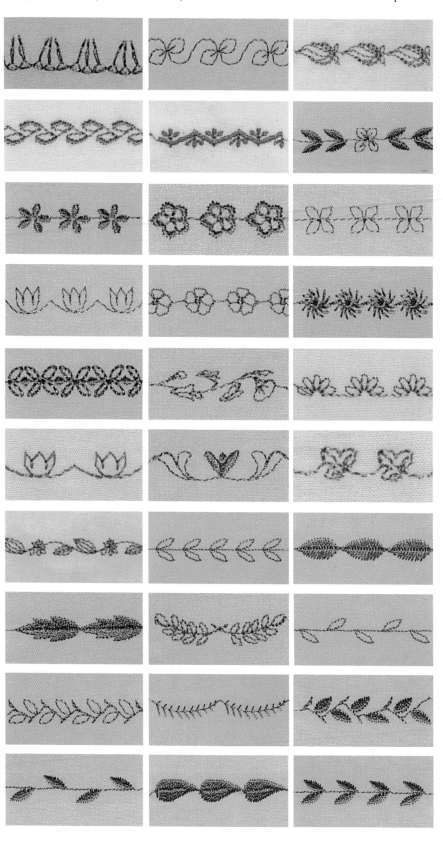

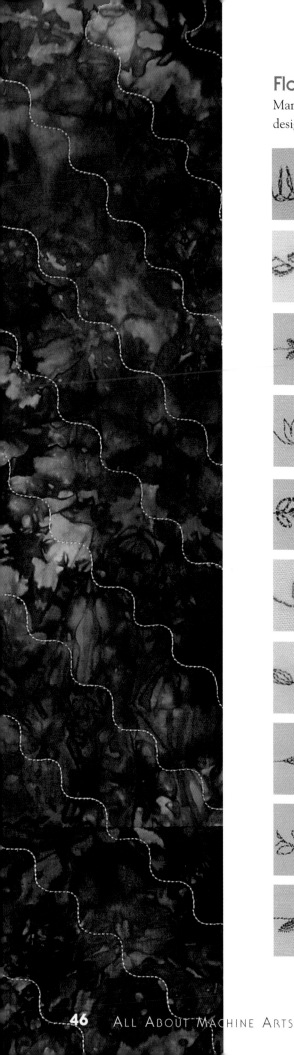

# Geometric Stitches

Many decorative stitches (both outline and filled) are geometric shapes. As with floral stitches, they also can be used alone or combined into sequences.

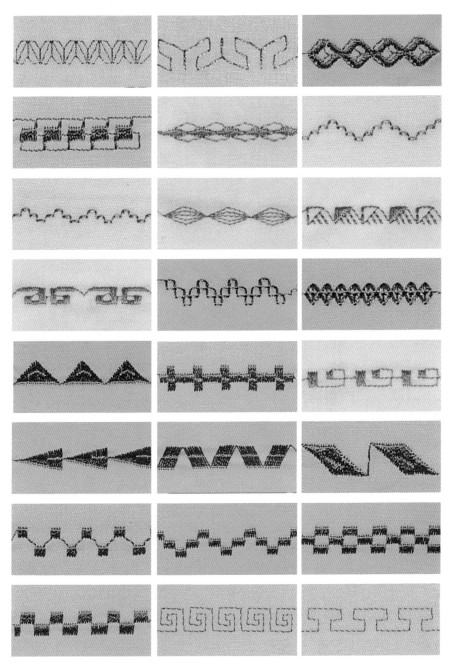

*(Continued on next page)*

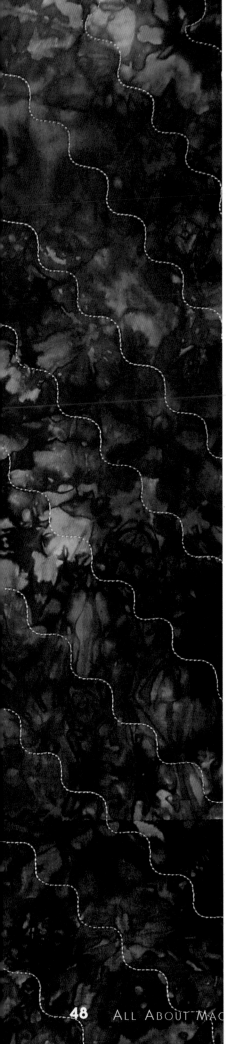

## Grid Stitches

Grid-like stitches are available in a variety of sizes, shapes, and fills.

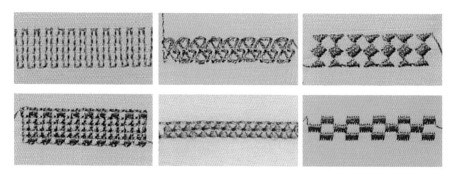

## Heart Stitches

As an outline or filled, use these stitches alone or combined with other stitches.

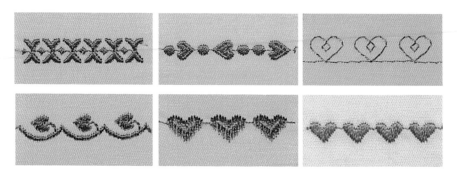

## Honeycomb Stitch

The honeycomb stitch is beautiful on its own and is often used for smocking. See pages 161–162 for honeycomb stitch.

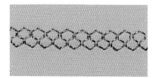

## Kids' Stitches

Decorative stitches designed for kids run the gamut from animals, to toys, trains, and more. Kids' clothes and quilts are the perfect canvas for these decorative stitches.

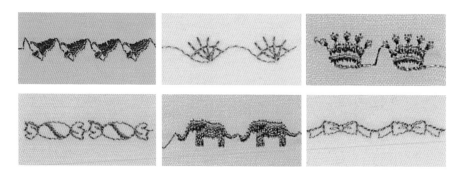

## Kids' Stitches Continued

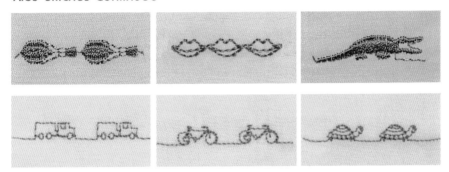

## Large-scale / Multi-directional Stitches

Some electronic and computerized machines offer large stitch patterns that are made by the combination of multi- or omni-direction needle movement, along with multi- or omni-directional movement of the fabric. You may need to adjust both the forward-reverse balance, and the side-to-side balance for these large-scale designs. Refer to your machine manual for instructions on balancing stitches.

## Lettering / Alphabets

Lettering or monogramming capabilities may be provided with your built-in stitches. If your machine has memory, you can string stitches into a sequence to write words, names, and dates. See page 173 for lettering and pages 178–179 for monogramming.

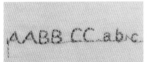
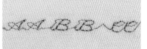

## Quilting Stitches

### Crazy Quilt Stitches

Many of the same stitches that can be used for bridging or fagoting are also perfect for crazy quilting. See page 127 for crazy quilt stitching.

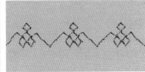
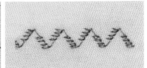

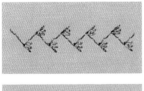
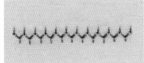

*(Continued on next page)*

### Hand-look Quilting Stitch

Some machines offer a mock or hand-look quilting stitch. To use this stitch, use monofilament thread in the needle, and your quilting thread in the bobbin. The top tension needs to be tightened and the bobbin thread may need to be loosened. The stitch works because the tight top tension causes the bobbin thread to be brought to the top of the fabric.

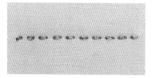

### Serpentine Stitch

The serpentine stitch can be used instead of a zigzag stitch to finish seams, and it is a wonderful stitch for quilting. Used in the same manner as a straight stitch, the slightly wavy lines provide interest and movement.

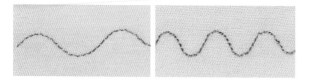

### Stippling Stitch

Some machines include a stippling or meandering stitch.

### Satin Stitches

Bold or delicate, satin stitches come is a variety of shapes and sizes. See pages 106–110 for satin stitch appliqué and pages 201–202 for satin stitching.

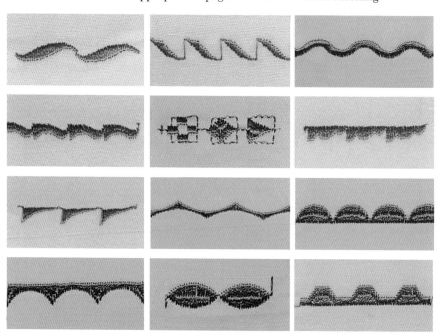

**Satin Stitches Continued**

## Scallop Stitches

Scallop stitches come in a wide range of designs and can be outlined or filled. They are perfect for hems, edges, and other decorative stitching. See pages 203–204 for scallop stitch ideas.

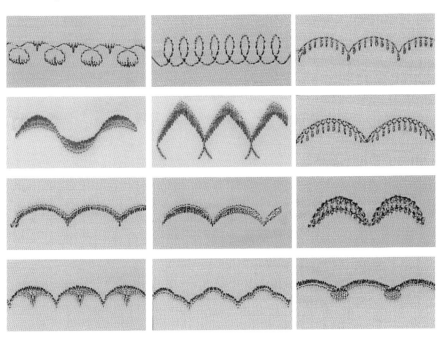

## Scrollwork Stitches

Scrollwork stitches provide delicate and elegant touches.

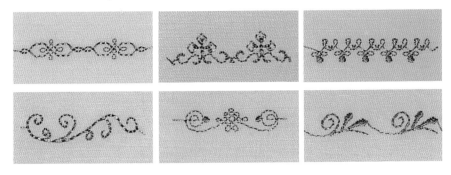

## Seam Finishing Stitches

As with stitches designed for hemming, seam finishing stitches such as overcast, overlock, and edge binding stitches are not only functional, but provide interesting patterns and textures for decorative stitching.

*(Continued on next page)*

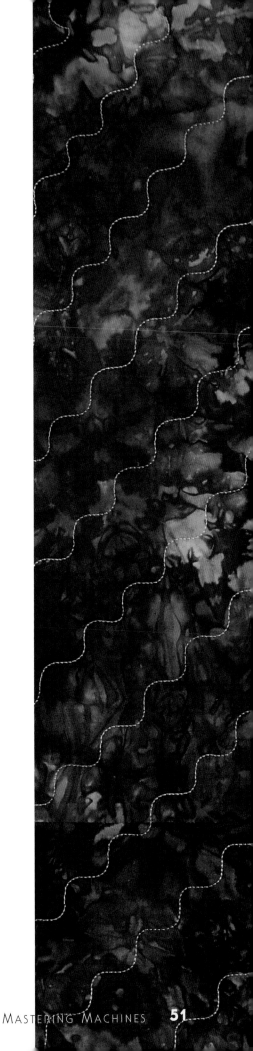

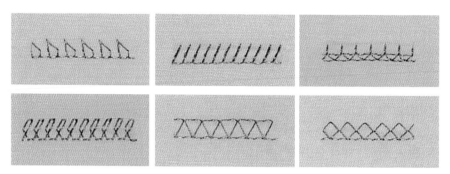

## Star Stitches

As an outline or filled, use these stitches alone or combined with other stitches.

## Straight Stitches

Straight stitching is used for sewing seams, as well as for topstitching and quilting. Use with decorative threads for a whole new look.

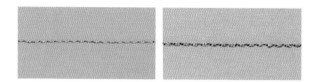

## Texture Stitches

A variety of stitches originally designed for hemming, finishing seams, and sewing elastic are available on many machines. In addition to their original functionality, they provide a wealth of interesting patterns and textures for decorative stitching.

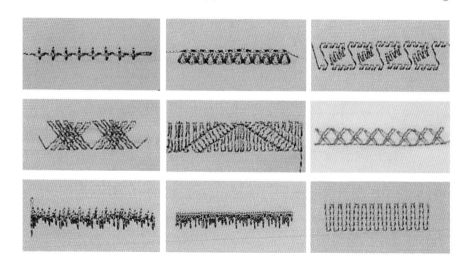

# Zigzag Stitches

The zigzag stitch is used for finishing seams so they don't unravel, satin stitching (see pages 201–202), satin stitch appliqué (see pages 106–110), hemstitching (see page 160), gathering (see page 159), and much more.

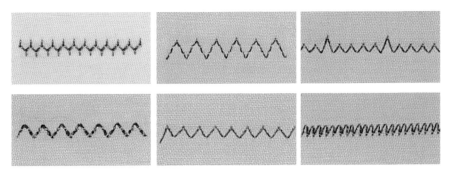

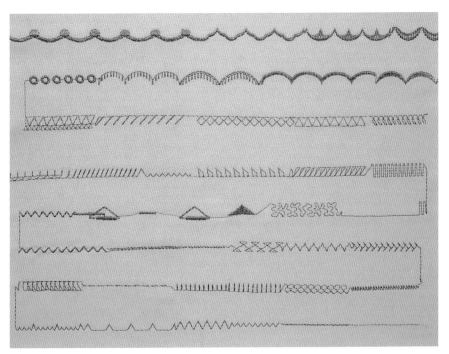

*Make your own stitch dictionary.*

# PRESSER FEET

*Presser feet are designed to help move fabrics and notions smoothly through the sewing machine. They come in all shapes and sizes—there's a special foot for just about anything you can imagine using your machine for. Here's a quick look at some of the feet that are perfect for decorative machine stitching.*

**Blindhem foot:** This adjustable version of the blindhem or blindstitch foot is designed to stitch a turned hem by catching folded fabric with a blind hem stitch.

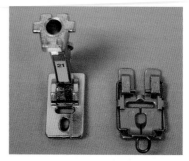

**Braiding foot:** The round opening in front holds narrow braids and cords in place for couching. Some versions of this foot have a loop to help feed the braid.

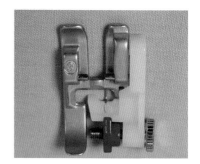

**Button foot:** The short, open toes hold flat buttons in place so you can attach them with a zigzag stitch. You can also use it to hold and attach rings, bows, and other embellishments.

**Edge stitching foot or edge joining foot:** The metal blade acts as a guide for edges or seams. Center the needle for perfect stitching-in-the-ditch. Adjust the needle right or left and use the vertical blade as a guide when topstitching, sewing narrow hems, and making tucks.

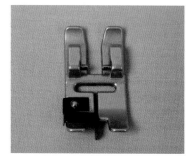

**Gathering foot:** Sometimes called a shirring foot, this foot gathers fabric evenly. Gathers are stitched into place, either on a single layer of fabric or onto another piece of fabric.

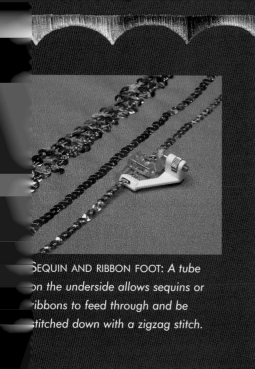

SEQUIN AND RIBBON FOOT: *A tube on the underside allows sequins or ribbons to feed through and be stitched down with a zigzag stitch.*

PEARLS AND PIPING FOOT: *A deep groove lets pearl strings or cording slide through and be stitched down.*

SATIN EDGE FOOT: *A guide and metal pin adjust for various size satin stitching.*

**DARNING/EMBROIDERY FOOT:** *Also called a free-form embroidery foot, the foot moves up and down with the sewing machine needle for free-motion stitching with the feed dogs dropped.*

*Multiple-hole cording foot:* The holes or grooves at the front of the foot guide multiple strands of decorative thread or cording so they can be stitched over for couching. The foot has an indentation on the bottom allowing room for the cords to pass easily under the foot. A foot with a moveable latch makes it easy to feed the cords through the foot.

*Open-toe or appliqué foot:* The open area at the front of the foot allows for greater visibility, helpful for many techniques including appliqué, satin and other decorative stitching, cutwork, and couching. The foot also has an indentation on the underside so it moves smoothly over raised stitches.

*Some older machines come with a darning plate if the feed dogs can't be dropped.*

*Pintuck foot:* Pintuck feet come in several sizes/number of grooves on the underside of the foot. When used with a twin needle, the multiple grooves aid in sewing uniform, evenly spaced pintucks. This foot can also be used to help hold the needles for charted needlework.

*Narrow or rolled hem foot:* The V-shaped scroll makes a narrow rolled hem in lightweight fabrics. Use a zigzag or blind hem stitch for a scalloped edge.

**EVEN-FEED/DUAL FEED/WALKING FOOT:** *The movement of the foot feeds the top layer of fabric at the same rate as the bottom layer of fabric, making it easier to keep layers of fabrics feeding evenly. This foot is recommended for quilting and other layered work.*

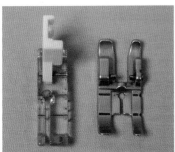

*¼" foot:* Also known as a patchwork foot, use the edge of this foot for an accurate seam allowance of ¼", perfect for piecing quilts.

*(Continued on next page)*

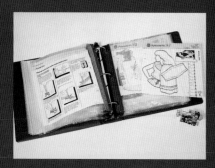

**PRESSER FOOT BOOK:** *Use a 3-ring binder and self-sealing storage bags to make a handy storage and reference book for presser feet. Reinforce the non-opening end of the plastic bag with a strip of cardboard, punch holes, and place in a binder. Keep feet and copies of instructions on using the feet in each plastic bag.*

*— Sue Barnabee*

**CIRCULAR SEWING ATTACHMENT:** *Different machines have different style attachments, but they all include a way to evenly pivot fabric around in a perfect circle. The attachments are adjustable so circles of different sizes can be stitched.*

**EYELET ATTACHMENT:** *The eyelet attachment provides an easy way to make perfectly round eyelets in different sizes. A plate, used to cover the feed dogs, may have a set size or may have a hole that can accomodate several sizes of "studs." An eyelet kit, may also include hole cutters of various sizes, and a special eyelet stitching foot.*

*Quilting or edge guide:* The guide is adjustable and is commonly used for quilting, but is handy whenever rows of stitching needs to be evenly spaced.

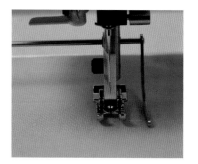

*Ruffler attachment:* Also called a pleater attachment, this foot stitches fabric into pleats for gathering, ruffling, shirring, pleating, and ruching. The frequency of the pleating can be adjusted using the lever at the top, and the depth of the pleats can be adjusted by using the screw on the side. The pleats are stitched into place, either on a single layer of fabric or onto another piece of fabric.

*Satin stitch foot:* Also known as an embroidery foot, this foot has an indentation on the underside to allow dense satin and decorative stitches to pass easily underneath.

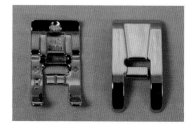

*Utility or Zigzag foot:* This foot is designed primarily for straight or zigzag stitching. The underside of the foot is flat to provide firm contact with the feed dogs. For the best straight stitching, use a straight stitch throatplate (see page 42).

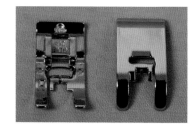

*Zipper foot:* The indentations on each side of the foot allow the needle to stitch very close to zippers and other raised seams such as piping. The feet are designed to allow a right- or left-hand needle position.

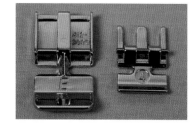

# UNDERSTANDING MACHINE TENSION

*Peggy Bendel*

*Is your sewing machine suffering from tension headaches? Banish stitch balance problems forever by learning how to adjust the tension—and when to leave well enough alone.*

Thread flow is the key to perfect machine stitches, and every machine has a carefully crafted thread delivery system. When threads move correctly through the system from the needle and bobbin, the stitches form perfectly.

## Top Thread Delivery

The top thread path is easy to follow. In a conventional machine, the thread leaves the spool, passes through a series of guides and enters the tension discs; it then passes through one or more additional guides and the take-up lever before entering the needle eye.

The two metal or synthetic tension discs, a key system part, are joined back-to-back. On some machines there are three discs to accommodate two top threads for twin-needle sewing. They squeeze the thread with varying pressure, depending on the setting you have chosen using the tension regulator (or the tension key on a touch screen); the higher the number, the more the thread is restrained and the tighter the tension.

According to experts at sewing machine companies, threading the machine with the presser foot down is the most common cause of tension problems. The tension discs slacken when the presser foot is up and become engaged only when the presser foot is down. For the thread to properly seat between the discs, you must raise the presser foot when threading the machine. Improperly threading the machine—such as skipping one of the thread guides—is also a frequent error.

The latest machine models have newly-engineered tension systems for efficient and dependable thread delivery, necessary for features such as extra-wide stitches, multi-directional stitch patterns and high-speed hooped embroidery. Guides to prevent the thread from shuttling from side to side or backlashing are embedded inside the machine, and the tension discs are usually hidden. On some models you can remove the front plate from the machine if a thread gets caught inside the discs, but others warn you not to attempt this on your own—you'll need an authorized service person to gain access to the tension discs. Check your manual or call your dealer.

Many of these sophisticated models also have automatic or self-adjusting tension, and exactly how this feature works varies from brand to brand. Some machines have sensors which "read" the thread as it goes through the system and release the right thread amount for a perfect stitch; others have computer chips which respond to the presser foot height as it rides on multiple fabric layers; still other react directly to the built-in stitch pattern

## Tip

### Overriding Automatic Tension

Even if your machine adjusts the tension automatically, you can often override it by using the tension regulator. On other machines, the tension is affected by selection of fabric type. Check the manual for your machine.

## Bottom Thread Delivery

The bobbin thread path in the delivery system is obvious on front-load machines. After the thread leaves the bobbin, it passes under the bobbin case spring. If the bobbin thread is seated properly in the spring, you should be able to suspend the bobbin case by the thread; when you give the thread a tug, the spring should release a short thread length.

The bobbin spring is adjustable by means of a small screw at its base (on top-loading machines, the screw is found on the bobbin shuttle or there is a dial for bobbin tension). A small turn of the screw can make a big difference in the bobbin tension. Turning the screw clockwise increases the tension; turning it counterclockwise decreases it.

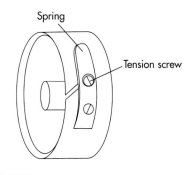

*Bobbin case*

*(Continued on next page)*

The factory-set tension will cover most sewing tasks, but problems can often be solved by using the regulator to change the needle thread tension. Always adjust the top tension first when correcting a tension problem. It's much easier to return to the original setting for the top tension than for the bobbin.

Bobbin tension adjustments most often apply when using unusual threads for creative embellishments or sewing especially heavy or very thin fabrics.

## Bypassing the Bobbin Tension

You may want to bypass the bobbin tension entirely for special effects. If you'd like to use a thick, decorative thread in the bobbin for irregular, textured embellishments, skip the bobbin spring.

## Balanced vs. Unbalanced Stitches

Most modern machines will sew a balanced stitch—a stitch with equal top and bottom tensions—on a range of fabrics using all-purpose threads without any tension adjustments. A row of balanced stitches looks smooth and even, without puckers, and the seam is strong enough not to pull apart easily.

Needle Thread

Bobbin Thread

Sometimes an unbalanced stitch works better than a perfectly balanced one. For example, a looser top tension will give you better buttonholes, smoother satin stitch embroidery, and more raised couching. Creative effects requiring different threads in the needle and bobbin also may call for unbalanced tension, such as the hand-quilted look you can achieve when using clear monofilament thread on top and cotton thread in the bobbin. For this stitch, tighten the top tension so the bobbin thread is pulled up visibly to form the "quilting" stitch. You may also need to loosen the bobbin tension.

## Troubleshooting

The wide variety of fabrics, threads, and special stitches we enjoy can influence thread tensions. If simple tension adjustments don't produce balanced stitches, there are other factors you can address before throwing in the towel:

*Thread quality:* Poor-quality threads aren't uniform, and the thick and thin areas can cause tension problems, not to mention lint build-up that clogs the tension discs. If the discs on your model are accessible, "floss" them with a smooth thread or lint-free cloth.

*Thread color:* Believe it or not, color matters. Darker colors can sometimes produce unevenness.

*Thread brand:* Some machines are calibrated at the factory using a specific thread brand. Ask the dealer what brand was used for your machine.

*Thread elasticity:* Some threads stretch more than others, especially during sewing, then relax after you've sewn with it, which causes puckers. Monofilament thread stretches easily; you may need to decrease the top tension for a satisfactory seam with this and other stretchy threads.

*Needle size:* Texturized nylon and heavyweight machine embroidery threads require a large-eye needle. If the eye is too small, it will resist thread flow. When using metallics, increase one or two needle sizes, or use a needle specifically made for metallic threads, and loosen the top tension to avoid friction and breakage.

*Stitch length:* If basic tension adjustments don't correct problems on slippery or thin fabrics, try a shorter stitch length.

 *Tips*

### Taming Bobbin Tension

Some machine models have an extra thread guide built into the bobbin case to increase the bobbin tension without touching the screw. Although manufacturers provide the screw to make bobbin tension adjustments possible, many experts recommend purchasing a second bobbin case for novelty uses so you can keep the original at its factory setting. Mark the secondary case with a dab of nail polish to avoid mix-ups.

### Winding Bobbins

Winding the bobbin at racing speed can stretch thread, so make it a habit to fill bobbins at a steady, medium speed.

## Adjusting Tension

Tension is like a tug-of-war—both threads should be equally strong.

If the bobbin thread pulls through to the top of your piece, loosen the top tension (or tighten the bobbin tension).

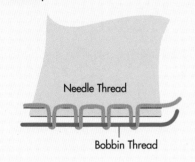

Needle Thread

Bobbin Thread

If the needle thread pulls through to the underside of your piece, tighten the top tension (or loosen the bobbin tension).

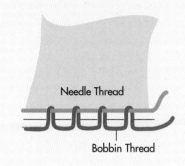

Needle Thread

Bobbin Thread

# How to Shop For a Machine

Regardless of the type of machine you are buying (sewing machine, embroidery, serger, or longarm), you should take a "test-drive" on prospective models, in addition to watching demonstrations.

***Fabrics:*** Bring your own fabrics so you can test sew on the variety of fabrics you use or plan to use.

***Feet and attachments:*** If you have specific sewing needs, try out the special feet or attachments to accomplish these types of sewing.

***Stitches:*** Try different stitches, varying length and width. Test the effects of speed on stitches, fabric feed, and tension.

***Threads:*** Bring your own thread along as well. Try decorative as well as utilitarian threads. Slippery rayons and finicky metallics will test any machine.

***Price:*** Although it shouldn't be your only criteria, you want the most for your money. It may be wiser—and less costly over time—to pay a bit more for the benefits of a full-service dealership. Do comparison shop at dealers in your area—many dealers will meet a competitor's lower price.

***Service and repairs:*** Ask questions about where repairs will be done, if shipping is required, and who is responsible for charges, yearly maintenance costs, and loaner machine availability during service periods.

***Warranties:*** Clarify exactly what is covered, for how long, and by whom.

***Other services:*** Ask if the dealer provides classes or other instruction on how to use your machine. For sewing and embroidery machines, there also may be monthly clubs to provide further instruction and inspiration. Find out what the dealer carries in attachments, embroidery cards, software updates, and specialty supplies available for use with your machine.

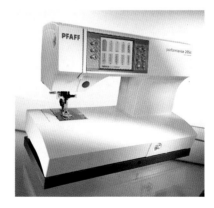

# COMPUTERIZED EMBROIDERY MACHINES

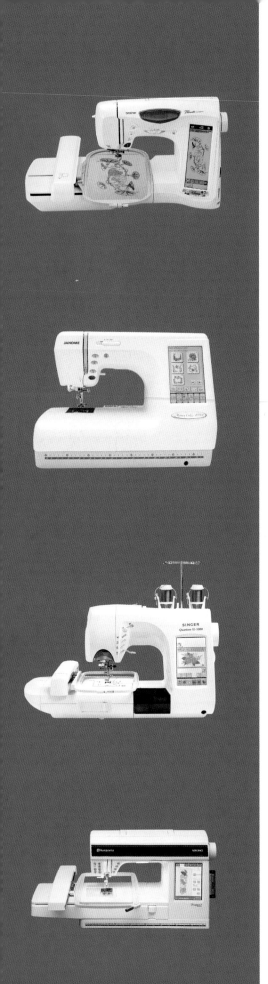

**Sew News *Staff***

*Most major sewing machine manufacturers offer models that come with computerized embroidery units designed for home use. Many embroidery designs are available on preprogrammed cards, disks, or CDs. You can also purchase software to create (digitize) your own designs. Here's a guide to some common terms and functions specific to embroidery.*

**Automatic thread cutters:** These clip the upper and/or lower threads at the end of each color in the design, or after each color in the stitching sequence.

**Built-in embroideries:** Available on some machines, many designs are exclusive to one brand and/or model.

**Built-in frames:** These allow you to make your own patches and crests. Many patterns are available to outline the frames. Some models offer frame patterns on embroidery cards or as a part of their machine-specific software.

**Built-in memory:** Save customized designs within the machine's program with this function.

**Color order information:** The color stitching sequence for each design can be seen on-screen and/or within the embroidery card booklets.

**Color skipping:** This feature allows you to stitch out specific parts of an embroidery pattern. It is also helpful for fixing areas that didn't stitch out properly.

**Combining designs:** On some machines, designs or text may be combined and stored in memory. Other machines allow designs from cards and text to be combined in a memory.

**Design area tracing:** This function instructs the machine to outline the embroidery area prior to beginning the actual stitching so you know the exact placement of the design. With this feature it's possible to place the tip of a water-soluble marker within the embroidery foot opening and trace the actual sewing area onto the item to be embroidered to ensure exact placement. It's also useful for appliqué embroidery.

**Design placement:** This function allows you to center a design precisely within the hoop area, even if it wasn't hooped perfectly. The amount of area available for adjustments will depend on the design and hoop size.

**Design rotation:** With rotation you can turn a design in the sewing field to properly position it regardless of which direction the project was hooped.

**Design scaling:** Changing an embroidery design while maintaining the same stitch density as the original size embroidery is a feature on some machines. Increasing or decreasing the design size will proportionately increase or decrease the number of stitches in the design.

**Design sizing:** This function allows you to change the stitched design size while the number of stitches in the design remains the same. Unless the machine has design scaling, a design made larger will have the stitching spaced farther apart, and a design made smaller will have more condensed stitching.

**Digitizing:** The process of creating a computer file that tells the sewing machine how to stitch out an embroidery design.

**Embroidery lettering fonts:** Text editing capabilities and fonts vary greatly between brands. Some models have several fonts built in; others require embroidery cards to access fonts. Scanners and machine-specific software may offer additional lettering options, such as arcing (placing letters on a curve) and kerning (adjusting the spacing between letters). Software is also available to create letters from computer fonts.

**Estimated embroidery time:** The approximate stitching time for a design may be available on-screen and/or within the embroidery card booklets.

**Low bobbin indicator lights:** Some machines have these warning messages that help prevent the possibility of sewing through a color only to discover that a portion of the color didn't stitch out.

**Maximum embroidery area:** When selecting designs you need to know the largest embroidery size that can be stitched in one fabric hooping. Every machine can embroider larger areas by hooping multiple times.

**Multiple-hooping alignment:** This allows you to re-hoop your design and still keep your design elements perfectly joined.

**Pattern size information:** This information may be available on screen and/or within the embroidery card booklets and tells exactly how large your finished design will be so you can determine if it fits within your intended space.

**Specialty hoops:** These accessories allow you to embroider baseball caps, pockets, and cuffs. Some brands also offer extra-large hoops that reduce the number of times a large design needs to be re-hooped, thus increasing accuracy.

**Stitch skipping:** This helps repair design areas that were removed and need to be restitched. It can be used for moving backward in a design after the needle thread breaks or frays. This feature also is useful for skipping over design parts you don't want to include.

**Upper thread monitors:** This feature stops the machine within a few stitches if the upper thread breaks or the thread runs out. Some machines allow the user to turn this function on or off.

## Want to Surf the Internet From Your Sewing Machine?

The newest embroidery machines not only have touch-screens that may look like your computer, some now have accessories that allow you to connect your machine to the Internet so that you can download embroidery designs and other stitches. You won't actually be able to "surf the net," but you will be able to connect to a dedicated Internet site or portal that will allow you to access that manufacturer's embroidery designs and stitches and download them to your sewing machine.

To use this feature, you'll need to purchase a modem from your sewing machine dealer or the manufacturer and will need access to an Internet provider.

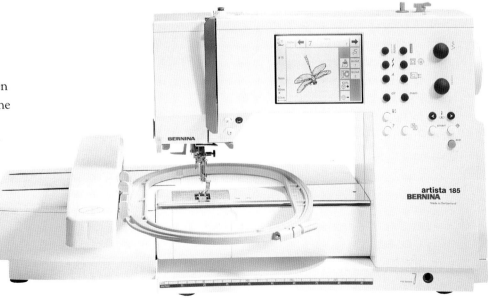

# Embroidery Software

*The term "embroidery software" is often used to refer both to computer software that allows you to download and manipulate embroidery designs, as well as the designs themselves.*

## Machine-specific Software

Most sewing machine manufacturers have their own software packages for use with their embroidery machines. You can use this software to create your own designs or modify existing designs as well as download designs to your machines.

## Independent-vendor Software

In addition to embroidery software specific to your brand of machine, you can purchase software to expand your embroidery cababilities. Software is available to allow you to catalog your designs, convert between embroidery-formats, resize designs and make other changes, and digitize your own designs.

## Embroidery Designs

Embroidery designs are available from a variety of sources including sewing-machine manufacturers and independent designers. Designs are generally available either on a CD, memory card, or computer diskette, or as a computer file downloaded from the Internet. With the wide variety of designs and formats available, it's best to talk to your dealer about what format you need to use for your machine, and what hardware or software you may need to transfer designs.

## Understanding Copyrights

As the use of home embroidery machines grows and the availability of embroidery designs expands, it is important to understand what's okay and what's not when it comes to copyrighted embroidery designs.

## Purchased Designs

Your purchase of embroidery software and designs grants you a license to:

- Embroider any item for personal use.

- Install the software on one computer or sewing machine of your choice.

- Modify the size and color of designs for personal preference.

- Stitch out licensed designs (like Sesame Street, Disney, Precious Moments, etc.) on garments and items for *personal use only*.

Restrictions involving the sale of sewn-out designs may be listed. Be sure to check the packaging for copyright information.

## Benefits of Purchasing Versus Copying Software

- All product documentation is included, and customer support is usually available.

- Registered users receive free update information.

- Helps keep your computer virus-free.

- Supports future product development while holding down the cost of goods.

## Copy Wrongs

When you purchase software or designs you may not:

- Duplicate the software or designs to sell, share, or distribute.

- Distribute any modified copyrighted computer files or designs.

- Install the software on more than one computer, sewing machine, or disk for multiple users.

- Upload, download, email, or transfer electronic files of copyrighted designs on the Internet, computer network, or direct connection.

Be sure to check the individual products you have purchased for additional restrictions.

Information on copyrights is provided by the Embroidery Software Protection Coalition, a nonprofit group of embroidery product manufacturers. Their purpose is to educate and help the consumer with copyright issues. Contact them toll-free at (888) 921-5732, or visit their website at www.embroideryprotection.org.

# SERGERS

Sergers are most commonly used in garment construction and to finish fabric edges so they don't unravel, but sergers offer a wealth of opportunities for decorative stitching. You should always refer to the manual for your specific machine as you explore new directions in decorative serging, but here's a quick guide to some of the common terms, functions, and features of today's machines.

*Differential feed:* Differential feed helps control puckering or stretching. Dual sets of feed dogs, one in front and one in back, control the fabric flow by moving at different speeds. (See pages 65–66 for more information on differential feed.)

*Loopers:* The moving metal "arms" under the needle plate that carry the threads responsible for forming the overlock stitch "loops."

*Looper threading:* Some machines are nearly self-threading, while others require you to carefully follow diagrams and/or color-coded or numbered pathways and use tweezers to get into different areas of the serger.

*Needle system:* Some sergers use household sewing machine needles, and some use shorter, round-shank industrial needles. Depending on the serger, the machine can use a single needle, two needles, or even three needles at a time for creating specialty stitches.

*Number of threads:* Sergers typically are manufactured in three-, four- or five-thread versions. Today, some top-of-the-line machines have as many as ten threads. The number of threads determines the types of stitches the serger is capable of. Three- to four-thread sergers are capable of basic overlocking stitches. Five-thread sergers are capable of chain and cover-stitching. Sergers with six to ten threads are capable of multi-needle coverstitching, decorative thread couching, and more.

*Roll-edge adjustment:* Most, but not all, sergers can make a narrow rolled edge. Conversion may require changing the throatplate and/or foot, or simply selecting a narrower stitch width and adjusting the looper tensions.

*Stitch finger:* The metal prong(s) on the needle plate that helps keep the stitches from drawing up the fabric edges during stitching.

*Stitch width and length adjustments:* The latest sergers have dials, levers, or touch-screen options to adjust the stitch width (or "bite") and length. Some older models are adjusted with a screwdriver or an internal mechanism.

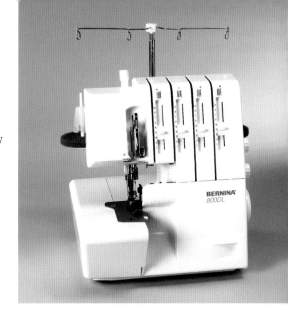

*Tension release:* This function allows pulling unchained thread lengths through the serger guides and eyes—handy for tying on new threads to "rethread" the machine without having to actually rethread each looper from scratch. On some sergers, a lever releases the tension; on others the tension releases when the presser foot is raised.

*Tension system:* Tension can be adjusted with a dial, a button, or on a touch screen. A few computerized and electronic models have automatic tensioning, where the serger sensors adjust according to the thread type and the stitch selected.

*Speed control / Stitching speed:* Consider these features if you do production sewing, dressmaking, or if you simply like to sew fast. Top speed is similar among sergers—usually 1,200 to 1,500 stitches per minute. If accuracy at slower rates is crucial, investigate dual speed and electronic controls.

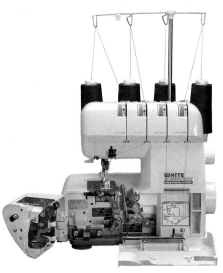

# SERGER STITCH DICTIONARY

*Garment construction, decorative edges, heirloom sewing, quilting, and more can be done quickly and easily with a serger. Here is a look at some of the basic stitches that are commonly available.*

### 3-Thread Stitch (Overlock)

This stitch is recommended for stretch seams to provide a durable edge finish. When balanced, the looper threads lock along the edge of the fabric.

For ideas for decorative uses see page 208–209 to make serger braid; pages 212–214 for double-sided serging; and page 220 for tucks.

### 4-Thread Stitch (Overlock)

The 4-thread stitch provides stabilization for light-weight edge finishes. When balanced, the looper threads lock along the edge of the fabric.

Decorative uses are similar to that of the 3-thread stitch.

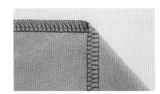

### 5-Thread Stitch

This stitch provides a durable seam and edge finish by combining a 2-thread chain stitch to create a seam with a 3-thread stitch to finish the edge.

### Blanket Stitch

The blanket stitch uses a 2- or 3-thread stitch with decorative threads in the needle and one looper to form the "blanket" stitches on the right side of the fabric.

For ideas for decorative uses see page 206.

### Chainstitch

The chainstitch functions like a conventional lockstitch (on a sewing machine) but forms a chain on the underside of the fabric. This stitch can also be used to make serger chain that can be used like any other decorative cording.

For ideas for decorative uses see pages 210–211 for creating chain; and page 217 for decorative chainstitching.

### Flatlock Stitch

This stitch provides a flat seam without bulk. The threads interlock forming straight "ladder" stitches on one side of the fabric.

For ideas for decorative uses see pages 215–217 for basic flatlocking; page 218 for decorative flatlocking; and pages 218–219 for flatlocked patchwork embroidery.

### Coverstitch

The coverstitch is a finishing stitch that looks like twin- or triple-needle stitching on the right side of the fabric. It is often used to hem knit garments or to join ribbing to a garment. It is also used to apply elastic and lace.

For ideas for decorative uses see pages 211–212.

*2-needle coverstitch*

*3-needle coverstitch*

### Rolled Edge Stitch

This stitch provides a very dense line of stitching to cleanly finish edges.

For ideas for decorative uses see page 214 for double-sided serging; pages 217 and 221 for lettuce edges; page 221 for pintucks; and page 221 for gathered shirring.

# SERGER PRESSER FEET

You'll find serger feet differentiate by machine brand. Check with your dealer to find out what feet are available for your machine. Some feet you may find are:

- Beading / pearl / sequin
- Blind hem
- Chainstitch
- Cording
- Cover hem
- Elastic
- Lace
- Narrow rolled-hem
- Piping
- Ribbon / tape
- Shirring / gathering

## Serger Needles

Some sergers use specialized serger needles, while other sergers use standard sewing machine needles. Check your manual to find what type is recommended for your brand of machine. Check with your dealer if in doubt.

# UNDERSTANDING DIFFERENTIAL FEED

*Naomi Baker*

*Differential feed used to be an optional feature, but it's now standard on almost every household serger. Using differential feed can be functional—perfecting basic serged seams and edges—or for purely decorative applications.*

## How It Works

The function of differential feed is to easily control the serged fabric using two sets of feed dogs: one that pushes the fabric under the presser foot and one that pulls the fabric from the back of the presser foot. Each set operates independently. Adjusting the differential feed determines how much the feed dogs will stretch or ease the fabric.

Back feed dogs move fabric out of presser foot

Front feed dogs move fabric into presser foot

The stitch-length setting determines how far the feed dogs move, so the movement of the back feed dogs is always determined by the stitch-length adjustment.

The differential feed adjusts the distance the front set of feed dogs moves, making shorter or longer strokes to affect how the fabric is moved. It is controlled by a knob or lever located on the serger front or side. Always test this feature on your chosen fabric before beginning your project. The numbers on the differential feed feature are ratios:

- When the differential feed is set on "N" or "1," the feed dogs move at the same ratio. Fabric is taken under the presser foot and released at the back of the presser foot at the same rate.

- When the differential feed is set on .5, below "1," or the "minus" setting, the front feed dogs move the fabric approximately half the distance of the rear feed dogs. The fabric is held taut or stretched; this setting prevents puckering of lightweight, sheer, or slippery fabrics.

- When the differential feed is set on the "positive" setting at 2, or above "1," the front feed dogs move approximately twice the distance of the back feed dogs. The fabric is fed under the foot faster than it's released from the back of the foot to avoid stretching; this setting can also ease or gather lightweight fabric. It prevents stretched or ruffled seams on knits, loosely constructed wovens or bias edges.

*(Continued on next page)*

## Setting Your Serger for Success

- If the lower layer ends up shorter when serging long sections, adjust the differential feed to a minus setting to make the lower layer fit.

- To ruffle stretchy fabrics, such as knit, bias, puckered, or crinkled fabrics, adjust the differential feed to the lower minus setting with a short length stitch. Stretch the fabric in front of and behind the presser foot while serging to ruffle.

- When serging outside curves or circles, such as tablecloths or napkins, adjust the differential feed to a plus setting to prevent stretching.

- Use differential feed to ease one fabric layer to another when one piece is longer, such as sleeves to a garment, shoulder seams, and elastic and ribbing applications. Serge with the longer layer on the underside. Adjust for a medium to long stitch length and a plus setting. The feed dogs will ease the underlayer to the upper layer without stretching the upper layer.

- Differential feed on a plus setting easily gathers lightweight fabric and finishes the edge in one step. Use a wide, medium to long, balanced stitch. The longer the stitch, the more the fabric will gather. Set the differential feed at 2 for maximum gathering.

- Gather or ease one layer when serging two layers. Lengthen the stitch and adjust the differential feed to 2. Hold the upper layer taut, away from the underlayer as you serge. The underlayer will gather as it's serged.

To produce additional gathers, especially on heavier fabrics, serge-gather a second time over a previously gathered edge, being careful not to cut the original gathering stitches.

## Gathering Foot

Most sergers have an optional foot available to gather one fabric layer while serging it to a straight edge, all in one step. Check with your dealer for availability. The gathering foot may also be called a separator attachment or fabric separator. This foot separates the fabric layers, keeping the upper layer flat and gathering the underlayer by adjusting the differential feed to a plus setting. It may also be used for gathering a single layer.

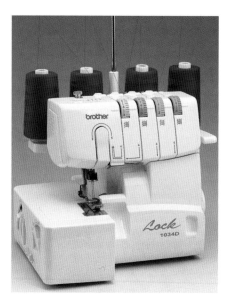

# Everything & Essential

Thread that doesn't break, needles that glide through fabric, embroidery that never puckers, colors that glow. . . . It's all possible when you understand the essentials.

# OH, THOSE THREADS

*Lynn Koolish*

*What is decorative stitching without thread? With so many different types of threads, it's hard to know where to begin when choosing.*

*For an overview of types of thread, there's a Thread Quick Reference chart on page 69, for more complete descriptions, you can read on about each type of thread and how it's made. To understand thread sizes see page 74. Read about tips and techniques for troubleshooting decorative threads on page 77. And don't miss the Thread size and Needle Quick Reference Chart on page 75.*

*If you have access to the Internet, thread manufacturers' websites often contain a wealth of information, including answers to frequently asked questions, tips, and techniques. See page 250 for a list of thread manufacturers and their websites.*

## A Few Things to Know

Sewing machines are adjusted at the factory for typical home sewing using medium-weight cotton thread for both the top and bobbin threads. With the ever-increasing variety of threads available, the more you know, the more successful you'll be when using decorative threads. If you are using thread or fabric you haven't worked with before, make some samples using the same fabric and thread you plan to use in your finished project. You may need to adjust either the top or bobbin tension (or both). See pages 57–59 for everything you need to know about machine tension. And finally, treat the samples as the finished item will be treated—iron, launder, press, et cetera so you know what to expect and won't be disappointed with the results.

Keep in mind that for machine arts, using decorative thread through the needle is only one of a number of techniques—decorative thread can also be used in the bobbin, couched, or made into thread lace or other embellishments.

## Types of Thread
### Cotton Thread

Cotton thread is used for all types of sewing. It is commonly suggested that the thread used to sew an item together should not be stronger than the fabric itself because it is generally easier to repair a ripped seam, than it is to repair torn fabric. This makes cotton thread appropriate for sewing woven fabrics for garments, quilts, and home décor.

When it comes to decorative stitching, cotton is also a good choice for those who prefer matte finish thread. Cotton comes in wide array of colors and thread weights. It has a soft hand and thread manufacturers are creating many exciting cotton threads that work well for quilting and decorative stitching. Hand-dyed cotton thread is also available in a range of sizes as well as wonderful colors and color combinations.

Cotton thread varies from very fine to very heavy. Some of the heavier weights of cotton (such as perle cotton) can be used as a top thread with a large

needle, or in the bobbin. Other heavy cotton threads can be used in the bobbin, or couched. These heavier-weight cottons, including crochet cotton, are great for decorative serging where they can be used in the loopers rather than through the needle.

To ensure high quality, look for cotton thread that is uniform in thickness, 100% long staple fibers, and mercerized. In addition to being stronger and more uniform, higher quality thread produces less lint in your sewing machine.

Cotton is not completely colorfast and items made with decorative cotton stitching should not be laundered with chlorine bleach.

### Rayon Thread

Rayon thread is a favorite for all types of decorative stitching. It comes in an almost endless array of colors and color combinations (twists, ombrés, multi-colors, and variegated), with new colors and combinations being created all the time. It is a soft thread with high sheen and creates beautiful stitches for all types of decorative techniques and machine embroidery.

Rayon is not durable for construction, but strength usually isn't a factor in most decorative stitching.

*(Continued on page 70)*

## THREAD QUICK REFERENCE

| Type | Characteristics |
| --- | --- |
| COTTON | Matte finish, good for general construction as well as decorative techniques |
| | Comes in many sizes; from extra fine for bobbins, to heavy for topstitching and couching |
| | Available in many colors, variegations, and hand-dyes |
| | For the best quality, look for long staple fibers, mercerized thread |
| | Avoid washing with chlorine bleach |
| RAYON | High sheen, good for many types of decorative stitching |
| | Comes in many sizes for embroidery, as well as serging and couching |
| | Not as strong as some other threads |
| | Avoid washing with chlorine bleach and detergents with optical brighteners |
| POLYESTER | *Spun* polyester has a matte finish, good for general construction and serging, as well as decorative techniques |
| | *Filament* polyester has a high sheen, good for embroidery and other decorative techniques |
| | *Texturized* polyester has a matte finish, provides soft and stretchable finish used primarily for serged edge finishes |
| | Comes in a variety of weights, including extra fine for bobbins |
| | Available in many colors and variegations |
| | Strong, durable, colorfast |
| COTTON-COVERED POLYESTER | Matte finish, more often used for general sewing than for decorative stitching Has strength similar to that of polyester, with the softer hand and matte finish of cotton |
| ACRYLIC | High sheen for embroidery, texturized for serging |
| | Colorfast even in bleach, good choice for items that will be laundered |
| NYLON (TEXTURIZED) | Matte finish, used primarily for serged-edge finishes |
| | Available in a variety of weights, even metallic and variegated |
| | Provides soft and stretchable finish |
| MONOFILAMENT | Available in clear and dark or smoke |
| | Nylon monofilament has low heat resistance, can become brittle and yellow |
| | Polyester monofilament has higher heat resistance than nylon monofilament |
| METALLIC | Available in a variety of finishes including matte, shiny, iridescent, pearlescent, flat laminates, and holographic |
| | Comes in a variety of sizes from very fine to heavy and textured, perfect for couching |
| SILK | High sheen |
| | Available in a variety of weights and colors |
| WOOL AND ACRYLIC BLEND | Matte finish, soft fuzzy feel |
| | Use as a top thread or in the bobbin, can be used for machine embroidery |
| BOBBIN | Lightweight cotton or polyester, made especially for bobbins |
| FUSIBLE | Melts when ironed, use for basting or holding materials in place |
| WATER-SOLUBLE | Dissolves in water, use for basting, trapunto, and other temporary stitching |
| GLOW-IN-THE-DARK | Glows in the dark |
| SOLAR-REACTIVE | Changes color in the sun |

Heavier weight rayon threads and narrow rayon ribbons are excellent for decorative stitching with sergers (use in the loopers), bobbinwork, or for couching.

Rayon thread is not completely colorfast and items made using rayon shouldn't be laundered with bleach or detergents with optical brighteners. Rayon thread can also shrink if laundered. Items made with rayon thread can be dry-cleaned.

## Polyester Thread

Spun polyester is strong, durable, colorfast, and has a matte finish. In addition to general sewing, polyester thread is often used as an all-purpose serging or overlock thread.

Filament polyester, the newer trilobal polyesters in particular, have a high sheen that makes them a good choice for decorative stitching. Filament polyesters are also a little stiffer than rayon thread so they may stand out a little more, providing more depth or texture, making it a good choice for satin stitching as well as other decorative uses.

Filament polyester maintains the characteristics of spun polyester; it is strong, colorfast, and more resistant to UV fading than cotton or rayon. It is not as strong as spun polyester but, as with rayon, strength is usually not an issue with decorative stitching. Trilobal polyester in particular produces less lint, keeping your machine cleaner.

Texturized polyester is similar to texturized nylon (see below) but has the colorfast and heat-resistant characteristics of other polyesters.

Polyester thread comes in a number of weights and a wide variety of colors and variegations. Polyester is a great choice for kids' clothes because it's strong and colorfast.

## Cotton-covered Polyester Thread

Cotton-covered polyester is a blend of fibers and as a result has a blend of each fiber's characteristics. It provides strength similar to that of polyester, with the softer hand and matte finish of cotton. It is more often used for general sewing than for decorative stitching.

## Acrylic Thread

Acrylic thread can be used for serging and for decorative stitching. Sometimes you'll find it combined with other fibers such as polyester or wool. Acrylic thread is colorfast even in bleach so it is a good choice for items that will be laundered. Acrylic thread can have a matte finish or a high sheen.

## Nylon Thread

Nylon is used either as a monofilament or as a texturized thread such as Woolly Nylon for serging a soft and stretchable seam. Texturized nylon comes in a variety of weights and in metallic for decorative serging.

Nylon thread is strong, but is not heat resistant and can melt when ironed. Nylon can yellow and become brittle over time and with laundering.

## Monofilament Thread

Monofilament threads, made of polyester or nylon come in two "colors," clear, and dark or smoke. Polyester monofilament is softer and won't melt with ironing. Use clear on light colors and smoke on dark colors.

Monofilament can be used as a top thread for couching, quilting, invisible appliqué, as well as a faux hand-quilting stitch available on some newer sewing machines (see page 50).

Monofilament can also be used in the bobbin. Try using monofilament in the bobbin when using metallic thread. The monofilament is slick and won't grab the metallic thread, resulting in smooth, even stitches. When winding bobbins, wind them slowly and don't load too much thread. Too much thread on a plastic bobbin can cause it to break.

## Silk Thread

Silk thread is smooth and has sheen unique to this fiber. It is strong, and available in a variety of colors and weights. It is more expensive that other threads, but may be worth considering for a special project.

## Wool-blend Thread

Several wool and acrylic blend threads are available and are great for a folk-art look or a soft and fuzzy feel. They can be used either as a top thread or in the bobbin. You can even use them for machine embroidery.

# Metallic Thread

There's nothing like metallic thread to add sparkle and shine. Like other decorative thread, metallics now come in an ever-increasing variety of colors, variegations, iridescents, and pearlescents. Metallic thread is also available in a variety of sizes and textures that range from smooth and fine to heavy and textured, perfect for couching.

A subcategory of metallic threads is the laminate or flat thread. These are made of combinations of polyesters, acrylics, and metallic materials to provide other sparkling looks, including holographic.

More than any other decorative thread, metallics have a reputation for being difficult to work with. For trouble-free stitching, buy high-quality thread (look for thread that is uniform in size and unwinds smoothly from the spool without kinking or tangling). Be sure to use the correct needle type and size adjust the top tension. See Troubleshooting Tips on page 77 for more suggestions.

*(Continued on next page)*

There are many metallic threads to choose from. Here's how some of the different threads look on the spool and stitched out. The best way to see the differences is to buy several types to make your own thread reference sampler. Then you can decide which you like best for the type of stitching you do.

Rayon is included for comparison.

*Rayon*

*Shiny metallic*
*(Sulky Metallic)*

*Metallic luminous*
*(Glow-in-the-dark)*
*(YLI Brilliance)*

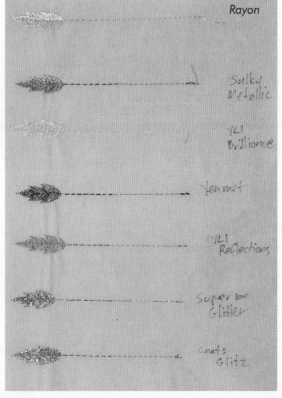

*Stitch reference sample*

*Pearlescent metallic*
*(Yenmet Pearlessence)*

*Translucent metallic*
*(YLI Reflections)*

*Flat holographic*
*laminate metallic*
*(Superior Glitter)*

*Flat laminate metallic*
*(Coats Glitz)*

## Bobbin Thread

It is often recommended that light-weight cotton or polyester thread be used in the bobbin to prevent a build-up of thread on the underside of the fabric when doing decorative stitching and machine embroidery. It can also help alleviate problems specific to metallic threads. Bobbin thread is available on spools, cones, and as pre-wound bobbins.

## Specialty Threads
### Fusible Thread

Fusible thread melts or fuses when ironed. One use for fusible thread is to replace basting to hold fabric or other materials such as ribbons and other trim in place prior to couching or stitching them down.

There are also decorative threads that are fusible. Fusing allows these threads to be precisely positioned and fused in place to make it easier to couch or otherwise stitch them down. Some fusible thread may be secure without stitching

### Solar-reactive Thread

Solar-reactive thread is a fun thread that changes color when exposed to sunlight. The thread appears colorless or pastel on the spool, but changes to a brighter color in the sun.

### Water-soluble Thread

Water-soluble thread dissolves in water. It is commonly used to temporarily hold fabric or trims in place as with basting or machine trapunto (see pages 234–235).

## Variegated Thread

Many types of variegated thread are available. Some change quickly from one color to the next, some have longer sections of each color. Whether the thread is cotton, polyester, or metallic, variegated threads add a colorful touch to your stitching.

Here are some examples of what the thread looks like on the spool, and what it looks like when it's stitched out. Notice how the spacing of the variegation differs.

Even though two spools of thread may look different (because of the way they're wound or the size of the spool), they can stitch out exactly the same.

### Quick Trick
#### Water-soluble Thread for Basting
*Ricky Tims*
Use water-soluble thread for basting quilts, either by hand or by machine. When the quilting is done, wet or block the quilt to dissolve the thread, and you don't have to worry about pulling out all the little basting threads.

## Glow-in-the-dark Thread

Yes, there is actually thread that glows in the dark after being activated by a light source. These threads can be used for fun or safety.

*(Continued on page 74)*

# How Thread Is Made

Thread is made by spinning natural fibers or by extruding synthetic filaments into yarn. The individual strands of yarn are twisted for strength and flexibility. These twisted strands of yarn are referred to as plies. Two or three plies are then twisted together to create the finished thread. You may be surprised to know that the direction of that final twist can have a major impact on how easy the thread is to use in your machine.

## Twist

Threads specifically designed for sewing machines are made with a "Z" or left twist. As the thread goes through the machine, the twist increases, and as a result, reduces the possibility of the thread untwisting during sewing.

Some threads are made with an "S" twist, which can untwist as it goes through the machine, causing it to fray and break.

If you have a choice, a thread with a Z-twist will be easier to use. Threads with an S-twist can be used in the machine, but require more care.

One way to determine the twist is to hold the thread in your left hand, and roll the thread with your right hand. Z-twist thread unrolls when thread is rolled to the right, S-twist thread unrolls when rolled to the left.

## Spun Threads

Cotton, some polyester, and a few rayon threads are made by spinning lengths of fiber called staples into the yarn or plies. The plies are then twisted together to create the thread. Most sewing threads are 3-ply while purely decorative threads are often 2-ply.

Spun threads have a fuzzy or fibrous surface that results in a soft hand and low sheen. This also minimizes thread breakage and makes them good sewing threads.

The longer the staple length of the fibers, the better the quality of the resulting threads. Long staple fibers also produce less lint in the sewing machine.

Mercerization is also a sign of quality. Mercerized thread has gone through a process that treats cotton fibers so they are more uniform. This increases the strength of the thread and allows it to accept dyes more readily, giving the thread more luster.

## Filament Threads

Polyester, acrylic, and most rayon threads are made by extruding a continuous filament or ply. Each ply is twisted, and two plies are twisted together to form a thread that is strong and uniform.

Filament threads are not as soft as spun threads. This can make the threads stand out more from the fabric, which can be a plus in decorative stitching. They also have a higher sheen.

## Core-spun Threads

Core-spun thread, such as cotton-covered polyester, is a combination of spun and filament threads. This combines the strength of filament threads with the softness of spun thread. The component yarns are made using a filament polyester core and covered with either cotton or spun polyester. The composite yarn is then twisted into 2- or 3-ply thread. Core-spun threads often have greater strength than other threads of comparable thickness.

## Monofilament Threads

A single filament of polyester or nylon is extruded to create monofilament thread. For home sewing, very fine thread, size .004 or .005, is most common. Monofilament is sometimes called invisible thread because it is so fine that it is hard to see.

## Metallic Threads

Metallic threads are made either by using a metallic wrapping or coating around an inner core of nylon, rayon, or polyester; or as a flat film, cut into specific widths. Look for thread that is smooth and consistent in size.

Flat film threads or laminates are made by bonding together layers of polyester and other materials and slicing to the desired width. These threads are very bright and reflective and can be made to have a holographic look.

Metallic threads are generally heat resistant, so they can be ironed—but make a sample to test first.

## Textured Threads

Textured threads such as Woolly Nylon, textured polyester, or textured acrylic are created using a process that creates softness and bulk. These provide excellent coverage for edges and are most often used in sergers.

# Thread Size

Thread size is a key factor in selecting appropriate needles. Thread size is also important when selecting threads for specific purposes. For example, you know an embroidery design works well with a 40-weight rayon, but you'd like to use a matte cotton thread instead. What equivalent cotton thread should you use to get the same stitch density?

Unfortunately different sizing systems are commonly used for different types of thread making it somewhat difficult to compare the thickness of one type of thread to another.

Fortunately, a sizing system called Tex that was introduced to standardize references to thread thickness, is becoming more prevalent making it easier to compare threads (see next page for a Tex comparison chart).

## Cotton Thread (Spun Thread)

Cotton threads are denoted by thread count number and number of plies, for example 50/3 is all-purpose sewing thread.

### Cotton Count

Cotton Count is the standard sizing system for spun threads such as cotton. It is based on how many yards of thread it takes to equal 1 pound of thread. The thicker the thread, the fewer yards needed, consequently the lower count number. The number of plies comes into play when comparing equivalent weights of thread: The same size thread can be made by using different thread count (thickness) yarns and different numbers of plies: a 30/2 thread (thicker thread, fewer plies) is equivalent in size as a 45/3 thread (thinner thread, more plies).

Cotton threads designed for construction are generally 3-ply threads. For example: 100/3 is very fine thread, 50/3 is a standard sewing thread, 40/3 a common quilting thread, and 18/3 is a heavyweight jeans or topstitch thread. You'll notice in these sizes, that *the higher the thread count number, the finer the thread.*

There are also 2-ply cotton threads designed for decorative stitching. A 60/2 is a fine thread that is good for machine embroidery or satin stitching, while a 12/2 is a heavyweight thread that is good for bold quilting or top stitching.

## Rayon and Polyester (Filament Thread)

Rayon and polyester threads for embroidery and decorative stitching are generally 2-ply and often denoted by a weight. As with cotton, the higher the weight number, the finer the thread. A 30-weight rayon or polyester is thicker than a 40-weight thread. Most embroidery designs are intended to be stitched out using 40-weight thread.

### Denier

Denier is the sizing system for continuous filament thread such as polyester and most rayon thread. Denier is the gram weight of 9,000 meters of thread, consequently, the thicker the thread, the more it weighs, the higher the denier. However, if you look at your spools of rayon or polyester thread, you'll often see a weight number rather than denier number. This is because

for most filament threads, the denier is converted into a weight which works in a manner similar to the cotton count with a higher number denoting a thinner thread.

## Metallic Thread

Metallic threads created by winding metallic material around a core may be numbered in a manner similar to filament threads such as rayon and polyester, or may have no number. Many flat or ribbon metallics don't have a number, size, or weight on them.

## Tex

In an attempt to standardize the sizing systems for thread, the thread industry is slowly adopting the Tex system. It is a more logical system because it is based simply on the weight in grams of 1,000 meters of thread—the lower the Tex number the finer the thread.

With this system, all the different types of thread, regardless of how they are made, can be compared to each other using the Tex number. Formulas are available to convert all the different sizing systems to Tex numbers, but for your convenience, on the next page is a Quick Reference chart that includes the most commonly used threads.

## THREAD SIZE AND NEEDLE QUICK REFERENCE

| Thread Type/size, weight, or denier | Tex size | Needle Size Recommendation |
|---|---|---|
| **Lightweight Threads (Tex 10 – Tex 24)** | | |
| Monofilament .004 | 10 | 60/8 - 90/14 |
| Silk #100 | 12 | 75/11 - 80/12 |
| Cotton embroidery 60/2 | 18 | 65/9 - 75/11 |
| Acrylic embroidery 40-weight, 120/2 | 24 | 90/14 embroidery |
| Metallic embroidery 40-weight, 120/2 | 24 | 80/12 - 90/14 metallic |
| Polyester embroidery 120/2 | 24 | 90/14 embroidery |
| Rayon embroidery 40-weight, 40-weight | 24 | 75/11 - 90/14 embroidery |
| Woolly Nylon 220 denier | 24 | Use in serger loopers |
| **Mediumweight Threads (Tex 27 – Tex 35)** | | |
| Cotton, all-purpose 40/2 | 27 | 70/10 - 80/12 |
| Polyester/Cotton, all-purpose 35/2 | 27 | 70/10 - 80/12 |
| Polyester, serger 42/2 or 60/3 | 27 | 70/10 - 90/14 |
| Rayon embroidery 35-weight | 27 | 90/14 embroidery |
| Silk #50 | 27 | 80/12 - 90/14 |
| Cotton embroidery 30/2 or all purpose 50/3 | 35 | 75/11 - 80/12 |
| Polyester, all-purpose 50/3 | 35 | 75/11 or 80/12 |
| **Heavyweight Threads (Tex 40 – Tex 90)** | | |
| Cotton 25/2 or quilting 40/3 | 40 | 90/14 - 100/16 |
| Polyester quilting 40/3 | 40 | 75/11 - 80/12 |
| Rayon embroidery 30-weight | 40 | 90/14 - 100/16 embroidery |
| Cotton topstitching 30/3 | 50 | 90/14 - 100/16 |
| Polyester topstitching 30/3 or 530/1 | 50 | 90/14 - 100/16 |
| Cotton topstitching 12/2 | 60 | 90/14 - 100/16 |
| Silk #30 | 60 | 90/14 - 100/16 |
| Cotton top or jeans stitching 18/3 | 90 | 100/16 |

## Threads and Spools

*Thread is wound onto spools in one of two ways: parallel or cross-wound. The way thread is wound onto the spool, affects how it should come off of the spool when you are sewing. Read on to find out why it matters whether the spool pin is horizontal or vertical.*

## Parallel-wound

Thread that is wound straight or parallel (the strands of thread are all parallel to each other) works best when used on a vertical spool pin so the spool turns and the thread unwinds. When used on a horizontal spool where the thread is pulled over the end of the spool, the thread can twist and kink causing it to fray or break.

## Cross-wound

Thread that is cross-wound (the strands of thread cross over each other) works best when used on a horizontal spool pin or a thread stand so the thread can pull up over the top of the spool. Cross-wound thread can be used on a vertical spool pin, if that is all that is available on the machine.

## Spool Pins

Spool pins on sewing machines are designed to hold standard home-sewing size spools of thread. Some sewing machines come with both a vertical and horizontal spool pin; some machines come with one type of spool pin and an accessory that provides the other type of spool pin orientation. Other sewing machines, especially older models, may come with only one type of spool pin. If your sewing machine has only a horizontal spool pin and you're using decorative threads, you may want to look into purchasing a thread stand so that the thread can unwind properly. Thread stands can also accommodate the larger spool sizes that are becoming more common.

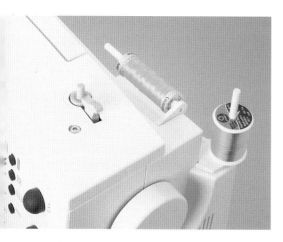

## Spool Sizes

Thread comes in a number of spool sizes. Some are designed for regular sewing machines, some for sergers, some for commercial applications (but that doesn't mean you can't use them with your home machine.) The amount of thread on a spool or cone varies. Some specialty thread spools contain as little as 5 yards, while cones can hold up to 6,000 yards of thread.

Whether you buy a small spool or a large cone will depend on how much thread you use. Thread can dry out and become brittle so you shouldn't buy more than you are going to use within a reasonable amount of time, which depends on your working environment and thread storage. See below for more on thread storage.

You may also need a thread stand and/or cone adaptor to use the cones or mini-cones. Wooden inserts are also available for the larger spools and mini-king spools. (See page 98 for thread stands and other accessories.)

## Storage

To extend the life of your thread, store it in a dust-free location away from direct sources of heat and ultra-violet (UV) light. Sunlight and many types of indoor lighting are sources of UV light, so thread is best kept in drawers or covered bins. If you live in a climate with low humidity, your thread is also likely to dry out faster, so you may also want to keep it in sealed plastic bags.

Some people advocate keeping the more fragile threads (such as rayons and metallics) in a sealed plastic container and storing the container in the freezer as a way to extend the life of the thread. If you choose to put your thread in the freezer, be sure the thread is warmed to room temperature before using.

When it comes to storing thread in your sewing room or studio there are many options. Some people like to keep their most-often-used threads on the wall in thread racks, and some use plastic storage containers designed specifically for thread. Others use plastic tubs designed for food storage, craft

supplies, or even containers designed to hold toy cars. Thread can also be kept in baskets, tins, bins, drawers, or any other type of container that suits your style and budget.

To keep thread tidy, some spools are designed with a way to secure the loose end of the thread—it may be a slit cut into the edge of the spool, a groove around the top of the spool, or a special ring that fits into the top of the spool. You can also wrap clear self-sticking tape or clear, thin vinyl around the spools to keep the thread neat.

*Clear self-sticking tape*

If you are using older cotton thread that breaks while you are sewing, it has probably dried out. You may be able to re-moisturize it either by spritzing the thread with water so it can re-absorb moisture or putting it into the refrigerator where it may pick up moisture. Be sure thread is dry and at room temperature before using.

For thread that just can't be used in the machine, use it to make, thread and ribbon scarves (see page 172), or tassels (see pages 233–234).

*Oh, Those Threads* was compiled from information provided by thread manufacturers, conversations with experienced thread users, and other published material.

# Troubleshooting Tips For Decorative Threads

**Rosemary Eichorn**

*Decorative threads have an undeserved reputation for being difficult to use.*

**For trouble-free decorative sewing refer to your machine manual as needed and make sure:**

- The machine is clean and free of lint. Clean and lubricate your machine after every two bobbin changes.

- The machine is threaded properly. Top thread must be firmly seated between the tension discs.

- The needle is inserted all the way and facing the correct direction.

- The top tension is adjusted correctly. You often need to loosen the top tension when sewing with decorative threads.

- The bobbin is inserted into the case correctly and the bobbin case is inserted completely and correctly into the machine.

- You are using the correct needle for the type of thread. If a universal needle doesn't work, use a Metallica or Metalfil needle for most metallic threads. Use a titanium coated needle for flat metallic threads. Alternatively, use a top stitch needle.

Use the smallest needle that will work with the threads and fabric you've chosen. A size 80/12 needle works for most circumstances. If you are not sure, check with your local quilt or fabric store, or the thread manufacturer's website.

**If all of the above are okay, and you are still having trouble with your thread, here are some things to try:**

- Sew at an even, moderate speed. If your machine has a half-speed, slow speed, or speed control, use it. Sewing with decorative threads builds up friction causing heat with fast stitching. This can cause fraying and breakage.

- When using metallic and rayon threads, avoid tiny stitches to obtain the most visual luster from the threads.

- Replace needles when they become dull or burred. Recommendations vary, but a good rule of thumb is to replace your needle with every new project. If you hear a popping sound when you sew, try a new needle.

- Use a horizontal spool pin only with cross-wound threads. If you're having trouble with the thread spinning off too fast, use a vertical spool pin. Use a vertical spool pin with all parallel wound threads. The way the thread comes off the spool can affect your sewing. If your thread seems to be over-twisting as you sew, turn the spool over so that it unwinds in the opposite direction.

- Use a thread stand—especially one with an arm that raises the thread above the level of the machine to reduce tension. Set the stand as far away from your machine as possible.

- Use Sewer's Aid or other silicone product—check with your dealer first to make sure it's okay to use such a product directly on thread that will go through tension discs. If you are not sure, apply the product to a part of the machine past the point where the thread passes through the tension discs, such as above the last thread guide before the thread enters the needle. (See pages 78–79 for more on using thread lubricants.)

- When using a spun metallic thread, bypass the last thread guide before thread passes through the needle. Metallic threads can file a groove in the needle clamp.

- Try another spool of similar thread. If the problem goes away, it is most likely a problem with the thread. If the thread is old, it may have lost its strength. Make little tassels with the faulty spool and buy a new spool for sewing.

- Use the thread in the bobbin. If you do much bobbinwork, consider buying a separate bobbin case that you can adjust for your special threads. If your thread is quite heavy, try bypassing the bobbin case's tension altogether.

# THREAD LUBRICANTS

*Peggy Bendel*

*Is thread lubricant a magic elixir that solves stitching problems or a poison potion to a sewing machine's delicate inner parts? It depends . . . on your sewing machine brand, which lubricant you choose, and how wisely you use it.*

## Types of Lubricants

Currently, there are three types of thread lubricants available for consumer use:

- Silicone suspended in a fluid (Sewer's Aid)

- Silicone suspended in an evaporating medium that includes a cleaning agent (Lube-It-All)

- Teflon suspension in an evaporating medium that includes a petroleum component (Tri-Flow)

## How They Work

In theory, these products all work in a similar way. If you could see a magnified close-up of a metal surface, such as the eye of a needle or a sewing machine bobbin hook, you'd notice it has very tiny pits; these pits are present on even the finest metal sewing tools and equipment. Silicone or Teflon particles act as microscopic ball bearings to fill in these pits, making the metal smoother and reducing friction. This is of special importance when using a metallic thread (metal on metal creates more friction than fiber on metal) or a weak thread, such as rayon; when stitching through fabrics such as vinyl or tapestry that tend to drag on the needle; or when embroidering a dense

motif through fabric backed with multiple stabilizer layers. With less friction, the needle stays cooler, and the thread is less likely to shred, and the machine is less likely to skip stitches.

When thread lubricants were first introduced to home sewing, the favored application method was to "stripe" the spool by applying a thin line of lubricant from top to bottom, then letting it bleed into the surrounding thread. Now other, more effective thread treatment methods are available as there are several other ways to apply the lubricants. One way is a thread stand that applies the lubricant immediately after it leaves the spool. Another way is an applicator that attaches to the sewing machine just above the needle and applies the lubricant just before it enters the needle's eye. (See page 98 for details on thread stands.)

Some sewing machines have rubber or plastic parts in the tension assembly that can be damaged by lubricants, and some have computerized tension systems that become "confused" when lubricated thread passes through them. Check with your dealer before choosing a thread lubricant applicator. Ask whether applying lubricant before or after the tension assembly is recommended for your model. Also ask which lubricant brand is recommended, as some machine manufacturers claim certain lubricants deposit damaging residues on their machines' moving parts.

## Smooth Solutions

With the many thread types and machine stitches in use today, even the most ardent thread lubricant fans claim it's only part of the solution when you encounter stitching problems. Check the following before applying a single drop of lubricant.

- *Needle:* There are specialty needles for use with metallic threads, microfiber fabrics, heavy-duty fabrics, and very fine threads, as well as quilting and machine embroidery needles. The right needle can make a big difference in stitching success. (See pages 80–82 for more on needles.)

  A new, sharp needle can make all the difference in your sewing. If you're having trouble, try changing to a new needle.

- *Tension:* Many decorative threads are pretty, but not always strong enough to sew seams. Many of these novelty threads stitch more smoothly when the tension is reduced. (See pages 57–59 for more on adjusting tension.)

- *Thread Feeding:* Thread should unwind from the spool and enter the first tension guide on the machine without kinking, twisting, or puddling. Switching from a horizontal spool holder to a vertical spindle may be all you need to do to stitch successfully with metallic thread. Slippery threads often feed better when you cover them with a thread net, or if you are using a serger, use a horizontal spool holder. Various thread management

accessories are available for both sergers and conventional sewing machines to help you modify how the thread feeds. (See page 75 for more information on the correct use of horizontal and vertical spool pins.)

Some thread brands feed fine from the first two-thirds of a spool, but the remainder causes problems because of the way the thread is wound or curled onto the spool; in these cases, you may have to discard the end of the spool.

- *Machine Condition:* Have you recently broken a needle? Burrs on the throatplate may cause the thread to catch before a stitch forms. Is the timing due for adjustment? A tune-up may be needed to keep the delicate dance between needle and bobbin hook in perfect step. (See page 77 for more tips on sewing with decorative threads.)

## Important Note

Be sure to check with your dealer before using any type of thread lubricant. Some sewing machines have rubber or plastic parts in the tension assembly that can be damaged by lubricants. Ask if thread lubricants can be used, what brand they recommend, and how to apply the lubricant.

# NEEDLES

*Laurie Baker*

*Sewers used to have two choices for needles—a sharp for wovens, and a ballpoint for knits. But that's not the case any more. Picking up a packet of needles for your next project isn't as simple as it used to be. Even when you follow all the guidelines, make a test sample using the fabric, thread, and needle you plan to use.*

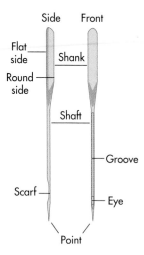

## Parts of the Needle

All needles have the same parts, but the configurations differ.

**Shank:** The upper portion of the needle is called the shank. For home machines, it's usually round on one side and flat on the other. Check your sewing machine manual for instructions on properly inserting this portion of the needle into the machine. Improper insertion can cause skipped stitches, no stitches at all, or broken needles.

**Shaft or Blade:** The lower portion that extends from the base of the shank to the point is called the shaft. The groove, eye, scarf, and point are all parts of the shaft.

**Groove:** The groove is the indentation on the shaft, on the rounded side. It acts as the last thread guide and provides a protective channel for the thread as the needle passes through the fabric to form the stitch.

**Scarf:** The scarf is an indentation on the flat side, right above the eye. The scarf allows the bobbin case hook to get close to the needle eye and catch the thread to form a stitch.

**Eye:** This is the hole above the point of the needle through which the needle thread passes. Its job is to carry the top thread into the bobbin case so the stitch can form. The size of the eye varies with the needle type to accommodate different thread types and weights. Select a needle with an eye that is the appropriate size for the chosen thread; otherwise, stitches may not form properly or the thread may be damaged. (See next page for a quick needle and thread compatibility quiz.)

**Point:** The point is the tip that pierces the fabric. Needle points are specifically designed to pierce a particular fabric type.

*From top to bottom: Universal, Embroidery, Metallic, Quilting, Sharp, Stretch, Ballpoint, Jeans/Denim, Jeans twin, Leather, Topstitch, Self-threading, Twin, Twin, Triple, Wing, Spring, Serger*

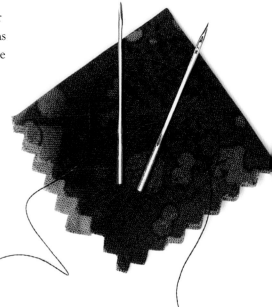

## Needle Sizes

Needles are sized according to two systems: European and American. Usually, both numbers are marked on the packaging, with the European (larger) number first. Some brands use a color-coding system in addition to the numbering system so the needle size can be easily identified. The numbers refer to the diameter of the needle shaft ranging from 60/8 (the finest) to 120/19 (the thickest).

## Needle Types

The basic rules for selecting a sewing machine needle still hold true: sharp point for woven fabrics, ballpoint for knits, and universal point for both wovens and knits. However, options now also include needles for specific fabrics and specialty threads. (See chart on page 82 for information on available needles.)

## Needle Selection

Thread, fabric, and the needle all work together in stitch formation, so all must be considered before taking the first stitch. Selecting a needle point based on the fabric type—woven or knit—is key, but fabric weight, which will determine the needle size, is also a factor.

The general rule for needle size is: the finer the fabric, the finer the needle. For example, when sewing on lightweight cotton, an 80/12 universal needle would be appropriate. But for sewing on denim, you might need a sharp-point needle or jeans needle, size 100/16 or 110/18. Just because both garments are made from a cotton fiber doesn't mean you can use the same needle.

Next, consider the thread selected for the project. The needle descriptions on the next page are a good place to start. Several needles are made for specific types of threads, and selecting one of them from the outset can make your sewing go more smoothly. There isn't a specific needle type for every fabric/thread combination, but knowing this basic information will make it easier.

If the eye of the needle is too small for the thread to pass through, the thread will shred. If the eye is too large, the holes created by the needle will be visible because the thread isn't heavy enough to fill them. The needle eye should be about twice the size of the thread.

After weighing all the factors, stitch some samples on fabric scraps comparable to the project fabric. Take the time to find the right fabric, thread, and needle combination for the best results in your stitching ventures.

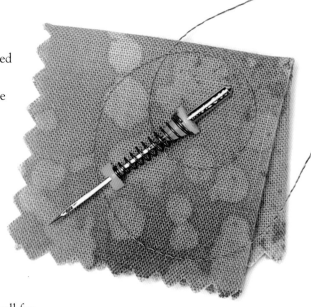

## Compatibility Quiz

To test the thread/needle compatibility, thread a 12" length of the desired thread through the needle you think is the correct size. Hold the thread vertically and fairly taut with the needle at the top of the thread. Spin the needle. If it slips down the thread, you're on the right track. If not, you need a larger needle.

| NEEDLE SIZES | |
| --- | --- |
| European | American |
| 60 | 8 |
| 65 | 9 |
| 70 | 10 |
| 75 | 11 |
| 80 | 12 |
| 90 | 14 |
| 100 | 16 |
| 110 | 18 |
| 120 | 19 |

# NEEDLE QUICK REFERENCE

| NEEDLE TYPE | DESCRIPTION | USES | SIZES |
|---|---|---|---|
| Ballpoint | Medium, slightly rounded tip that goes between threads rather than piercing them | Knit fabric | 70/10 - 100/16 |
| Sharp | Sharp point to pierce threads | Woven fabrics; heirloom sewing; when perfectly straight stitching is desired | 60/8 - 90/14 |
| Universal | Point is slightly rounded for use with knit fabrics, yet sharp enough to pierce woven fabrics | Most woven and knit fabrics; all household sewing machines that accept a flat shank | 60/8 - 120/19 |
| Denim/Jeans | Extra-sharp point and stiff shank | Stitching denim, or other densely woven fabrics; stitching through multiple fabric layers | 70/10 - 110/18 |
| Leather | Wedge-shaped point easily penetrates tough fabrics | Leather; heavy, faux leather; suede; and other heavy, nonwoven fabrics | 80/12 - 110/18 |
| Machine embroidery | Specially designed scarf and large eye prevent shredding and breakage | Rayon, metallic, and other machine embroidery threads; dense embroidery designs | 65/9 - 90/14 in ballpoint and sharp |
| Metallic | Fine shaft and sharp point eliminate thread breakage; elongated eye accommodates thread, large groove prevents threads from shredding; specially designed scarf prevents skipped stitches | Metallic threads; monofilament threads | 70/10 - 90/14 |
| Quilting | Tapered point sews through thick layers and crossed seams | Piecing a quilt; machine quilting layers together | 75/11 and 90/14 |
| Self-Threading/ Handicap | Slot on one side allows thread to slide into the eye | General-purpose | 80/12 and 90/14 |
| Spring | Spring around needle acts like a flexible presser foot, lowering and raising as the needle enters the fabric | Free-motion machine embroidery; quilting; monogramming | universal 70/10 - 90/14 stretch 75/11 & 90/14 denim 100/16 embroidery 75/11 & 90/14 quilting 75/11 & 90/14 |
| Stretch | Deeper scarf prevents skipped stitches | Knit fabrics; synthetic suedes | 75/11 and 90/14 |
| Titanium | Titanium nitride layer on surface extends life of needle up to five times that of conventional needle | All-purpose | 70/10, 75/11, 80/12, and 90/14 in ballpoint and sharp |
| Topstitch | Extra-sharp point, extra-large eye, larger groove | Topstitching thread; using two strands of all-purpose thread | 80/12 - 100/16 |
| Twin or Triple | Two or three shafts on a crossbar that extends from a single shank; twin currently available with two denim, two stretch, two embroidery, one wing and one universal, or two metallic shafts; triple available with three universal points only | Heirloom and decorative stitching; multiple, parallel stitching; machine must have zigzag capabilities and front-to-back threading | Sizing slightly different: the first number is the distance between needles, the second number is the European size |
| Wing/Hemstitch | Sides of shank are flared and look like wings | Decorative openwork stitching on tightly woven fabrics such as linen and fine batiste | 100/16 and 120/19 |

# Fabulous Fabrics

*Fabrics abound for machine arts creations. And you can always create your own embellished fabric. There's never a need to waste—scrap quilts and crazy quilts are the perfect way to use up those odds and ends.*

## Cotton

Long a standby for garments, quilting, and home décor, cotton comes in an almost endless array of colors, patterns, knits, wovens, and textures. Don't forget flannels for quilts and garments.

## Home Décor

Often overlooked for garments and quilting, home décor fabrics such as romantic chintzs, dramatic tapestries, and rich moirés offer a world of options. Fabrics with large motifs provide a ready guide for free-motion quilting.

## Fleece

Nothing beats fleece for warm and cozy. Edges require little finishing and many decorative techniques take on a new look when stitched onto fleece.

## Lamé

Look for two categories of lamé—those with a backing such as tricot, and those without, such as tissue lamé. The tissue variety unravels, frays, and snags, and it melts under the heat of an iron. It must be handled carefully, but the sparkle and shine are worth the extra effort.

## Linen

One of the strongest of all natural fibers, linen is a great choice for up-to-the-minute fashion, table linens, and even quilting. It shapes beautifully and maneuvers easily. Traditionally known for a palette of solid colors, you can also find linens and linen blends in checks, stripes, and plaids.

## Rayon

A man-made fiber made from natural plant fibers, rayon has many of the same qualities as cotton. Rayon is strong, extremely absorbent, and available in a variety of styles and weights. Rayon can withstand the heat of a warm (but not hot) iron.

## Sheers

Sheer fabrics come in many fiber contents (cotton, silk, synthetics) and have many names: organza, organdy, georgette, voile. The finish may be matte, shiny, metallic, or opalescent. They find their way into many decorative stitching techniques. They are also great for shadow appliqué, creating your own designer fabrics, making chenille, and as an overlay to tone down a loud or too-bright fabric.

## Silk

One of the oldest textile fibers known to man, silk is the strongest natural fiber available. Silk absorbs moisture, making it cool in the summer and warm in the winter. Because it's highly absorbent, it can be easily dyed. Silk retains its shape, drapes well, and is a wonderful choice for home decorating, garments, and sumptuous quilts.

## Velvet

Several types of velvet are commonly available for machine sewing, including cotton, silk, rayon, acetate, polyester, and blends of these fibers.

## Wool

A natural fiber, wool absorbs moisture, is durable, and drapes nicely. Wool fabrics come in a variety of textures and weights, making it a good choice for tailored garments and warm, cozy quilts. Felt made from wool is also available; it is easy to work with for appliqué because cut edges don't fray.

# STABILIZERS

*Jeanine Twigg*

*When it comes to machine arts projects, the right stabilizer can make all the difference. Whether you are doing machine embroidery, decorative stitching, or free-motion thread painting, understanding which type of stabilizer is best for your fabric and stitches is the key to success.*

There are two categories of stabilizers: backings and toppings. Backings are the most common and are used on the wrong side of the fabric to help maintain the shape of the fabric and to hold the stitches. A topper (usually a water-soluble stabilizer) is used on the right side to prevent stitches from embedding into the fabric. (See pages 87–88 for details on toppers.) When an embroidery hoop is used, stabilizers can be hooped with the fabric. For some techniques, a hoop is not needed and stabilizer can be pinned or basted to the fabric.

## Stabilizer Types
### Tear- and Cut-away

Tear- and cut-away stabilizers are available in several weights. Sometimes it's more effective to use two layers of a lightweight stabilizer rather than one heavyweight.

*Tear-away stabilizers* are torn away from the design after stitching. The fabric must be able to support the design after the stabilizer is gone.

Remove by working on a flat surface and tearing the stabilizer close to the design edge and then pulling gently outward to tear away the excess. The stabilizer should remove easily; tugging distorts the threads. If necessary, cut away the stabilizer and allow garment laundering to remove the remaining pieces.

*Cut-away stabilizers* are permanent after washing. A cut-away stabilizer will hold the design during and after the stitching process.

Remove excess by cutting away the stabilizer carefully with paper scissors approximately ¼" away from the design. Note that cut-away stabilizer can dull fabric scissors over time.

## Disappearing

Disappearing stabilizers are temporary and disappear with the aid of water or an iron. Be sure the chosen fabric can tolerate the water or iron temperatures needed to remove the stabilizer.

*Water-soluble stabilizer* is the most popular of the disappearing stabilizers. Often used as a topper (see page 87), water-soluble stabilizers are also used as backings, perfect for lacemaking or specialty stitching techniques. Store these stabilizers in a resealable plastic bag to prevent them from drying out.

Before removing, tear or cut away as much of the excess stabilizer as possible. Follow the manufacturer's directions to either mist, soak, or launder to remove. A damp washcloth can also be used to dab the stitching until the stabilizer disappears.

### Quick Trick
#### "No-mark" Stitching

Stitching designs and guides can be drawn on water-soluble or very light tear-away stabilizer and pinned or basted to fabric as an alternative to marking directly on fabric. When stitching is complete, the stabilizer can be dissolved or torn away—no worrying about marks left on fabric! Use for any type of design in quilting or decorative stitching.

*Heat-away stabilizer* can be used when making or working on lace or other delicate stitching where tearing away the stabilizer will disturb the stitching. It can also be used on fabrics that can't be washed in water.

Remove by heating with an iron from the wrong side of the fabric to turn the stabilizer black. The stabilizer disintegrates so it can be brushed away. Be careful not to touch water to the stabilizer before removing it completely from the fabric—it can mix with the residue and stain the fabric. If necessary, rub the back of the design together to loosen any excess stabilizer from under the stitches.

*Melt-away stabilizer* can also be used for delicate stitching on fabrics that can't be washed.

Remove by heating with a dry iron. This stabilizer will literally melt away or melt into nuggets that can be brushed away from the design. It won't adhere to the iron sole plate so there is no messy clean up. Set the iron temperature to accommodate the fabric.

## Water-activated

*Water-activated adhesive stabilizer* has a strong bond when dry and is available in cut- or tear-away styles. To use, gently run a damp sponge over one side of the stabilizer to activate the adhesive, then smooth the fabric over the stabilizer to secure. Either stabilize the fabric before hooping, or hoop only the stabilizer, and then stick the fabric to it.

It may be necessary to re-moisten the stabilizer to remove the excess from the fabric. Once the fabric is separated from the stabilizer, follow the instructions above for removing cut- or tear-away stabilizers.

## Self-sticking

*Self-sticking stabilizer* is another form of adhesive stabilizer. It is a tear-away stabilizer that has a sticky surface. It's great for hard-to-hoop items such as socks, velvet, and synthetic suede. Use a hoop with a large outer flange to secure the stabilizer, then score, and remove the protective paper within the hoop. Or, tightly screw the inner and outer hoops together, peel the protective paper, then secure the stabilizer to the back edge of the hoops. Secure the item to be stitched onto the stabilizer and stitch the design.

Remove by lifting the adhesive stabilizer away from the fabric and then follow the removal instructions for cut- or tear-away stabilizers.

## Iron-on

*Iron-on stabilizers* are great for any fabric that stretches, including knits, or for any fabric that just needs a little additional support. Simply iron a piece of stabilizer onto the wrong side of the fabric. Fabric with iron-on stabilizers can be hooped or not.

Remove by peeling the stabilizer off of the fabric.

## Liquid

*Liquid stabilizer* can be used as an alternative to spray starch to stiffen fabric. It can be purchased as a ready-to-use product or you can make your own by dissolving a water-soluble stabilizer in a small amount of water. The liquid is brushed on and allowed to dry before stitching.

Remove liquid stabilizer by rinsing the fabric in water.

## Choosing a Stabilizer

It's important to choose stabilizers with the same weight and feel as the fabric to be stitched. Be sure to choose quality stabilizers made specifically for high-speed machine stitching. Stabilizers shouldn't stretch—even on the bias—because they could warp the fabric and design, yielding unsuccessful results.

If the stabilizer weight is too heavy the result will be a stiff design, and if it's too light the design may warp or pucker.

As a general rule—use a tear-away stabilizer with woven fabrics, and a cut-away if the fabric stretches.

- Denim and corduroy are woven fabrics, but they stretch when worn, so stitch them using a *cut-away stabilizer* to hold the fabric during and after the stitching process.

- Loosely woven fabrics such as linen should be stitched with a *cut-away stabilizer* because the fabric weave isn't dense enough to hold the design on its own. On linen, use a *water-soluble stabilizer* on top for added stability.

- Knits, including fleece, are best stitched with a *mesh cut-away stabilizer* to support the stitches. Add a *water-soluble stabilizer* on top to keep the stitches on top of the fabric surface while stitching. They also benefit from an *iron-on interfacing*, such as tricot fused to the wrong side, perpendicular to the fabric stretch. The interfacing will prevent the fabric from stretching during the hooping and embroidery process.

- Tightly woven fabrics, such as poplin, shirting, some wool, synthetic suede, rayon, and canvas, are best stitched with a *tear-away stabilizer*. In most cases, a *water-soluble stabilizer* on top isn't necessary.

 *Tip*

## Spray Adhesive

Make any stabilizer tacky with a temporary spray adhesive. If the fabric and stabilizer will be hooped, you can hoop the stabilizer, and lightly spray the stabilizer inside the hoop with adhesive, or secure the fabric and stabilizer together with the spray adhesive before hooping. Spray only the stabilizer—the fabric could have an adverse reaction to the adhesive ingredients. In addition, read the label to determine whether it's permanent, water-soluble, or will dissipate over time, and to be sure the product is compatible with the fabric or project.

Spray adhesive can be particularly helpful when making thread lace with loose strands of threads and other embellishments.

*Be careful not to allow overspray to come in contact with your embroidery machine.*

# STABILIZER QUICK REFERENCE

| TYPE | USE/REMOVAL |
| --- | --- |
| Tear-away | Use for embroidery, appliqué, and other decorative stitching.<br><br>Very light-weight stabilizers that are easy to tear are good for fagoting and other heirloom sewing.<br><br>*Tear away after stitching.* |
| Cut-away | Use for embroidery, appliqué, and other decorative stitching on woven and knit fabrics where the fabric weave isn't dense enough to hold the design on its own.<br><br>Use for denim and corduroy because they stretch when worn.<br><br>*Cut away excess after stitching.* |
| Cut-away (Mesh) | Use for embroidery, appliqué, and other decorative stitching on knits, including fleece.<br><br>*Cut away excess after stitching.* |
| Iron-on | Use like a tear-away stabilizer for any fabric that stretches, including knits, or for any fabric that needs a little additional support.<br><br>*Peel off / tear away after stitching.* |
| Water-activated | Use for embroidery for hard-to-hoop items such as socks, velvet, and synthetic suede.<br><br>*Re-moisten with water to remove.* |
| Self-sticking | Use for embroidery for hard-to-hoop items such as socks, velvet, and synthetic suede.<br><br>*Peel off / tear away after stitching.* |
| Heat-away | Use for lacemaking and specialty stitching, especially with fabrics that should not get wet.<br><br>*Heat with dry iron to remove.* |
| Melt-away | Use for lacemaking and specialty stitching.<br><br>*Heat with dry iron to remove.* |
| Water-soluble | Use for lacemaking, fagoting, and other specialty stitching; can also be used as a topper.<br><br>*Soak in water or wash to remove.* |
| Liquid | Use as an alternative to spray starch to stiffen fabric, especially when using a wing needle or doing dense decorative stitching.<br><br>*Rinse in water to remove.* |

# TOPPERS

*Rebecca Kemp Brent*

*Toppers—special stabilizers placed on top of fabric prior to stitching—can make a design stand out and be noticed.*

## Types of Toppers

There are two types of toppers—temporary and permanent. When choosing a topper, consider the job it will do and the result of your project. Choose a temporary topper by its removal method—water- or heat-soluble. Pick a permanent topper by the design's finished appearance as well as the fabric care.

Although toppers add a light layer of stability to embroidery and other decorative stitching, it is important to remember that toppers do not take the place of stabilizers. Use a topper in conjunction with a stabilizer to match the characteristics of your fabric and design.

## Temporary Toppers

Unlike stabilizers used to back an embroidered design, temporary toppers are completely removable. Some dissolve in water, while others dissolve with the heat of an iron.

Temporary toppers are used to tame the nap of fabrics such as terry cloth and to support the threads of the design so they do not sink into the pile of velvet or the soft surface of a sweatshirt knit. A satin stitch design embroidered without a topper reveals loops of terry poking through the stitches. The same design embroidered with a layer of water-soluble stabilizer on top of the terry has an unbroken surface.

Without topper

With topper

Water-soluble stabilizers vary in weight depending on the manufacturer. Heavyweight styles can be used alone as a base for lace embroidery and specialty applications, but work well for toppers, too.

For the easiest removal after stitching, choose a lightweight topper.

Heat-soluble stabilizers can also be used as a stand-alone base for stitching or as a topper.

Be sure your base fabric and threads can withstand the temperature required for removing heat-soluble toppers.

To use a temporary topper:

- Position the topper on your base fabric and baste it in place. If the fabric is to be hooped, hoop the topper with the fabric to maximize its compacting effect on textured fabrics.

- Stitch the design and if a hoop was used, remove the fabric from the hoop. Cut or tear away as much of the extra topper as possible, but remember that tearing may distort the stitches of a delicate design.

- Remove the remaining topper with water or heat following the manufacturer's instructions. Thorough removal of water-soluble stabilizers may require several soakings or complete project washing.

*(Continued on next page)*

## Permanent Toppers

Sometimes a topper is needed to enhance the coverage of a stitched design, or to add texture to the surface of the stitching. Opaque, permanent toppers fill in the gaps between stitches, improving the appearance on fabrics that are patterned (for example, checks or stripes) or contrast sharply with the color of the thread (light over dark or bright).

Follow these tips when working with permanent toppers

- Use a piece of permanent topper slightly larger than the area to be covered. Use a light spray of adhesive to hold it in place on the fabric.

- Stitch the part of the design that will cover the topper and gently tear away the excess topper outside the perimeter of the embroidered area.

- Outline stitching will cover any bits of permanent topper visible around the design edges. A blast of steam from your iron can be used to shrink any remaining visible pieces of permanent topper in the design—do not place the iron in direct contact with the topper.

### Foam

Foam toppers are designed to become a permanent part of stitched designs and come in a variety of colors. They are placed on top of the fabric before a portion of the design is sewn then the excess is torn away.

Place it under a satin-stitched area to give a three-dimensional lift to the stitching as well as covering the background fabric.

*Without foam*

*With foam*

Foam is washable, but cannot be dry-cleaned.

For embroidery, choose designs that are digitized for foam. The satin stitching needs to perforate the foam around the entire perimeter of the design for easy removal. Keep these factors in mind when choosing a design or when digitizing your own designs for foam.

### Vinyl

Vinyl toppers are used to cover the surface of the fabric under stitching without adding dimension to the design and come in a variety of colors. Stitching designs over a layer of vinyl close to the color of the thread yields a solid appearance without increasing the density of the stitched fill.

### Nylon Organza

Nylon organza can also be used as a permanent topper. It comes in a variety of colors and is easily cut away from the outside edges of a design.

*Floral Embroidery Designs: Brother Card #23*

 *Tip*

### Not All Foam is Created Equal

Be sure to use foam designed for use with sewing machines. Craft foam can disintegrate and fall into the bobbin area.

# A New Look At Color

*Lynn Koolish*

*What strikes you first when you look at a quilt, a garment, or a pillow? Most likely what you notice first are the colors. But exactly what is it that attracts your attention? Is it the colors themselves? Is it the lightness or darkness? Is it the contrast of colors and values? Is it your emotional response? Actually, it is all of these.*

Color is what draws many of us to fabric and thread. To use color to your advantage, you need to understand it when you choose fabric, thread, and embellishments for your machine arts projects.

## Color Wheels

The color wheel is a helpful tool when working with color. It is based on the three primary colors, from which the other colors are created. Most of us have learned that blue, red, and yellow are the primary colors, and all other colors can be mixed from these primaries. This is true for paint and other pigments.

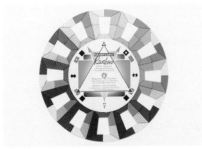

*Color wheels based on primary colors blue, red, and yellow*

However, in the world of color photography and printing (both on paper and fabric), the primary colors are cyan (also called turquoise), magenta, and yellow (commonly referred to as CMYK, where K stands for black).

*Color wheel based on primary colors cyan, magenta, and yellow*

Mixing together two primary colors creates the secondary colors, and mixing together a primary and a secondary color creates the tertiary colors

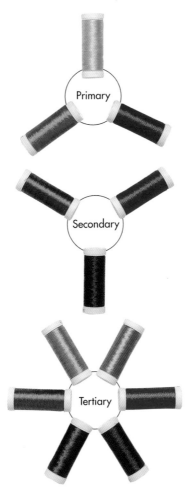

## Using a Color Wheel

Any color wheel is a good planning tool and will help you identify the specific colors in any of the color schemes described on pages 90–91. When working with fabric and thread however, you may be more successful if you use a CMYK color wheel. The colors used to print and dye fabric and thread are based on the CMYK color model, so these colors are more likely to match the actual colors of fabric and thread.

Use your color wheel at home to plan and design your project and to find the most effective color combinations. Take your color wheel with you to the fabric store, and use it to find the exact fabrics, threads, and embellishments you need for your chosen color scheme.

## Properties of Color

Colors are divided into "warm" (red, yellow, orange) and "cool" (blue, green, violet). As a rule, warm colors are vibrant and exciting. Cool colors are relaxing and soothing. Warm colors appear to advance, while cool colors recede.

*Warm colors*

*Cool colors*

*(Continued on next page)*

EVERYTHING ESSENTIAL **89**

Be aware however, that colors are affected by the colors around them. For example, a yellow-green will appear warm when placed next to a violet, but will appear cool when placed next to orange.

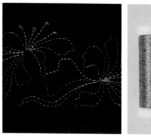

*Yellow-green appears warm next to cool color.*

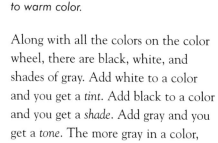

*Yellow-green appears cool next to warm color.*

Along with all the colors on the color wheel, there are black, white, and shades of gray. Add white to a color and you get a *tint*. Add black to a color and you get a *shade*. Add gray and you get a *tone*. The more gray in a color, the lower its *intensity*.

Color also has *value*—how light or dark it is. The value of a color is also relative. A medium-value color placed next to a very dark color will be considered the light value of the pair. If that same color is placed next to a very light color, it will be considered the dark value of the pair. This is true of thread on fabric, as well as two colors of thread next to each other.

When discussing color, many teachers say that color gets the credit, while value does the work. They mean that using value effectively is often more important that the actual colors used.

*Yellow-green appears dark next to light color.*

*Yellow-green appears light next to dark color.*

## A Good Value

You'll find it well worth the small price to purchase a value finder: a piece of colored plastic (usually red for viewing most fabrics and green for viewing red fabrics), available at fabric shops and some art-supply stores. Lay your fabrics out on a flat surface, and look at them through the value finder. You won't be able to see their color, only their value, so you can evaluate fabric groupings and selections just on that basis.

## Color Schemes

Why is all this important? By knowing how to use warms and cools; tints, tones, and shades; value; and intensity, you can control the look of your quilts, garments, and home décor projects. Color is often discussed in relation to fabrics or paint, but have you thought about how it affects your choice of thread as well? For embroidery, quilting, and decorative stitching in general, both fabric and thread are major components of your color scheme.

Spools of thread are included to show the entire color scheme in addition to stitched samples where one color is represented by the fabric.

*Monochromatic* color schemes use various tints, tones, and shades of a single color. When used effectively, this color scheme can be elegant and sophisticated. There can be subtle or high contrast depending on the values used. Monochromatic colors are always "safe" choices, but they can be bland when there is too little contrast. To blend stitching into the background, use a thread that is a tint, tone, or shade of the background fabric.

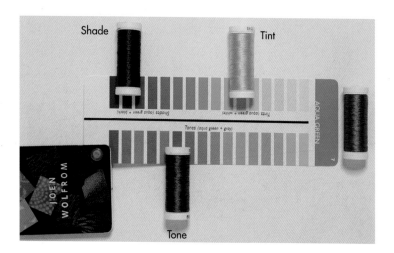

Shade

Tint

Tone

For more contrast, use a thread that is of a much different value—either lighter or darker.

*Analogous* color schemes use colors that are side by side on the color wheel, and are always harmonious when limited to one-quarter or one-third of the color wheel. Use a variety of tints, tones, and shades of the analogous colors to create a pleasing and interesting color scheme. For example, orange-yellow or yellow-green threads used on a yellow background will stand out without calling too much attention to the stitching.

*Complementary* color schemes use colors opposite each other on the color wheel and produce vibrant, high-contrast results. Think of violet and yellow pansies, or green holly leaves with red berries. Thread that is the complement of the base fabric will produce the most visible stitching.

*Split-complementary* color schemes use colors that are next to a color's complement. Split complements provide much of the pizzazz of complementary colors, but without such strong contrast.

*Triadic* color schemes use three colors that are equally spaced around the color wheel. Triadic color schemes increase the range of colors used and provide contrast while maintaining balance and harmony.

*Polychromatic* color schemes make use of all or many colors. Items made using polychromatic colors can be exciting, or they can be unbalanced and chaotic. Polychromatic colors are often used in quilts, especially scrap quilts.

Use tints, tones, and shades of colors to increase the variety in a color scheme and make it more interesting while maintaining its basic characteristics.

## Contrast— Putting It All Together

The properties of color and the various color schemes work most effectively when you tie them together with the concept of contrast. Contrast of color, value, and intensity affect visual perception. Monochromatic color schemes have the least contrast, while complementary color schemes provide the highest level of contrast. Within any color scheme you'll influence the level of contrast through your choices of value and intensity. High contrast creates vibrancy and energy, but it can also become overwhelming and uncomfortable. Low contrast, when done well, can be soothing, elegant, and sophisticated, but it can also look tired and boring.

For some, choosing colors is an intuitive and comfortable process. For others, it is more challenging. Whether you are selecting fabric, thread, or other elements of a machine arts project, these principles give you a place to start when you are considering how to use color to achieve your desired look.

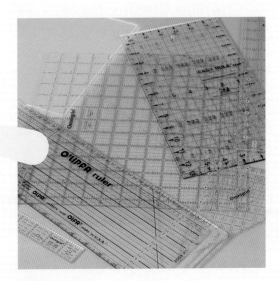

# Terrific Tools

Every good machine artist needs good tools. Here are basic tools and supplies to have on hand.

# TOOLS

## Chenille Cutting Tools

(See pages 122–124 for making chenille.)

Cutting fabric to make chenille is easy with one of two specialized tools, either a rotary cutter with a foot that prevents the base fabric layer from getting cut, or narrow cutting mats designed to slip into the stitched chenille channels.

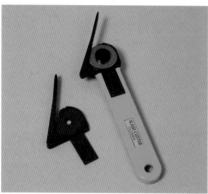

## 3-in-1 Color Tool

(See pages 89–91 for more on color.)

The 3-in-1 Color Tool helps you choose and match fabric, thread, and embellishment colors by providing visual guides of the most commonly used color schemes.

## Hand-guided Quilting Systems

(See pages 152–158 for free-motion stitching and quilting.)

A number of tabletop hand-guided quilting systems are available for use with home sewing machines. All are designed for free-motion stitching and include some type of frame that holds the quilt sandwich for stitching. Some systems provide tensioned rollers so the quilt doesn't need to be basted. In other cases, the quilt does need to be basted but the frame stretches the quilt for easier stitching.

With some systems, the machine is placed on a movable platform and the machine is moved while the quilt is stationary. With other systems the machine is stationary and the frame is moved.

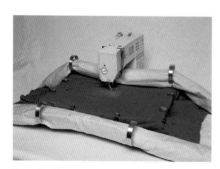

*Easy Quilter*

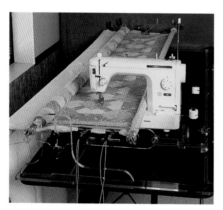

*Super Quilter with Handi Handles*

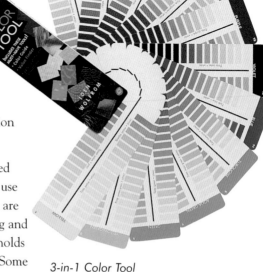

*3-in-1 Color Tool*

## Hoops

(See pages 162–163 for basic hooping techniques.)

A hoop holds fabric taut for embroidery and other decorative stitching. Some fit into computerized embroidery sewing machines, some are hand guided and fit under the presser foot.

## Machine Embroidery Hoops

Embroidery machines usually come with several sizes of embroidery hoops, and there are many more specialty hoops available. There are hoops for embroidering on hats and socks; frame hoops with large sliding sides to move the location of the embroidery without unhooping; and a variety of shaped hoops, such as circular, free-arm, mini-hoops, and extra-large hoops. Check online or with your local sewing and embroidery machine dealer to see what hoops and hooping accessories are available.

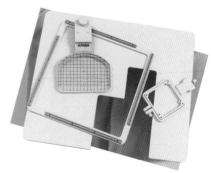

## Hooping Aids

Hooping a T-shirt or sweatshirt for embroidery can be frustrating when it comes to placement. Hooping boards have holes to accommodate universal brackets that can be adjusted to fit your brand of embroidery hoop. To use, the T-shirt or sweatshirt is placed over the board and is hooped with the stabilizer in a predetermined placement location

Other accessories are helpful aids for hooping and placement. For example, a cloth-setting device is available to help with the alignment of an embroidery design onto fabric. For hooping in general, a hoop holding device is available to help push the inner hoop into the outer hoop with ease.

## Hand-guided Embroidery Hoops

Many machine-stitching techniques (beading, thread painting, and machine lacemaking, for example) are easier when an embroidery hoop is used. When purchasing hoops, be sure they are thin enough to slip under the presser foot, or have a notch that will allow you to do so.

## Magnifiers

Whether you wear the magnifier, or have one mounted on your machine or table lamp, magnifying devices help you see all the details. Use when trimming stitches or doing detailed stitching or quilting.

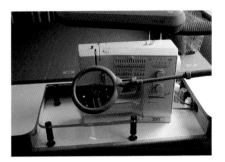

## Marking Tools

Many types of marking tools exist, some are easily removable and some are permanent.

When it is important that the marks be removable, test the marker on a sample of the fabric you are using. Always follow the manufacturer's directions—some removable markers may become permanent with heat.

Removable markers include water- and air-soluble, some chalks, specially designed fabric-marking pencils, and soapstone.

Permanent markers are often easier to see, but should only be used when the lines won't show. Permanent markers include permanent ink pens, colored pencils, and graphite pencils.

## Quilting and Stitching Aids
### Foam-backed Products
(See pages 152–158 for free-motion stitching and quilting.)

Foam-backed discs or open hoops help you move fabric for free-motion stitching or quilting. The foam grips the fabric making it easy to move through the machine.

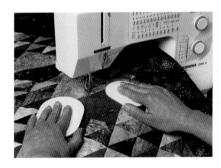

## Quilting Clips

When quilting a large quilt, it can be helpful to roll up portions of the quilt to get them out of the way. Quilting clips hold the rolled-up quilt securely.

## Quilting Gloves

Gloves help grip and move the quilt while free-motion stitching. Various types are available.

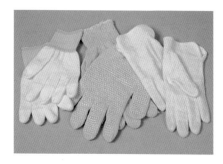

## Rotary Cutters, Rulers, Mats

Rotary cutters, gridded rulers, and cutting mats make cutting fast, precise, and easy.

## Rotary Cutters

Rotary cutters come in variety of sizes and styles, from small (18mm) to large (65mm). The small size is for small pieces and curves, the largest size speeds cutting. Some models are ergonomically designed to ease hand fatigue.

In addition to regular replacement blades, decorative blades are available for cutting pinked, wavy, scalloped, deckle edges, and more.

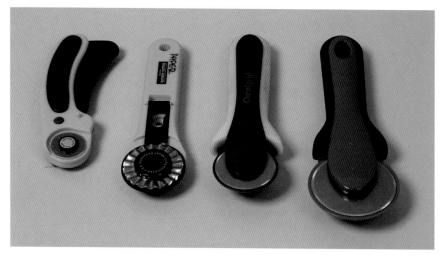

## Gridded Rulers

Rulers designed to be used with rotary cutters come in a wide array of sizes, grid styles, and colors. Select sizes and shapes that fit your specific needs.

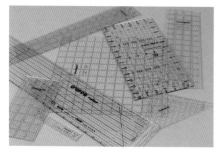

## Cutting Mats

Cutting mats come in several colors and a wide variety of sizes. Large mats are great for cutting large pieces of fabric, small mats are perfect for trimming, or taking to class.

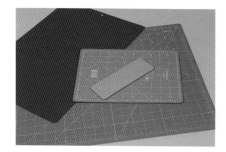

## Seam Ripper

Seam rippers have a sharp, curved edge for opening seams and a point to pick out individual threads. They come in various sizes and shapes; select a seam ripper that feels comfortable in your hand.

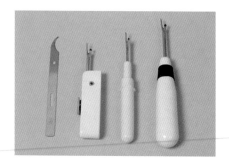

## Second Bobbin Case

(See pages 113–115 for bobbinwork, page 134 for embroidery basics, and pages 201–202 for satin stitching.)

The bobbin case that comes with your machine is adjusted for standard sewing by the machine manufacturer. By having a second bobbin case, you can adjust the tension and use it for a variety of thicker or thinner decorative threads without affecting the regular bobbin case tension.

Some manufacturers also make bobbin cases specifically designed for use with heavy threads for bobbinwork where a looser bobbin tension is required. A bobbin case with a tighter tension for embroidery or decorative satin stitching (where it's important that the bobbin thread pull the top stitches more to the back of the work) may also be available for your machine.

## Sewing Machine Extension Table

An extension table provides a larger surface area at the same height as the bed of the sewing machine to support quilts and other large projects. Extension tables make free-motion stitching much easier because the area to be stitched is on a flat surface and not draped over the arm of the machine.

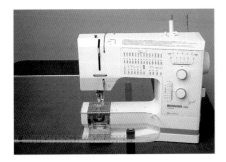

## Spool Adapter

Some larger spools will fit your spool pin more securely with a wooden spool adaptor.

## Stilettos

If you're a bit shy about getting your fingers near the sewing machine needle, these tools come to the rescue. Stilettos help hold yarns, ribbons, cord, or thread in place while keeping your fingers at a safe distance.

A run-in between a metal stiletto and a sewing machine needle can be disastrous. Some sewers prefer to use non-metal stilettos to avoid this possibility. Stilettos are as individual as sewers and can be purchased or home made. Stilettos are commonly made from metal, wood, plastic, and porcupine quills.

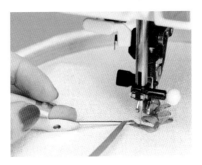

*Trolley needle*

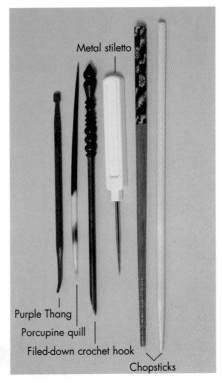

Metal stiletto

Purple Thang
Porcupine quill
Filed-down crochet hook
Chopsticks

## Stitch Remover

This gadget resembles a shaver, but is made for removing embroidery. Shave across the wrong side of the design or stitching to clip bobbin threads, then easily remove the unwanted threads from your fabric.

## Surge Protector

Sewing machines and sergers have become electronic, computerized, and expensive. A good surge protector is a small price to pay for protecting your investment. Many surge protectors look like power strips, but it is important to be aware that a power strip—even it if has a switch—is *not* a surge protector. You need to buy a product specifically designated as a surge protector.

For the best protection, look for a surge protector with a *protected equipment warranty* or *connected equipment warranty*. Read the packaging carefully or ask what type of equipment is protected to be sure your machine will be covered.

If you take your machine to retreats, classes, or seminars, take your surge protector with you.

## Thread Nets

With slippery decorative threads and larger spools, thread nets can help keep thread under control. Use with thread stands or horizontal spool pins to keep thread from slipping and tangling.

## Thread Stands

(See pages 76 and 77 for more on using thread stands.)

### Single-spool Thread Stands

Thread delivery is critical to smooth sewing and thread stands can help provide the proper orientation for spools of all sizes. Some thread stands also include a method for applying thread lubricants. (See pages 78–79 for more on thread lubricants.)

## Cone Adapters

Cone adapters are available to make it easier to use larger cones that don't fit on home sewing machines.

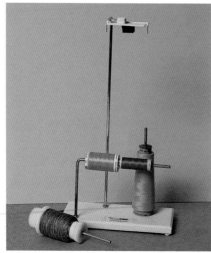

## Multi-spool Thread Stands

A multi-spool thread stand provides a place to hold the numerous spools of thread that are often used in embroidery, quilting, and thread painting. A thread stand can also help thread flow smoothly from the spool to the machine.

## Tweezers

Good tweezers are invaluable. Use them for:

- Pulling up jump threads in order to trim close to a stitched embroidery design

- Holding on to ribbon for silk ribbon embroidery

- Holding thread, ribbon, or cording in place for couching

Choose a pair that can grip thread at the tips and have a long handle that is easy to hold.

### 🌸 *Quick Trick*

#### Quality Tweezers

When purchasing tweezers, squeeze them shut and hold them up to the light. If you can see light between the blades at the tips, then you won't be able to get a good grip on thread.

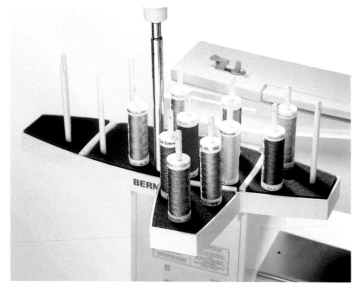

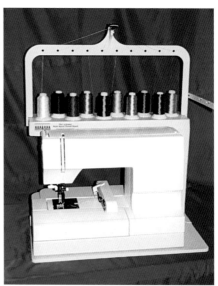

*Multi-spool Thread Stands*

# SUPPLIES

## Basting Spray

See Spray Adhesive.

## Batting

Batting has many uses in machine arts, especially for quilts, quilted garments, and trapunto. Quilting adds depth and texture, and the choice of batting can make a substantial difference in the finished look.

There are many types of batting available. Most common are cotton, polyester, and cotton/polyester blends, but you can also find wool and silk batting. If you're new to quilting, talk with the sales people at your local quilt shop, and ask for recommendations for your specific project. You may want to buy a small quantity of several different types of batting and make samples. Follow package recommendations on how closely you need to stitch. Also read the label to see if any pretreating is recommended.

Batting is generally available prepackaged in common bed sizes (crib, twin, double, queen, and king), as well as by the yard. It is available in white, off-white, and sometimes black or gray. Fusible batting is also available for those who don't want to baste.

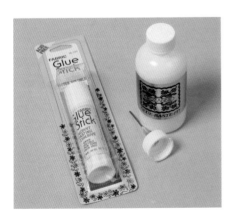

## Fabric Glues

In stick or liquid form, fabric glues are available to temporarily hold anything from appliqués to zippers. For most fabric applications, you want to use a product that washes out with water. If you need a precisely controlled application, look for products in a squeeze bottle that can deliver a fine line of glue.

## Fusible Web

Fusible web is commonly used for appliqué, and is available in several weights. The webs contain a bonding agent that adheres to fabric when heat is applied. They can be purchased in packaged, precut lengths, or by the yard. Some fusible web is adhesive on one or both sides making it easy to position and reposition.

## Fray Preventive

See Seam Sealant.

## Needles

See pages 80–82 for detailed information on needles.

## Seam Sealant

Usually referred to as seam sealant by those who serge, and fray preventive by quilters and other stitchers, this liquid stops fabric edges and ends of seams from unraveling. Several brands are available, so it's best to try them out to see which you prefer. Some dry more stiffly than others do, some soak into the fabric, while others bead up.

## Spray Adhesive

Temporary spray adhesives, also known as basting spray, have many uses in machine arts. Some are removable with water, some dissipate over time. You can usually reposition sprayed fabric, allowing you to fine-tune your placement. They can be used to:

- Hold fabric to hooped stabilizer

- Hold a topper in place

- Make tear-away or cut-away stabilizer adhesive. This is especially helpful on fabrics such as fleece that shouldn't be ironed with a hot iron.

- Hold together layers of fabric and batting for quilting

- Hold appliqués in place

- Hold together layers of fabric for chenille

- Hold together layers of stabilizer when making machine lace

Be sure to follow product directions and use only in well-ventilated areas.

## Stabilizers and Toppers

See pages 84–88 for detailed information on stabilizers and toppers.

## Thread

See pages 68–77 for detailed information on thread.

## Thread Lubricant

See pages 78–79 for detailed information on thread lubricants.

Appliqué

Bent-handle

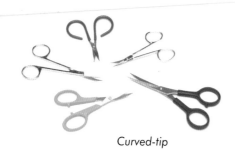

Curved-tip

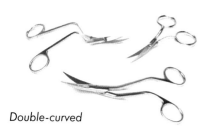

Double-curved

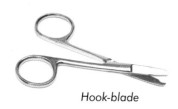

Hook-blade

Micro-tip

# SCISSORS

*Sue Barnabee*

*Scissors are necessary for any machine arts project. Here are the choices that will help you cut right.*

## Types of scissors

*Appliqué scissors* are sometimes referred to as "duck bill" or "pelican bill" because of the extended large blade that protects under-layers of fabric from being cut. The extended bill lifts the fabric to be cut and allows a close trim without nicking the fabric or embroidery. Some are spring-action and have soft, padded handles. The spring-action automatically opens the blades after each cut to reduce pressure on the finger joints.

*Bent-handle scissors* have a straight blade that is parallel to the embroidery with the handle raised above the work.

*Curved-tip scissors* have slender blades that curve up at the tip. They have fine points that allow close and precise cutting of threads while the embroidery is still in the hoop. The finer the blades, the greater the cutting precision. Curved tip scissors cut tight curves and corners accurately when working with cutwork and lace.

*Double-curved scissors* have several bends to reach over the hoop without obstructing the cutting view. Your hand can rest comfortably above the embroidery, decreasing fatigue and increasing precision. One curve is near the finger holes, which is high enough to go over the embroidery hoop, and the other curve is at the tip so the loose threads remain visible. The tips cut flush with the fabric. Some curved tips are finer than others. The finger bows can curve low, angled, or high.

*Hook-blade scissors* allow you to easily get under one stitch and cut close to the embroidery. They are also helpful for clipping stitches from the reverse side. The scissors has a tiny curved prong on the bottom blade that is used to lift a thread and snip one stitch at a time.

*Micro-tip curved scissors* provide a very slender extra-fine blade.

*Snips and clips* are available with one finger hole, without a finger hole, or with very short blades and spring action. These scissors have sharp points for selecting, pulling, and snipping threads. The versions with no finger holes provide quick snipping action for those with hand and wrist ailments. Snips and clips are perfect for trimming threads from the front or back of the work, but should never be used for cutting or trimming away stabilizer.

*Spring-action, double-curved scissors* are the same as the double-curved embroidery scissors except that the handle opens effortlessly because of the spring.

*Steeple-tip curved scissors* provide a very slender blunt tip with a sharp blade to get under stitches without fear of clipping the fabric.

*Straight-tip scissors* have slender blades and fine points so the threads can be cut close to the fabric. Some blades are finer; some are spring-action with micro-tips.

*Vintage-look scissors* are available for those who like quality vintage-look tools. Consider the various reproductions of antique scissors from museums and private collections. These scissors may be pewter-like, sterling silver, or gold-plated, some may be shaped like storks or hens to duplicate those of past generations.

*Snips and clips*

## Care and cleaning

Good quality embroidery scissors will stay in sharp working condition and last a lifetime, if you properly care for your investments.

- Clean with rubbing alcohol and a soft cloth if fusible or spray adhesives build up on the surface.

- Place scissors where they cannot be easily knocked to the floor, which can cause damage to the cutting edge and/or tips.

- Take care not to cut into pins, which can damage the blades and tips.

- Keep the cutting blades sharp. The blades should cut cleanly from the pivot point to the tip. Cutting with dull blades can quickly stress you and the tool!

- If scissors resist cutting, don't complete the cut. The added pressure can force the blades out of alignment.

- Protect blades by storing fine scissors in a leather case, plastic pouch, or sheath provided by the manufacturer. Or place scissors in a protective box, in a soft cloth wrap, or in custom-sewn storage sleeves for protection.

- Keep scissors in a safe, cool, and dry place. In high-humidity areas, regularly wipe the blades with a light coating of oil to prevent rust or corrosion. Wipe blades thoroughly before using.

- Cutting paper, metal, plastic, or cardboard dulls scissors, as does cutting synthetic fibers and threads such as polyester and nylon. The abrasive synthetic lint clings to blades after cutting. To minimize wear and tear on the blades, wipe the inside of the blades with a clean, dry, soft cloth to restore smooth cutting action.

- Some stabilizers tend to dull the blades of scissors quickly—consider designating a pair specifically for cutting interfacing and stabilizers.

- Scissors that become too loose or too tight may need to have the tension adjusted by turning the screw clockwise to tighten or counter-clockwise to loosen. If a lock nut is used in the assembly, you must loosen the lock nut before adjusting the screw and retighten the lock nut to hold the tension.

*Spring-action, double-curved*

*Steeple-tip curved*

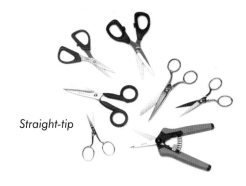

*Straight-tip*

*Vintage-look*

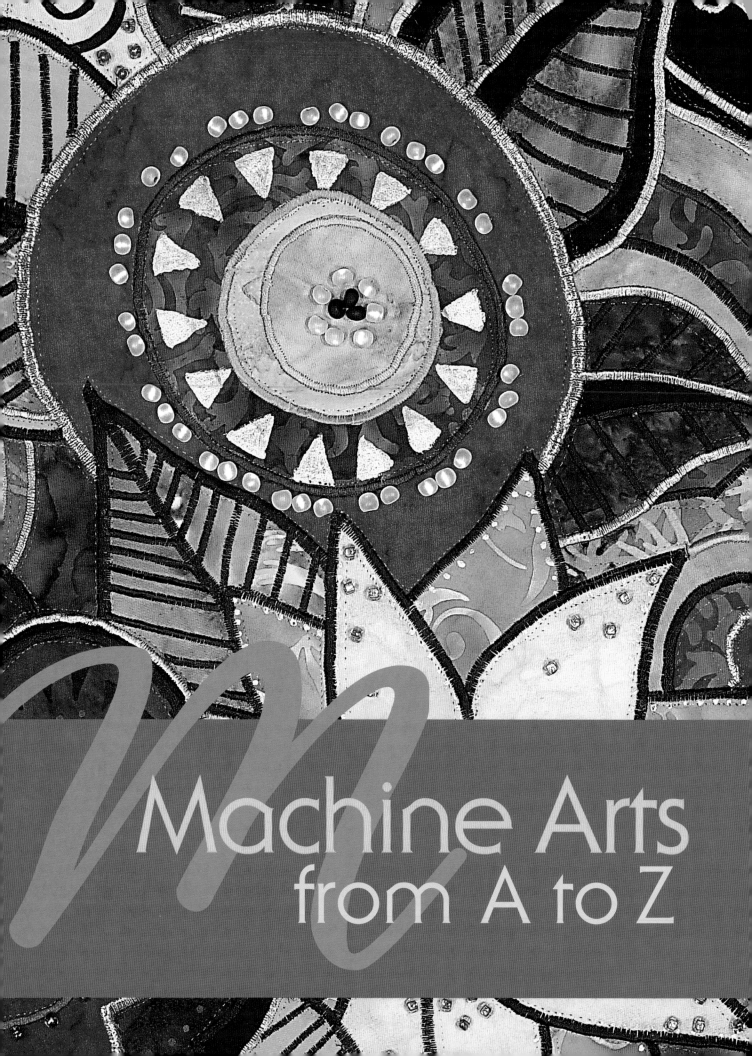

Machine Arts
from A to Z

# APPLIQUÉ

## Follow this Thread

See pages 43–53 for a visual
   guide to decorative stitches.
See pages 80–82 for needles.
See pages 68–77 for threads.
See pages 54–56 for presser feet.

## Blanket Stitch Appliqué

### Harriet Hargrave

*Blanket stitch appliqué, also known as buttonhole stitch is a wonderful decorative finish on items such as wall hangings, that won't receive hard use or constant laundering, and gives a country touch to any quilted item.*

Check your sewing machine manual to see if your machine has a blanket stitch (it may also be called a hemstitch, point de Paris, or pin stitch). The structure of the stitch is easy to recognize: a straight stitch forward, then a perpendicular stitch to the left and back again, then another stitch forward. (If your machine stitches to the right, use the mirror image function for ease of handling.) The straight stitches will lie exactly along the edge of your appliqué shape, and the perpendicular stitches will anchor your shape to the background.

*True forward-motion blanket stitch*

(Continued on next page)

## Shopping Tip

### Don't Be Fooled

If you are shopping for a new machine, check the stitch configurations offered and be sure that a true blanket stitch is available. Some machines have stitches that are similar to the blanket stitch, such as the double stitch blanket stitch, which just doesn't work as well because it doesn't fill in well along the edge of appliqués.

*Double-stitch blanket stitch*

The more complicated multiple stitch blanket stitch is difficult to guide around curves and points.

*Multiple-stitch blanket stitch*

Some overlock stitches are similar to the blanket stitch but have an angled side stitch, which makes it difficult—if not impossible—to stitch around points and curves.

*Overlock stitch*

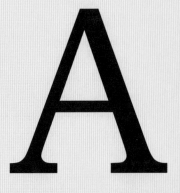

## Stitch Width and Length

The longer the stitch length, the greater the distance between the perpendicular stitches, and the less securely attached your appliqué will be. If the appliqué has very tight curves and lots of corners or points, use a shorter buttonhole stitch. To be visually pleasing, the length of the perpendicular stitch (which you set using the stitch width) should be just a hair shorter than the stitch length.

For large appliqués or for a very country look, a larger stitch length and width will looked better proportioned; for small appliqué shapes or ones with many tight curves or points, use a smaller stitch.

## Preparing Appliqué Shapes

There are two ways to prepare appliqué shapes: finished size (with a raw edge), or with an added, turned-under seam allowance. If the edge is raw, use short stitches to secure the edge in place and prevent fraying.

If you prefer raw-edge appliqué and want to ensure the edge won't fray, stitch the raw edge first using a tiny zigzag stitch and invisible thread, then blanket-stitch the edge.

## Stitching a Reference

Use an open-toe appliqué foot so you can see each stitch. Experiment with needles, threads, and the machine settings to find the ones that create the look you want. Sew a line of stitches, then use a fine-point permanent marker to note next to it the stitch length and width, type of top and bobbin threads, and needle size. If you adjusted the tension settings, note that as well. Refer to this sample whenever you want to blanket-stitch appliqué.

### Tip

## Sewing Test Samples

When you're sewing a sample, start with 30-weight, 2-ply cotton embroidery thread and a 90/14 universal needle in the top, a 60-weight thread in the bobbin, and the pre-programmed stitch settings.

## Needle Position

If your machine has a "pattern begin" or "pattern start" function, engage it so you always start at the same point of the stitch. It's easiest to begin the stitch with the straight part. Sew some sample stitches with this function to see where your machine begins the stitch.

## Starting and Stopping

There are several ways to start and end a line of stitching so you secure the tails:

- Take two or three short, straight stitches just at the edge of the appliqué ("in the ditch"). Cut off the thread tails or leave long tails to knot by hand later.

- Use the "fix-lock-tack" option if your machine has one.

- Set your machine for a three-step zigzag stitch (the stitch that takes three tiny stitches in each zig and each zag). Keep the width set as it was for the blanket stitch, and set the length to 0. Let the needle zig, then zag.

## Stitch Placement

The straight part of the stitch should be as close to the edge of the appliqué as possible. As you sew, the needle should rub the edge but not "hop" onto the appliqué. The perpendicular part of the stitch should go straight from the edge into the appliqué shape. For accurate stitching, learn to look at the fabric edge and the needle, not the presser foot, as you sew.

## Outside Corners and Angles

The trick here is to end the stitches exactly at the outside corner.

Create a measuring device by stitching a straight line of stitches the same size you will use in your project. Use it to mark where a stitch should begin a few stitches before a corner, then "fudge" the stitch length to "land" the needle at that spot. This also works well for matching up the beginning and end of a round of stitches.

Begin on a straight portion of your appliqué shape. Use the measuring device to space your stitches so a straight stitch will end exactly at the corner; end with the needle down.

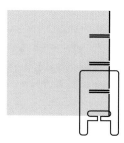

Lift the presser foot, and pivot the fabric so that the perpendicular stitch will go "straight into" the outside angle, dividing it exactly in half. Sew in and out of the corner, ending with the needle down exactly at the corner again.

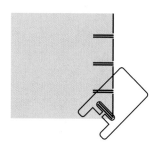

Lift the presser foot, and pivot the fabric so that the next straight stitch will fall exactly along the new straight edge. The needle will be already lined up when you pivot, ready to sew the next straight portion.

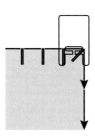

*Tip*

## Stitching Accurate Corners

If the stitches on the sides of the corner overlap, decrease your stitch width or increase your stitch length. If your appliqués have sharp angles, use a shorter stitch length and width to prevent overlapping stitches.

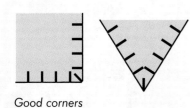

*Good corners*

*Stitches too wide*

*Feline Fairies* (detail), from *Laurel Burch Quilts* by Laurel Burch. Quilt by Nancy Odom.

## Inside Corners and Angles

You can treat your inside corners as you did the outside corners, or "fill in" the stitching a bit with starburst corners (see next column).

Begin on a straight portion of your appliqué. Use the measuring device (see previous page) to space your stitches so a straight stitch will end exactly at the corner; end with the needle down.

Lift the presser foot, and pivot the fabric so that the perpendicular stitch will divide the corner angle exactly in half. Sew in and out of the corner, ending with the needle down exactly at the corner again.

Lift the presser foot, and pivot the fabric so that the next straight stitch will fall exactly along the new straight edge. The needle will be lined up, ready to sew the next straight portion.

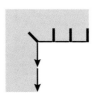

### *Starburst Corner*

Sew to the corner, then sew the perpendicular stitch at the corner without pivoting.

Lift the presser foot, and pivot the fabric so that the perpendicular stitch will divide the corner angle exactly in half. Drop the feed dogs—the machine will take an "extra" invisible stitch in the same hole as the perpendicular stitches, then sew the perpendicular stitch in and out of the corner, ending with the needle down exactly at the corner again.

Lift the presser foot, and pivot the fabric so that the next straight stitch will fall exactly along the new straight edge. Sew one more perpendicular stitch, stopping with the needle down along the new straight edge.

Raise the feed dogs, and continue sewing along the edge of the appliqué as usual.

(Continued on next page)

## Inside and Outside Curves

The trick to curves is to keep all the perpendicular stitches "pointing" exactly to the center of the curve. You will need to constantly stop sewing and pivot the fabric to evenly distribute your stitches along the curve.

Begin sewing on the straightest portion of the curve. When you need to turn, stop with the needle down after a straight stitch, lift the presser foot, and pivot the fabric until the perpendicular stitch is pointing toward the center of the curve.

Sew the perpendicular stitch in and out of the curve, stopping with the needle down. Raise the presser foot, and pivot the fabric until you are sewing straight along the edge. Sew a straight stitch. Repeat until the curve is completely sewn.

Sew along curves with shorter stitches; they make the curve look smoother.

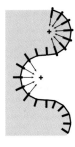

## Tip

### Heavy Stitches

Some types of appliqué, such as folk-art and felted wool, look especially good with a very heavy thread. If your machine won't handle thick thread, use two spools of 30-weight thread on the top of your machine. Check your manual for threading and tension requirements, and use a size 90/14 topstitching needle. Make sure to sew a sample first.

### Follow this Thread

See pages 80–82 for needles.
See pages 68–77 for threads.
See pages 84–86 for stablizers.
See pages 54–56 for presser feet.
See pages 201–202 for satin stitching.
See page 244 for serger appliqué.
See pages 57–59 for adjusting tension.

## Satin Stitch Appliqué

### Harriet Hargrave

*Satin stitching—particularly around appliqué—is an all-purpose decorative technique that's great for quilting, home décor, and garments (quilted or not). Use a contrasting color or specialty thread for a "wow!" effect, or a matching color for a more understated look. Satin stitch is a durable finish, so it's perfect for items that will be laundered frequently.*

A satin stitch consists of zigzag stitches set closely together so they appear as a solid line, but not so close that they bunch up and jam under the foot. The satin stitch completely encloses the raw edge, preventing unraveling. It has a crisp, durable-edge finish that results in a well-defined appliqué shape.

Knowing how to set up your machine is the key to successful satin stitching. The needle position for the majority of satin stitch appliqué is the center position. An open-toe appliqué foot will let you see the stitches as you go and help avoid snagging the thread. Use the same weight thread in both the top of the machine and the bobbin.

*Drift III* (detail) by Libby Lehman.

## Stitch Width

The ridge of satin stitches should be wide enough to completely encase the raw edges of an appliqué piece. This will prevent unraveling through multiple launderings. Each swing of the needle should catch approximately five to seven threads of the appliqué fabric, plus one or two threads of the background fabric. Start with a stitch width of ⅛", then experiment. Stitches that are too wide will have a bulky, heavy look; you want to just hold the edge securely and prevent unraveling. If the stitches are too wide, curves, corners, and points are more difficult.

*Carlotta in the Secret Garden* (detail) from *Laurel Burch Quilts* by Laurel Burch. Quilt by Barbara Baker and Jeri Boe.

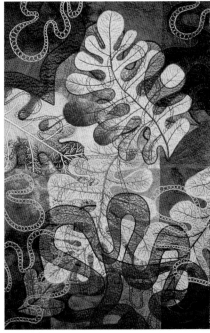

*Drift III* (detail) by Libby Lehman. See page 18 for another quilt by Libby.

## Quick Trick

### Watch the Needle

Train your eye to watch the needle as it swings to the right with each stitch, and keep it just a hair outside the appliqué edge. If the needle is too close to the edge, a frayed, fuzzy edge results. If the needle is too far from the edge, the edge won't be secured adequately and the satin stitch won't appear smooth.

## Stitch Length

Adjust the length to the shortest stitch your machine has and try the zigzag stitch. If the fabric or thread jams up, try a slightly longer stitch. The machine should feed the fabrics evenly without help—don't pull on the fabric or you will distort the stitches.

## Tension

When you have width and length settings you are happy with, adjust the top and bottom tensions. You want a tight stitch, where top thread color shows on the bottom but no bobbin thread shows on the top. Check your manual for a buttonhole tension setting for the top thread. This will draw the top thread to the underside, giving a smoother appearance along the edges, and you won't have to constantly change the bobbin thread to a color that matches the top thread.

Sew a line of stitches and look at them. If bobbin thread shows on the top, tighten the bobbin tension, but loosen the top only slightly (if the top tension gets too loose, the stitch will loop). Look on the back of the fabric. If the tension is adjusted adequately, there will be a bar of bobbin thread running down the center of the stitching, with top thread color showing on one or both sides.

## Tip

### Sewing Test Samples

Adjust only one setting at a time, then sew another line of stitches and check again. Too much tension adjusting is never a good thing—and it's hard to undo.

Check and readjust the tension for different sewing conditions. The weight and thickness of the fabric, number of layers, thread size and quality, spool size, and even how the thread is wound on the spool all affect thread tension. Regularly check the back of your work to be sure that the threads remain properly balanced.

Use 60-weight cotton embroidery thread for the needle and bobbin, a size 70/10 universal point needle, your open-toe appliqué foot, and the stabilizer of your choice. Start with a thread color that contrasts with the fabric of your test sample so you can clearly see the stitches as you go.

## Stabilizer

Stabilizer underneath your appliqué will add some stiffness to the fabric and help keep the stitches smooth and flat. Test different stabilizers before any new project, and practice satin stitching with different combinations until you feel comfortable. Generally, a heavy fabric needs a lightweight stabilizer, and a lighter-weight fabric needs a sturdier, stiffer stabilizer.

## Starting and Stopping

Begin stitching in the center of a straight line or very gentle curve. Pull the bobbin thread to the top. Hold both threads as you start stitching, and take several very small, straight stitches to lock the thread in place. Cut the thread tails close to the surface of the fabric. When you return to the starting point, stitch on top of the starting stitches for 2 or 3 stitches, then set the stitch width to 0 and sew several tiny, short stitches "in the ditch."

If you stop at the edge of another fabric, stitch three or four stitches into the next fabric, stop, and cut the threads. When you satin stitch around the next fabric, you will cover the previous stitches and lock them in.

## Outside Corners

There are three methods for satin-stitching outside corners.

### Crossover corner

This results in a very secure corner. Sew down one straight side. When you get to the corner, end on a right swing, with the needle down exactly outside the corner of the appliqué. Pivot the fabric; the needle is in position to sew along the new edge.

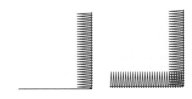

Sew slowly when you turn corners—your needle has to sew through the previous satin stitches as well as the fabric and stabilizer.

*(Continued on next page)*

### Butted Corner

This results in less bulk at the corner, but it is not as secure as a crossover corner. Use it when you need the corners of two opposite sides to match. Sew down one straight side. When you get to the corner, end with a left swing, with the needle down exactly at the next edge of the appliqué. Pivot the fabric until it is positioned to sew down the new side. Turn the hand-wheel, hold the fabric in place, and take one stitch in the same hole the last stitch made. The needle is now on the right swing, and you can continue your stitching down the new edge.

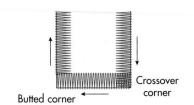

Butted corner      Crossover corner

### Mitered Corner

This method is slightly less bulky than the crossover corner, but holds securely. If your machine has both right- and left-hand needle positions, you can make mitered corners. Set your machine to the full right needle position. Sew down one straight side. When you get to the corner, end on a right swing, with the needle down exactly outside the corner of the appliqué. Pivot the fabric under the needle, which is already in position to sew along the new edge.

Set your stitch width to 0, then stitch slowly, gradually increasing the stitch width until you are back at your original setting. (Because of the right-hand needle position, the width will increase to the left, angling out as you stitch.) Continue along the new edge.

### Inside Corners

It's best to use a crossover corner, similar to the outside corner technique, to securely stitch all edges of inside corners. Stitch past the turning point of the corner, ending on a left swing, the same distance past the corner as your stitch width.

Stop stitching and pivot to gauge your distance past the corner.

Pivot the fabric. Stitch slowly along the new edge, aligning the stitches carefully, until you have sewn over all the previous stitches.

Continue stitching down the new edge.

## Curves
### Outside Curves

Pivot when the needle is in its right-hand swing, on the outside of the appliqué piece. Stop sewing with the needle down, lift the presser foot, and reposition the fabric slightly so the needle will sew directly toward the center of the curve, perpendicular to that portion of the curve.

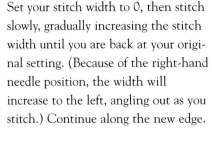

*Pivot points for outside curves*

### Inside Curves

Pivot when the needle is in its left-hand swing, inside the appliqué piece. Inside curves are often tighter than outside curves, so you will need to pivot more often. Go slowly—you'll see the needle beginning to angle away from perpendicular and know it's time to take a slight pivot.

*Pivot points for inside curves*

## Points
### Inside Points

Draw a light pencil guideline that extends from the second edge of your point into the body of the appliqué. Eventually, you will be able to do this by eye.

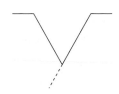

### Blunt Points

Stitch along the first edge, stopping with a left swing when the needle is at the guideline. Use the handwheel to guide the needle up and down again into the same hole it just left. Reposition the fabric so you are ready to continue sewing along the new edge. Continue stitching.

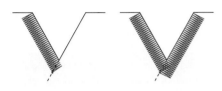

### Pointed Points

Draw light guidelines as wide as your stitch width to show your point. Sew along the first side until the right swing of the needle hits the guideline. Pivot the fabric slightly so that the foot aligns with the point. Sew one stitch at a time, reducing the stitch width to stay within the guidelines. At the end of the point, you should be at 0.

Pivot the fabric, and continue along the second side, gradually increasing the stitch width.

Pivot slightly to stay within the guidelines.

## Outside Points

### Mitered Points

These points aren't as secure as the pointed method, but they have a more formal look.

Draw a guideline that divides the point in half. Stitch along the first side until the needle hits the guideline. Begin decreasing the stitch width, and stitch so the needle swings from the guideline to the fabric edge. End at the very point at 0 width. Pivot, then sew along the second side, increasing the stitch width as you go, until you are back to the original width. Continue along the new edge.

### Tapered Points

This technique works especially well on long, thin points. Stitch along the first edge, and stop when the right swing of the needle goes outside the other edge of the point. Pivot slightly so the point is in the center of the presser foot. Continue sewing slowly, and gradually decrease the stitch width as you sew—the needle swing should rub both raw edges with each stitch.

At the very tip of the point, you should be at 0 width, and the point should be totally encased with stitches. Pivot the fabric, and stitch along the second edge, increasing the stitch width at the same rate that you decreased it. When you are back at the original stitch width, pivot slightly and continue stitching.

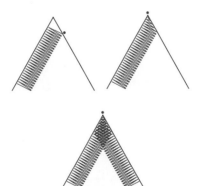

## Practice

Practice these techniques until you can easily and comfortably control the fabric with your left hand and make width adjustments with your right hand as you sew.

## Pivoting

Satin stitches should always be perpendicular to the cut edge of the appliqué, even along curved edges. Without pivoting, you will get gaps or sew slanted stitches, not perpendicular ones, giving the edge a messy finish.

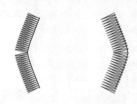

*Gaps from pivoting on wrong side of needle swing.*

*Slanted stitches*

When you are first learning to pivot, sew a few stitches, then pivot slightly, repeating this slowly until the curve is complete. Pivot more frequently on tighter curves, less frequently on gentler curves.

# 5 Ways to Use Satin Stitching in Appliqué

*Jane Sassaman*

**1. Defining:** To reinforce and emphasize the line between a shape and the background, use matching thread and a slightly open satin stitch so the edge of the fabric is still visible. The needle follows the edge of the shape as a guide.

**2. Blurring:** Use a neighboring color of thread with a slightly open satin stitch. The stitch overlaps both the shape's perimeter and the background to blur or distort the definite silhouette of the shape.

**3. Drawing:** A tight or closed satin stitch creates a solid line of color. This line is so strong and definite that it adds a whole new design element. It also creates additional texture and interest because of the raised thread on the fabric's surface.

**4. Electrifying:** A contrasting color of shiny rayon thread makes the shape seem to glow and vibrate. This effect adds vitality and enlivens the design.

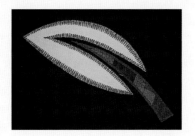

**5. Painting and Sculpting:** Use a lighter thread on one side and a darker thread on the other side to create the illusion of dimension and depth. This implies sunlight because the shape is outlined with light and shadow.

## Shadow Appliqué

In shadow appliqué, shapes are stitched or fused to a base fabric, and a sheer fabric such as voile, organdy, or organza is stitched on top, allowing the shapes to show or "shadow" through the sheer layer.

A lovely variation on shadow appliqué uses silk flowers stitched to a base fabric to create subtle images under a layer of sheer fabric. Vest by Annrae Roberts.

## BARTACKS

Follow this Thread

See pages 43–53 for a visual
guide to decorative stitches.

## A New Look for Bartacks

*Pauline Richards*

*Ordinary embroidery floss takes on a new
use and dimension when small skeins are
machine-bartacked to fabric. Clip and
fluff the ends after stitching for a unique
play on floss.*

### Prepare the Skeins

Secure one end of the embroidery floss
to one end of a piece of 1" x 3⅓" cardboard with your thumb.

Wrap the floss lengthwise around the
cardboard 10 or 11 times and cut the
floss end. Slide the mini skein off the
cardboard and set it aside carefully.
Don't wrap the floss too tightly or it will
be difficult to slide off the cardboard.

Prepare as many mini skeins as desired
from each floss color.

### Tip
### No Bartack Stitch?

A bartack stitch is often used to
reinforce areas of stress in garments
such as belt loops or the end of a zipper. If your machine doesn't have a
bartack stitch, use a closely spaced
zigzag stitch.

### Apply the Skeins

Avoid positioning the skeins within 1"
of all seamlines and within 2" of a
hemline. Pin each skein into position.
Thread the machine with thread
matching the floss color. Set your
machine for a 4mm to 5mm bartack.

Gently twist the coordinating color
mini skein to force
the threads together.
Position the twisted
skein parallel to
the crosswise grain
under the presser
foot and bartack
over the first
floss color.

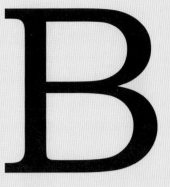

Turn the fabric 180°, bringing the
completed bartack behind the presser
foot. Realign the mini skein with the
crosswise fabric grain. Twist the skein
again, straightening and smoothing
the floss strands as necessary. Position

the first bartack
about 1" behind
the needle and
secure the twisted
floss with another
bartack.

Secure all the other mini skeins with
matching thread and bartacks. Clip,
trim and even out the floss ends.

The secured mini
skein should meas-
ure about 3".
Apply a dab of
seam sealant or
fray preventive to
the wrong side of
each bartack.

# BEADING

**Follow this Thread**

See pages 80–82 for needles.
See pages 68–77 for threads.
See page 54 for beading feet.
See pages 162–163 for hooping.

## Beading by Machine

**Pauline Richards**

*Beaded projects look intricate, but if you can thread a needle and plug in a machine, you can bead by machine. Here are three techniques to try.*

## Free-motion Stitching

Beads can be applied one at a time using free-motion machine stitching.

Select beads, such as large seed beads, that have holes large enough for a fine machine needle (such as 60/8) to fit through.

Secure the fabric in an embroidery hoop. Drop the feed dogs and follow the instructions in your machine manual to set up the machine for free-motion stitching.

Use extra-fine monofilament thread for stitching that is basically invisible.

To begin, take several stitches in place to secure the thread. Then, place a bead on the needle, stitch through the bead center, then stitch to the side of the bead. Repeat, moving the hoop as desired to free-motion stitch to the next bead location. Finish by taking several stitches in place to secure the thread.

## Couching

Use a zigzag stitch to apply rows of cross-locked beads to fabric. A beading, cording, or special "pearls and piping" presser foot (with a channel to guide the beads automatically as you stitch) makes these machine methods especially quick and easy. *Note: Cross-locked beads are strings of beads where each bead is locked in place and are generally available from bead-craft suppliers.*

To stitch beads, thread the needle with extra-fine monofilament thread. Wind the bobbin with thread to match the project. Adjust the stitch length and width to create a long, narrow zigzag stitch that slips between the raised beads.

You can also leave the machine set to a straight stitch and stitch along two beads. Jump over the beading thread to the other side and stitch along two beads.

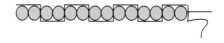

## Serging

To serge beads, thread the loopers and needle with monofilament thread. Adjust the machine for rolled-edge stitching or flatlocking. (See pages 215–216 for details on flatlocking.)

Apply the beads, then use a seam sealant or fray preventive on the wrong side at the beginning and end of each row of stitches.

## Quick Trick

### String Your Own Beads

If you don't have pre-strung beads, you can string your own.

Thread a beading needle (or other needle that will go through the beads) with Nymo beading thread or other strong thread. Do not cut the thread yet; leave it attached to the spool.

String a length of beads.

From the right side of the fabric, insert the needle where you want to start beading, and securely tie off the end of the thread.

Snug the beads to the starting point and use one of the machine stitching methods.

When you reach the end, slide any unused beads back toward the spool. Cut the thread, leaving a 6" tail.

Thread the tail onto a hand-sewing needle, and insert the needle into the fabric. Secure the thread with a few hand stitches.

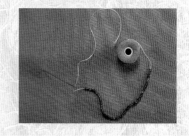

## More Ideas

### Beaded Edges

Strings of beads can also be zig-zagged onto edges for a quick and elegant finish.

# BINDING

See pages 43–53 for a visual guide to decorative stitches.

## Decorative Stitched Bindings

**Lynn Koolish**

*Tired of the same old binding? Don't want to stitch it by hand? Want something fun for a child's quilt? Try stitching down bindings from the front with built-in decorative stitches.*

You can add decorative stitching to a binding that has already been sewn down simply by stitching over it, but you can also make the decorative stitching a part of the binding process.

## Selecting Stitches

Select stitches that fit the width of the binding. It's okay if the stitch doesn't cover the entire binding, but you don't want the stitching to be wider than the binding itself.

The stitching doesn't have to be continuous along the entire edge, but select stitches that will secure the binding enough to withstand washing and handling.

Look for open or outline stitches. Dense stitching may cause puckering.

Have fun matching stitches to the fabric motifs: flower and leaf stitches for floral fabrics, playful stitches for kid's fabrics, geometric stitches for graphic, geometric fabrics, and so on.

## Quick Trick

### Ideas for Quick Bindings
**Sarah Dunn**

1. Cut the quilt backing ½" bigger than the quilt front. Wrap backing around to the front, fold under, and stitch down with a decorative or topstitch.

2. Plan the quilt front to be ½" bigger than the quilt back. Wrap quilt front around to the back, fold under, and stitch down with a decorative stitch. If you stitch from the back, you can use heavier decorative thread in the bobbin for a bolder look. (See pages 113–115 for more on bobbinwork.)

## More Ideas

### Combining Stitches

For another look, use the machine's programming capabilities to combine several stitches into a new stitch. Use stitches that flow into each other in a logical manner.

Program words into the machine memory to stitch the binding with nursery rhymes, a new baby's name, or a favorite phrase.

# BOBBINWORK

See pages 43–53 for a visual guide to decorative stitches.
See pages 80–82 for needles.
See pages 68–77 for threads.
See pages 84–86 for stabilizers.
See pages 57–59 for adjusting tension.

## Stitching from Below

**Deborah Yedziniak**

*Bobbinwork is a method of sewing from the back side using a decorative thread or ribbon in the bobbin and standard sewing thread in the needle. Working with the right side of the fabric down, threads and yarns too thick to use in the needle become an available option when used in the bobbin.*

## Thread Selection

For the bobbin, look at the decorative threads available. Within reason, any decorative embroidery thread that can be sewn by hand can be tried in the bobbin. However, it's better to use a twisted thread, such as perle cotton, as opposed to a stranded thread, such as six-strand embroidery floss. Stranded thread can separate and feed unevenly, causing a thread jam.

Experiment with a variety of novelty threads and ribbons, including crochet threads, corded threads, and silk ribbons in 2mm or 4mm widths. Some machines don't sew well with the wider 4mm ribbon, so try a narrower ribbon or corded thread instead.

For the upper thread, use an all-purpose sewing thread. For an invisible look, match the upper thread and bobbin thread colors, or try a fine monofilament thread.

*(Continued on next page)*

When using monofilament thread, sew test samples to adjust the tension correctly. The fineness of the upper thread compared to the heavier bobbin thread will mean extra adjustments.

Another popular upper thread choice is 30- or 40-weight rayon embroidery thread. Match or contrast the embroidery thread color to the bobbin thread. This adds a highlight of color and an interesting dimension to the stitch.

## Tension Adjustments

The most important adjustment for bobbinwork is the tension for both the upper and bobbin threads. The bobbin thread is the passive thread that lies below the fabric. The needle or upper thread is the active thread that stitches or couches the bobbin thread in place. By adjusting the thread tensions, you can achieve an attractive stitch that shows off the decorative thread and gives greater texture to the stitching.

The bobbin thread is heavier than normal sewing thread; you will need to loosen the tension so the thread feeds with ease through the tension clip or bypass the tension

totally. The rounder cordlike threads need a looser tension than flatter ribbon-like threads. Some bobbin cases have a hole through which the tension clip is bypassed.

In effect, there's no real thread tension. Depending on your sewing machine, this could cause a thread jam. Check your owner's manual for advice.

The upper thread holds the bobbin thread in place. It can hold the thread firmly or loosely, which affects the look of the stitch. Increase the upper tension one number at a time until the desired result is achieved. Adjust the tensions, and then stitch a sample to determine the tension's effect on the stitch. The same thread and stitch can look very different at different tension settings.

The looser the upper tension, the more visible the needle thread.

A small screw usually controls the bobbin case tension. Turn the screw slightly (right to tighten; left to loosen) and pull the thread to see how the tension has been adjusted. Sew a test piece and check the stitching. The bobbin thread should be held in place by the upper thread. Adjust the tension as needed. Ribbons will lie flatter and look fuller with less tension, but beware, as less tension can cause a jam.

 **Quick Trick**

### Keep an Extra Bobbin Case
To avoid problems resetting the tension for normal sewing, purchase a second bobbin case for use with bobbinwork.

## Stitch Selection

Experiment with a variety of stitches on your machine.

Try the basic straight stitch and adjust the length from short to long.

Select the zigzag stitch and adjust both length and width. You'll achieve very different results with a short-wide zigzag, a long-wide zigzag and a long-narrow zigzag.

Use the basic straight or zigzag stitch to sew a variety of designs, such as scrolls and loops. These stitches also are good for forming flowers and letters.

Use decorative stitches to sew rows of stitches for outlining details, such as collars or pockets.

Free-motion sewing will produce interesting shapes or a stippling effect.

Experiment with other decorative stitches, such as a feather stitch, cross stitch, flower stitch, and an appliqué or blanket stitch. With the heavier bobbin thread, the stitch quality improves if you increase the length and width from the normal setting.

Experiment with the stitches on a sample fabric piece. Note the stitch and the length and width settings to help you learn which combinations are most pleasing to the eye.

Use bobbinwork to embellish any number of projects. For example, a shirt or jacket collar, cuffs and yoke offer ideal areas for decorative bobbin

*Time Warp* (detail) by Ricky Tims. See page 14 for quilt.

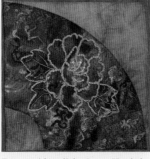

*Fantasy* (detail) by Lynn Koolish. See page 22 for quilt.

*Vest* (detail) by Rosemary Eichorn. See page 15 for vest.

stitching. Or simply embellish a piece of fabric with an eye-catching design, then cut out the fabric and make a pillow or use in a quilt.

## Stitching the Designs

Wind the thread onto the bobbin by hand or machine. If you use the machine, you may have to hand-feed the thread because the thread might not come on a traditional spool. When winding by hand, take care to firmly and evenly wind the thread on the bobbin. Not much thread will fit on the bobbin due to the larger thread size, so wind two or three bobbins before beginning to sew.

Stabilize the wrong side of the fabric with a fusible stabilizer or interfacing to avoid distorting the fabric while sewing. Draw the design on the stabilizer with pencil. Remember, the finished design will be the reverse image of the design drawn on the stabilizer. Although the fabric is sewn right side face down, let the machine feed the fabric normally.

Choose the needle size according to the fabric type you're sewing. For general purposes, use a ballpoint needle.

Choose the threads you want to sew with and experiment with both the upper and lower tensions to achieve the desired result.

When stitching is completed, cut the threads and use a large-eye darning needle or a chenille needle to pull the threads to the wrong side of the fabric; knot the threads.

## BRIDGE STITCHES

See page 44 for more stitches to use for fagoting.
See pages 80–82 for needles.
See pages 68–77 for threads.
See pages 84–86 for stabilizers.

## Bridging the Gap with Fagoting

### Sallie J. Russell

*By using one of the bridging (or fagoting) stitches on your machine, you can actually feature a seamline—or make it a focal point of your creations.*

Fagoting is a method of attaching fabric to fabric—or fabric to trim—with a row of threads, creating an open, lacy look. It is often associated with heirloom sewing. Although fagoting is too delicate to use in high-stress areas, it can be used to lengthen or decorate garments and table linens.

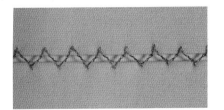

## Selecting Threads

For light- to medium-weight fabric, use cotton machine embroidery thread or rayon thread for extra sheen. For medium- to heavyweight fabric, use heavier topstitching thread.

## Basic Fagoting Stitch

Use an open-toe presser foot. Select the needle and thread according to the fabric weight.

Loosen the tension for the needle thread so the bobbin thread doesn't show on the right side of the project. Make a test sample to adjust the tension, stitch length, and stitch width. (The stitch length determines how much thread shows in the open space between the two fabric pieces.)

Create the fagoting space by pressing under the desired seam allowance, plus 1⁄16".

To keep the two fabric pieces an equal distance apart when stitching, draw two parallel lines 1⁄8" apart on a piece of water-soluble stabilizer.

Pin or baste the fabric pieces right side up onto the stabilizer, matching the folded fabric edges to the drawn lines.

Center the space under the presser foot and stitch, barely catching alternate edges with the bridging stitch.

*(Continued on next page)*

Remove the stabilizer and press.

For a heavier look, wind the bobbin with perle or crochet cotton. Pin or baste the fabric, wrong side up, onto the stabilizer and stitch.

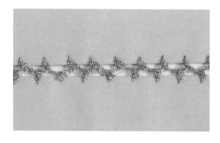

Fagoting is a beautiful way to hold together lengths of lace.

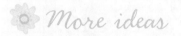

## More ideas

### Try Other Stitches
Some machines have a built-in stitch called a fagoting stitch, but many of the utility, as well as decorative stitches, are perfect for fagoting. Experiment with stitches and decorative threads for a unique look.

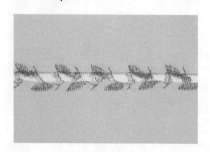

### Serger Fagoting
A serger flatlocking stitch can also be used for fagoting (see page 217).

*Bridge Stitch examples stitched by Lynn Koolish.*

## BUILT-IN STITCHES

### Follow this Thread

See pages 43–53 for a visual guide to decorative stitches.
See pages 80–82 for needles.
See pages 68–77 for threads.
See pages 84–86 for stabilizers.

## Using Built-in Stitches

**Rebecca Kemp Brent**
*Many sewing machines include a variety of built-in stitches. Older machines may have just a few; newer computerized machines may have hundreds, with the capability to program even more. The uses for built-in stitches are limited only by your imagination.*

*Start by becoming familiar with the shapes and sizes of your machine stitches, then play with the variations available.*

## Analyze the Stitches
Begin by thinking of the machine's decorative stitches in categories. Many stitches may fit more than one category.

### Filled or Open
Is the pattern filled with satin stitching, or is it shaped by a series of straight stitches?

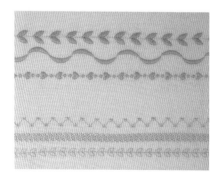

Pre-made shirt stitched with built-in stitches and embroidery by Elizabeth Tisinger.

*Embroidery designs: Cactus Punch, SIG 18*

*Built-in stitches: Husqvarna Viking*

### Straight or Meandering
As a whole, does the stitch pattern create a straight line, or does it weave back and forth?

### Straight or Shaped Edges
Stitch a sample several inches long and look at the pattern's upper and lower edges. Are they straight, or do they form a scalloped or peaked line? Is one side straight while the other is shaped?

### Narrow or Wide

Notice the stitch's default width and its appearance at that setting. Also observe if the machine uses lateral motion—feeding the fabric sideways under the presser foot—to form the stitch.

## Stitch Variations

Decorative stitches come with preprogrammed length and width settings. These are the settings that yield the result shown in the instruction book or on the machine's control panel.

Sometimes, changing the default settings can result in an unattractive appearance or create mechanical problems while forming the stitch. For example, shortening a satin stitch may cause thread to build up, hindering the fabric feed. In other situations, it may be necessary to change the default settings to accommodate an unusual thread weight or fabric texture.

Most of the time, though, varying the stitch is an enjoyable way to play. The most elementary stitch variations are length and width adjustments. Options vary by machine, from a small, medium, or large choice to incremental variations along a digital scale.

### Width

Try changing only the width. Sometimes the distortion creates a new design with a very different appearance.

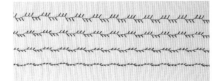

### Width and Length

Change the width and length proportionally to make a larger or smaller version of the original.

### Length

Lengthen a decorative satin stitch to create a lacy, open pattern, or decrease the stitch length to improve the appearance by preventing fabric show-through. Increase the length of a decorative stitch for the illusion of greater width.

### Combinations

Create and save stitch combinations and use them as building blocks. For example, alternate a leafy vine with a flower stitch. You can also create patterns using different lengths of the same stitch pattern.

### Mirror Image

Use a single pattern of a decorative stitch in combination with its mirror image. If your machine allows, experiment with mirroring the design both horizontally and vertically.

## Stabilizers

The secret to attractive decorative stitches is stabilizing the fabric. Some projects allow fusible interfacing under the stitched border, providing support for the stitches.

For areas that aren't interfaced, use a liquid water-soluble stabilizer or aerosol stabilizer such as spray starch to stiffen the fabric. Apply several light coats, pressing the fabric dry

between applications. This method provides a stable surface for stitching, and the stabilizer washes away, so there isn't any fabric or paper to be picked out by hand when the stitching is finished.

Satin-stitch patterns often require additional stabilizer to prevent the fabric from forming a tuck or tunnel underneath the stitches. A lightweight tear-away stabilizer provides additional support. When stitching multiple satin-stitched rows, remove and replace the stabilizer as each row is completed to avoid leaving tiny pieces between each row.

## Threads

To add variety to decorative stitches, consider using specialty threads as well as embroidery and all-purpose sewing threads.

### Metallic Threads

Use a needle designed for metallic threads. It may be necessary to loosen the tension and stitch at a slower speed. Some metallic threads are flat, like ribbon, and twist during stitching. Sometimes they lie flat and sometimes on edge, creating satin stitches with an uneven appearance. Try round metallic threads for satin-stitch patterns.

### Variegated Threads

These multicolored threads sometimes combine with a stitch pattern for wonderful results. For example, stitch multicolored blossoms along a vining stitch. If the colors look too patchy, try combining the variegated thread with a coordinating solid color thread through the same needle.

### Heavy Threads

Make the decorative stitch bolder by using a heavier thread in the needle, such as 12-weight cotton thread, quilting thread, or topstitching thread, or by using two threads in a single needle.

*(Continued on next page)*

Use with a larger needle (size 90/14 or 100/16) or one recommended for top-stitching, which is engineered to carry and protect the heavier thread. You may also need to reduce the upper tension and adjust the satin-stitch motif density to avoid thread buildup.

## Tension

Evaluate the tension setting for each stitch using the thread that will be used for the project. The needle thread should be pulled slightly to the wrong side of the fabric so no bobbin thread is visible from the right side. If a wide decorative stitch creates a tuck or tunnel along the stitch length, reduce the upper tension.

## Tips for Creating Stitched Borders

**Rebecca Kemp Brent**

*Have fun combining the decorative stitches on your machine into borders. Keep sample fabric handy to try stitch combinations and refine the settings for various threads and fabrics.*

To create a mock lace border, begin with two or three rows of honeycomb stitch positioned so their edges touch. Add a scallop on each side, slightly overlapping the honeycomb. Finish with a flower or meandering vine down the center, over the honeycomb. Use a satin stitch motif or a heavier thread for the final stitch pattern so it stands out against the honeycomb.

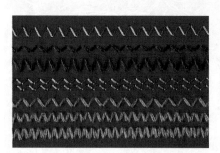

Repeat a single utility or decorative stitch to create a border. Change the length, width, and thread to vary the rows.

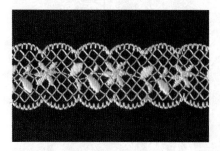

Stacked stitches can simulate ribbon beading. Set the machine for a 4mm satin zigzag and stitch along a guideline. Change to a contrasting thread and a 4.5mm to 5mm ladder stitch and stitch over the satin zigzag. To complete the illusion, add a silk ribbon bow.

To turn a border into an edging, position a satin stitch scallop along the desired finished edge. After stitching, draw a line of seam sealant or fray preventive along the scallops on the wrong side of the fabric. Cover with a damp press cloth and press dry. Trim away the excess fabric below the scallops.

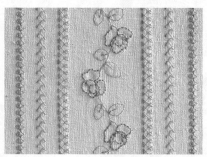

Combine floral and crazy quilt stitches for another look.

See pages 43–53 for a visual guide to decorative stitches.
See pages 80–82 for needles.
See pages 68–77 for threads.
See pages 84–86 for stabilizers.
See pages 10 and 13 for Kristen's vest and stitched block.

## Decorative Machine Stitching and Quilts

### Kristen Dibbs

*Add decorative stitching to the printed surface of fabric in quilts to create another dimension.*

### Using Decorative Stitching

Decorative stitching is most easily done after the quilt is pieced, but before it is quilted. Avoid distortion caused by intensive stitching by using either a fusible tear-away stabilizer or one or more layers of light, fusible quilt batting.

With a layer of quilt batting fused to the back of the fabric, the decorative stitching will sink down into the fabric, throwing the unstitched areas into relief. The shine of silky rayon and metallic thread provides a rich contrast to the matte surface of cotton fabric. Choose a line on the printed fabric and follow it with the stitch pattern of your choice.

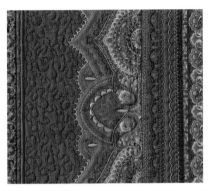

### Using Single Pattern Units

Most modern machines have a single pattern unit function, so you can program your machine to sew just one little heart or leaf shape, and you can place these wherever you want them on your fabric. Make sure you always secure your thread at the beginning and end of each individual pattern unit so there will be no chance of your threads unraveling.

### Quick Trick

#### Hooping Can Help

If you find that your fabric is distorting even when you use stabilizer, try using a hoop. (See pages 162–163 for hooping techniques.)

## Find Your Stitch Vocabulary   *Jane Sassaman*

Every quilter has a different style of working and individual ideas to express. Just as quilters are different, so are sewing machines. Each brand and model offers a unique selection of features and stitches. Discover for yourself which machine, features, and stitches are appropriate for your work. Explore your machine to use it to its fullest advantage. You may currently be using a few of many available stitches, but by experimenting you may be surprised to discover a new stitch that you can add to your visual vocabulary.

Test the stitches and effects of your machine by making a sampler and trying as many stitches and variations as your machine will perform. Some stitches will look better than others. Some will look good but will be inappropriate for your style of work. By trying them out, a stitch just may surprise you by being just what you're looking for.

*Resurrection* (detail) from *The Quilted Garden* by Jane Sassaman. Quilt by Jane Sassaman.

*Seeds* (detail) from *The Quilted Garden* by Jane Sassaman. Quilt by Jane Sassaman.

*Lily* (detail) from *The Quilted Garden* by Jane Sassaman. Quilt by Jane Sassaman. See page 15 for quilt.

# BUTTONHOLES

## Follow this Thread

See pages 43–53 for a visual guide to decorative stitches.
See pages 84–86 for stabilizers.
See pages 106–110 for satin stitch appliqué.

## Appliquéd Buttonholes

**Pauline Richards**

*Whether hidden behind a pleated placket or taking center stage with fun appliqués, buttonholes make an ordinary shirt interesting. Use these ideas to embellish a ready-made garment or when creating your own.*

If you are creating new buttonholes, make any necessary spacing adjustments so that one buttonhole is centered over the fullest part of the bust to prevent gaping.

When planning buttonhole appliqués, select fabrics with 1⅛"-wide or smaller motifs so they will fit within the placket width.

Look for unusual, eye-catching buttons or charms.

For more interest, alternate appliqué buttonholes with purely decorative appliqués.

Consider embellishing buttonholes on cuffs and pockets, too.

## Frayed Appliqués

If using a plaid fabric for these appliqués, choose a woven rather than printed plaid, since plaids may be printed off-grain.

Determine and mark the desired number of buttonhole and decorative appliqué squares. For an average blouse cut each appliqué fabric square 1¼" x 1¼" centering the desired motif. Fray ⅛" to ¼" on each fabric square edge.

Cut and center a ¾" square of fusible web on the wrong side of each fabric square. Fuse following the manufacturer's instructions.

Remove the protective paper from the back of each frayed fabric square and center an appliqué over each mark. Fuse in place.

Use a 2mm straight stitch to sew around each square ⅛" to ¼" from the edge.

Stitch the buttonholes and sew on the buttons.

## Satin-stitched Appliqués

Determine and mark the desired number of buttonholes and decorative appliqués. Depending on the width of the placket, cut shapes no larger than 1⅛" x 2" from the fabric, centering any motifs.

Follow the manufacturer's instructions to iron fusible web to the wrong side of each appliqué.

Center an appliqué over each mark and fuse in place. Use an appliqué foot and a narrow satin stitch to sew around the appliqué edges with matching or decorative thread. For added interest, use decorative stitches or add design elements, such as rays, to the edges.

Secure thread ends with a small dot of seam sealant or fray preventive applied to the wrong side of the stitches.

Stitch buttonholes and secure buttons.

## Decorating Buttonholes

**Sallie J. Russell**

- Make the buttonhole into a trim by stitching with embroidery thread or other suitable decorative thread.

- Buttonholes can form borders in place of more traditional trims. Kids will get a kick when you make a buttonhole mouth on an appliqué. Cut it open and show a tongue or teeth stitching out.

- Make a buttonhole face.

- Dress up a standard buttonhole with decorative stitches at both ends or surround the buttonhole with decorative stitches.

- Use a wide satin stitch—larger than a true buttonhole setting— to make an oversize buttonhole for use with a smaller button. Use a hoop to prevent the wide satin stitch from puckering.

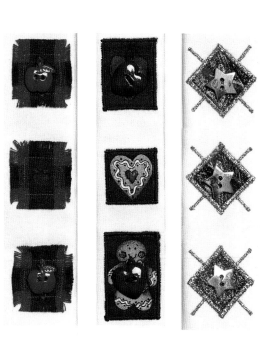

# CHARTED NEEDLEWORK

*Follow this Thread*

See pages 201–202 for satin stitching.
See pages 68–77 for threads.
See pages 84–86 for stabilizers.

## Charted Needlework by Machine

### Patsy Shields

*Charted needlework by machine is a unique technique using satin stitching over very small knitting needles to create a design that looks like hand stitching.*

## Getting Started

Use a commercial charted needlework pattern or create your own on graph paper.

Apply stabilizer to the wrong side of the fabric.

Tape the charted pattern in place on the right side of the fabric.

Thread the machine with the appropriate color needle thread for the top thread and a fine-weight bobbin thread in the bobbin.

Remove the presser foot from the machine. Lower the feed dogs. If you can't lower the feed dogs on your machine, set the stitch length to zero. The feed dogs no longer have the ability to move the fabric and you can control the fabric movement.

A foot with a deep groove such as a pintuck foot can also be used with this technique, see page 55.

## Stitching

Place the fabric under the machine needle at the design upper edge. You may start from either the right or left side of the design, whichever feels more comfortable to you.

With the needle thread in your hand, turn the handwheel to lower the needle into the fabric. Bring the needle up out of the fabric; tug on the needle thread to bring the bobbin thread to the top of the fabric. Straight stitch in place four or five times to secure the stitches; clip the beginning threads close to the stitching.

Lay a knitting needle on the pattern between two black pattern lines; lower the presser foot.

Set the machine for a zigzag stitch just wide enough to clear the knitting needle comfortably.

To anchor the charted needle, slowly zigzag over the needle, pushing the work away from you rather quickly to create an open zigzag stitch.

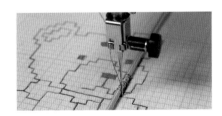

Go over this row of stitching again, this time pulling the fabric slowly toward you and stitching quickly so the stitching builds up and has a satiny appearance. *(Continued on next page)*

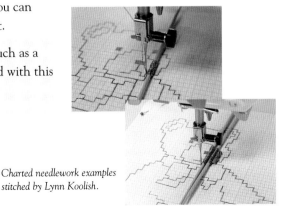

*Charted needlework examples stitched by Lynn Koolish.*

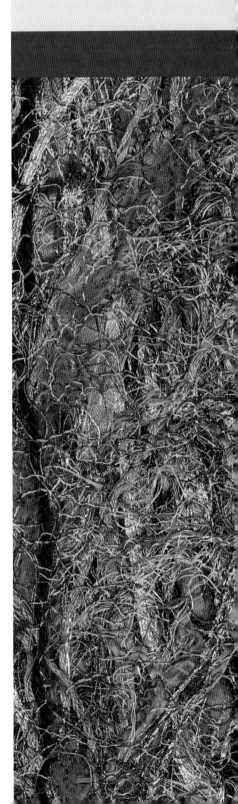

If your satin stitch isn't heavy enough, go over the row again. This will cover the needle completely and give the pattern a fuller look.

Follow the color pattern and fill in each color area, stitching all of one color before changing threads.

It's necessary to secure the stitches at the end of the row only when you're changing thread colors. To secure the stitches, return the machine to a straight stitch, and stitch in place several times. Raise the presser foot, clip the needle thread, rethread the needle with the new color, lower the presser foot, and stitch in place several times. Return the machine to a zigzag stitch and continue stitching the pattern.

Do not remove the charted needle until the row on each side of the needle has been stitched. If your pattern has more than one color in the same row, try to leave the needle in that row so you can go back later and stitch the remaining colors. If you must remove the needle before the row is completed, simply slide the needle back under the stitches.

Place the next charted needle beside the first one and repeat the process. As you become comfortable with the technique, you can eliminate the anchoring step and just satin stitch over each needle. Continue in this manner until all of the pattern is stitched.

When the design is completed, remove all of the charted needles and unthread the machine needle. Stitch around the design outer edge to perforate the paper. Remove the project from the machine and tear off the pattern and stabilizer.

# CHENILLE

See page 94 for chenille tools.
See page 124 for pictorial chenille.
See page 174 for stitching chenille on a longarm machine.

## Making Chenille Fabric

*Nancy Restuccia*
*Whether used as embellishment or for a whole garment or quilt, chenille can be everything from elegant to down-home cozy.*

## Foundation Fabrics

The foundation fabric is the one upon which the chenille is built. This layer remains intact after all the rest are slashed. For best results, the fabric needs to be strong enough to support the many slashed layers throughout construction, washing, and drying. Fabrics that are flat and densely woven, such as cottons, microfibers, and twills, will provide a firmer foundation than a loosely woven, nubbly, or crinkly fabric.

## Selecting Slash Fabrics

Slash fabrics are the ones that actually form the "fuzzy" chenille. When selecting slash fabrics, look for fabrics made entirely from cotton, rayon, or silk. Avoid polyesters and polyester blends (they don't bloom well) and wools (they shrink and felt). Generally, the looser the weave, the better the fabric will bloom. Don't overlook the upholstery section when searching for fabrics; tapestries and gauzes are possibilities. In particular, don't forget about flannels—they make especially cozy chenille.

There are exceptions to every rule. Tissue lamé is a synthetic fabric that adds wonderful sparkle within a slashed fabric construction. Other sparkly fabrics can work very well when layered with fabrics that bloom well.

The only way to know for sure how different fabrics will interact within your finished project is to test them. Wash and dry the test samples to see how individual fabrics will perform.

## Making the Chenille
*Preparing the Fabric*

It's not necessary to prewash most fabrics used in slashed fabric construction; the sizing in unwashed fabrics helps to make stitching easier, plus natural shrinkage often contributes a desired texture to the final effect. If you mix fibers or use fabrics you think will bleed, wash and press first.

Trim selvages from all fabrics and straighten the raw edges.

When making chenille, the fabric slashes need to be cut on the bias, so when planning a project such as a scarf, cut lengths of fabric on the bias and stitch and slash the channels parallel to the long edges (see photo above).

For other projects, such as quilt squares or a garment, cut fabric on the straight grain, and stitch and slash the channels on the bias (see jacket below). For larger projects, the foundation fabric can be pieced together if needed.

Work on a flat surface and layer the fabrics to be slashed on top of the foundation fabric. Pin the layers together or use basting spray. The layers to be slashed can be overlapped at the edges if necessary to create pieces large enough for your project.

### Stitching

Mark a center stitching line lengthwise on the top fabric. Stitch with a short, very narrow zigzag (or straight triple-stretch stitch). Remove pins as you sew. See tip at right for suggestions on channel width.

Stitch as many rows as needed on either side of the center stitching line. Stitch each row in opposite directions to minimize shifting.

Use an even-feed or walking foot and hold the fabric layers from side-to-side while stitching to prevent fabric shifting and stretching.

### Trimming and Slashing

Trim the raw edges on all sides.

Use a blunt-tip scissors or a rotary cutter and mat designed for chenille to cut between the stitching. Cut through the top layers only. **Don't cut through the fabric base layer.**

### Washing and Drying

Shake the slashed fabric well to get rid of any loose fibers. Trim any fabric that extends beyond the surface.

Machine wash and dry at least once, but washing and drying three times is preferable. To bring out the full bloom, include jeans, towels, sneakers, or other rough and textured items in the washer and dryer.

## Quick Trick

### Two-sided Chenille

It's a snap to make two-sided chenille that is perfect for scarves.

1. Place three or more layers of fabric (and shadow fabrics if desired—see more ideas) on top of the foundation fabric.

2. Pin through all the layers.

3. Turn the scarf over.

4. Add three or more layers and shadow fabrics, if desired.

5. Pin through all the layers and remove the original pins.

6. Stitch as with one-sided chenille.

7. To create fringe, after washing and drying, cut through the foundation layer for 5"– 6" at each end.

## More Ideas

### For Added Interest

Cut and add shadow fabrics between layers for subtle or obvious accents to the finished fabric surface. These may be strips, odd-shapes pieces, squares, rectangles, et cetera. Be sure that the shadow fabrics are cut and positioned with the straight grain and bias aligned with the slash fabrics.

Layer, pin and stitch as above.

## Tip

### Always Make a Sample

Because making slashed fabric is both time- and material-intensive, it's a good idea to make several samples to see how your fabrics will interact in terms of color and texture. Make as many samples as you need to determine the best fabric combinations, layering orders, and channel width (try stitching ⅜", ½", and ⅝" apart). Follow the instructions for Making the Chenille (on previous page) to make test samples as well as make yardage for finished projects.

Keep garment patterns simple and avoid fitted seams. Jacket by Katrina Lamken.

## Pictorial Chenille
**Leta Myers**

*Pictorial or large-scale prints can make beautiful chenille. Use as an appliqué, as part of a garment, or in a quilt.*

Select a design from a fabric that will fray (see previous page for selecting and testing fabrics). Plan to use four or five layers of fabric in addition to your base fabric.

Cut and stack the fabric, carefully lining up all the prints. Pin all the layers together. Mark the stitching lines on the top layer.

If you're making a chenille appliqué, place the stack on the selected background. (You may want to use a temporary spray adhesive to hold the chenille stack in place.)

Sew on the marked lines, then cut between the sewn lines. Wash and dry.

 *Tip*

### For Fluffier Chenille
The closer the stitching lines, the fluffier the chenille looks. Try using the presser foot width as a stitching guide.

# CIRCULAR STITCHING

*Follow this Thread*

See pages 84–86 for stabilizers.

## Sewing in Circles
**Barbara Weiland**

*It isn't difficult to stitch a perfect circle. You'll find countless uses for these embellishing techniques and more than one way to achieve perfect rounds.*

### Setting Up
If your machine has a circular stitching attachment, you're on easy street. Just follow the manufacturer's instructions to position the arm and determine the circle radius.

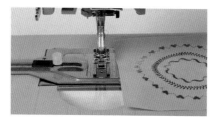

If you don't have this attachment for your machine, here's a low-tech way to get terrific circles: the tack method. You'll need a sharp household tack, strapping tape, and a pencil eraser. Push the tack through the strapping tape's sticky side, and tape it onto your sewing table the same distance as the radius of your circle from the machine needle.

Place a pencil eraser on the point to protect yourself from scrapes and your fabric from snags.

Select the desired stitch and adjust the stitch width and length for your fabric and thread. When using a satin-stitch motif, loosen the needle tension so the bobbin thread will pull the needle thread to the underside. You may want to test and adjust the stitch on a scrap of fabric before stitching the circle.

Mark the circle center in the desired location on the fabric. Back the fabric with an iron-on, tear-away stabilizer or place the fabric in a machine embroidery hoop with the fabric right side up; this will prevent the fabric from drawing up and puckering while you stitch.

Remove the eraser from the tack and position the circle center mark on the tack point. Gently force the tack through the fabric and replace the eraser. If using the circular stitching attachment, position the fabric as directed by your machine manual.

## Stitching

Stitch, allowing the fabric to pivot in a circle. Use your hands to lightly guide the fabric, but allow the feed dogs to do most of the work. Don't tug or pull on the fabric and don't let excess fabric surrounding the circle get caught, causing drag and distortion. If your design incorporates interlocking circles, you may need to coax the stitching when crossing previous stitching.

It's important to stitch at a consistent speed to keep motifs uniform. If speed control is available on your machine, use the slowest speed.

End the stitching when you reach the beginning point. Pull the threads to the wrong side and tie off, or stitch in place.

 *More Ideas*

### Design Alternatives

Use metallic or decorative thread to sew a circle. Decrease the radius and stitch again. Repeat several times for an interesting accent.

Overlap circular designs using different threads and sizes. Vary the stitch width, add additional decorative stitches over the basic satin stitch, or stitch partial circles.

Use a braiding foot and an open zigzag stitch to couch cording or fine, narrow trim in a circle. Pull the thread ends to the underside to secure.

Use an open-toe embroidery foot and a zigzag or decorative stitch to sew over ruffled lace, beading, or narrow trim while you stitch it in place. Trim the fabric close to the stitching on the underside.

Play with other special presser feet and stitches to create your own circular stitching variations.

# COUCHING

## Follow this Thread

See pages 43–53 for a visual guide to decorative stitches.
See pages 54–55 for cording feet.
See pages 84–86 for stabilizers.
See page 112 for couching beads.
See pages 204–205 for couching sequins.
See pages 245–246 for couching yarn.

## Couching by Machine

### Lynn Koolish

*Couching is a great way to put a decorative touch onto the surface of your project. By adding specialty threads, ribbons, yarns, and more to your fabric, you can create another dimension of texture and color. Special presser feet designed specifically for cording and braid make couching a breeze.*

Simply put, couching is stitching over cord, yarn, ribbon, decorative thread, et cetera. Good candidates for couching are:

- Cording
- Embroidery floss
- Yarn
- Specialty threads
- Ribbons
- Trims

Any type of stitch that will go over the material being stitched down can be used:

- Zigzag and triple (stretch) zigzag stitches
- Bridge or fagoting stitches
- Quilting stitches such as the feather stitch and feather stitch variations

- Decorative stitches with a zigzag movement, so the thread goes back-and-forth over the material being couched.

Stitching can be continuous and completely cover the material being couched or it can be open so the material underneath shows through.

Threads can range from unobtrusive monofilament to heavy decorative threads that add another decorative element.

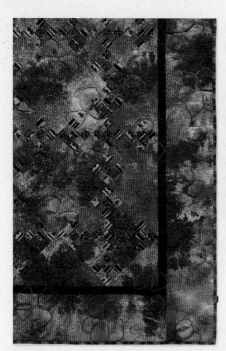

Quilted flower shapes are emphasized by couching with green and blue cord over the quilting lines. *Hot Stuff* from *Quilting Back to Front* by Larraine Scouler. Quilt by Larraine Scouler.

Leaf veins and stem were created by couching over cording. Tote bag by Lynn Koolish and Lyda McAuliff. See page 25 for tote bag.

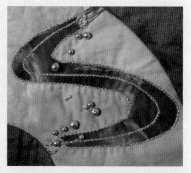

Decorative thread is held in place with decorative couching. *Fantasy* (detail) by Lynn Koolish. See page 22 for quilt.

Purple ribbon is held in place with gold couching. *Fantasy* (detail) by Lynn Koolish. See page 22 for quilt.

# CRAZY QUILT STITCHING

 Follow this Thread

See page 49 for crazy quilting stitches.
See page 68–77 for threads.
See pages 84–86 for stabilizers.
See page 134 for references to embroidery basics.
See page 126 for couching.
See pages 161–162 for honeycomb stitch.
See pages 167–171 for lace.

## Pieced Delight

**Rebecca Kemp Brent**

*Built-in stitches and machine embroidery are made for crazy quilting, which uses an assortment of fabrics, colors, sizes, and shapes. Try these ideas on your next crazy-quilted project.*

As a part of your crazy quilting, use machine embroidery and decorative machine stitching to dress up or blend together the elements of the project.

Pick your favorite machine stitches, and play with the way they look, changing the stitch length, width, and/or density for different effects. Use them in one of many ways:

- Embroider a border design over seams.
- Use metallic threads.
- Build a wide design by sewing multiple rows of decorative stitches side by side.
- Couch over heavy decorative threads.
- Use a multi-hole cording foot to couch over 5 or 7 threads at once, creating your own braid.
- Create lace by sewing 2 or 3 rows of honeycomb stitch side by side.
- Stitch ribbon over seams.

## Embroidery Designs

Use embroidery designs as you piece your crazy quilt blocks, or add them after your blocks are pieced. Choose your favorite designs and show them off with a contrasting color, or let them act as blenders across very different fabrics.

To avoid crushing napped fabrics with your stitches, use an adhesive stabilizer or a temporary spray adhesive. Hoop the stabilizer first, then adhere the fabric. You may also want to use a topper (see pages 87–88) to prevent your stitches from sinking into some fabrics.

## Even Out Bulky Seams

A bulky or textured fabric may result in a seam with a high side and a low side. Compensate by placing decorative stitches on the "low" side of the seam, so the presser foot travels on level ground.

*Lace embroidery designs: Brother card #29*

*Fancyworks embroidery designs: Brother card #45*

*Other embroidery designs: Artistic Designs' Lace & Romantic Designs by Sue Box*

*Decorative stitches: Brother's ULT2001*

## More Crazy Quilt Stitching

*Fantasy (details) by Lynn Koolish. See page 22 for quilt.*

# CROSS-STITCH

**Follow this Thread**

See page 45 for stitches
designed for cross-stitch.
See pages 68–77 for threads.
See pages 84–86 for stabilizers.

## Cross-stitch by Machine

**Lynn Koolish**

*Get the look of cross-stitch for monogramming, creating borders, and designing decorative motifs without the hand stitching.*

## Selecting Stitches

Sewing machines with built-in stitches often have a variety of cross-stitch patterns in several sizes and styles. Select single or multiple rows of cross-stitches, or choose stitches set into patterns. By changing the length and width of the stitches, you can create different looks and sizes.

Use the memory feature of your machine to create your own combinations.

## Stitching

If your machine has a half-speed or slow speed function, you may want to use it when using the cross-stitch stitches.

For delicate fabrics, use a stabilizer underneath your work. For heavier weight fabrics, you may not need a stabilizer depending on the density of the stitching. It's best to stitch out a few test samples.

Heavier threads will make a bolder statement, while finer threads can provide a delicate or subtle touch. Try stitching samples with different threads to see how they work for your planned project.

## Embroidery Designs

Cross-stitch embroidery designs are available from the same sources as other embroidery designs including sewing machine dealers and independent designers.

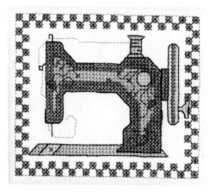

*Floral embroidery design: Pfaff Creative Fantasy Card #1*

*Sewing machine embroidery design: Tina's Cross Stitch Designs, Live to Sew*

# CUTWORK

**Follow this Thread**

See pages 84–86 for stabilizers.
See pages 162–163 for hooping.
See page 134 for references to
embroidery basics.
See pages 100–101 for scissors.

## Cutwork Embroidery

**Marlis Bennett**

*Cutwork is the technique of cutting away a portion of fabric and embroidering around the raw edges, leaving delicate open areas. Yesterday's cutwork was created by hand, and the raw edges were encased with a buttonhole stitch. Today, cutwork can be easily replicated using a satin-stitch design and an embroidery machine.*

## Designs

Cutwork designs are easy to find. Look for designs with solid satin stitching and intersecting lines to create holes that can be cut out.

## Test-stitch

As with any stitching technique, it is always best to test-stitch a design. The test-stitching process will provide you with the step-by-step method in which a cutwork design is embroidered. Choose ready-made designs, or digitize your own.

## Richelieu Bars

Connecting stitches are an option if your cutwork areas are large or abundant. These connecting stitches are called Richelieu bars and will hold the cutwork areas together.

## Position, Stitch, Cut

Print a template of the design, and mark the position of the motif onto your fabric. Positioning is critical for placement and when combining designs. If embroidering on a pre-made item, take care to avoid embroidering over seams.

To embroider, stabilize and hoop as appropriate for the fabric, placement, and design.

When the embroidery is complete, remove the hoop from the machine. Remove the fabric from the hoop, and use small curved scissors to cut out the desired areas.

Cutwork defines the yoke of the blouse. *Embroidery stitched by Elizabeth Tisinger.*

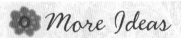

## More Ideas

### Satin Stitching for Cutwork
See Fleece Cutwork for another approach to cutwork using satin stitching rather than embroidery.

*Floral Embroidery Designs (left): Original designs by Marlis Bennett*

*Floral Embroidery Designs (above): Michelle Pullen Husqvarna Viking Card #26*

See pages 54–56 for presser feet.
See page 151 for sculpturing fleece.
See pages 142–143 for embroidering fleece.
See pages 201–202 for satin stitching.

## Fleece Cutwork
**Nancy Cornwell**

*Fleece offers many opportunities to push the limits of your imagination and your sewing machine's capabilities. Cutwork on fleece is an out-of-the-ordinary treatment that lends itself beautifully to quilts, garments, and more.*

Cutwork involves open, cut-out areas, so it's most suitable for items that won't be subjected to heavy use or frequent laundering.

## Getting Started
### Fabric
Choose high-quality, medium-weight, dense fleece with a tight knit and a flat surface to withstand the handling of this technique. Cutwork is not suitable for Berber or plush fabrics.

### Construction Threads
Use all-purpose thread in a color that either matches or is a shade darker than the fleece.

### Finishing Threads
Use decorative threads for satin stitching: 30- or 40-weight rayon is easy to use and is readily available in a wide range of colors. Its heavier, smoother texture results in even satin-stitching coverage. A thread color that blends with the fabric is very forgiving. Or try metallic or iridescent thread to add sparkle to the satin-stitched cutwork edge.

### Needles
You will need to use different needles for the different types of sewing. Use a 90/14 universal or ballpoint needle for construction. For decorative threads, choose a size 90/14 embroidery needle with a long eye. Use a metallic needle for metallic and iridescent threads.

When sewing multiple fleece layers, it may be necessary to change to a larger size needle to prevent skipped stitches or needle breakage.

### Stabilizers
Use iron-on, tear-away stabilizer to trace the cutwork motif, stitch-transfer the design, and stabilize the fleece for the multiple cutwork steps. Use water-soluble stabilizer as a base for the finishing satin stitching. Adhere the water-soluble stabilizer to the fleece with temporary adhesive spray.

### Presser foot
Use an open-toe or appliqué foot on your machine for the most visibility.

## Beginning the Cutwork
Make a sample to determine the stitch settings needed. If the edges ripple, increase the stitch length. Adjust the needle tension so the needle threads pull slightly to the wrong side when satin stitching.

*(Continued on next page)*

For garments, it's imperative to place the design properly. Use pins to mark all seamlines and anything else that may interfere with the cutwork design once the garment is assembled. If you are using a pre-made item, plan to keep stitching at least 1" away from seams and hems.

Trace the cutwork design of your choice onto the paper side of iron-on tear-away stabilizer. (Use a pencil; ink could smudge onto your fabric.) Shade in the areas that are to be cut out. *If the design has a definite right and left side, trace it reversed so it will be correct in the finished design.*

Use a press cloth, and a dry iron on a low setting to press the waxy side of the stabilizer to the wrong side of the fabric. Press approximately 10 seconds to adhere the stabilizer in the pin-marked area.

### Tip

### Pressing Prudence

- ▪ Press only the stabilizer, never the bare fabric.

- ▪ Don't overpress: The iron may leave a permanent imprint or melt the fleece.

- ▪ Practice with fleece and stabilizer scraps to find the lowest setting that will adhere the stabilizer to the fleece.

- ▪ Don't rub—gently place the iron on the stabilizer, then lift and replace it.

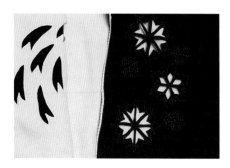

## Stitching and Cutting

Stitch around the entire design, using a 1.5mm to 2mm straight stitch. The stitching stabilizes the design while it stitch-transfers the design to the right side of the fleece.

Use sharp appliqué or embroidery scissors to cut out the designated areas, trimming close to the straight stitching line.

To further stabilize the cut edges, set the machine for an open zigzag stitch (2.5mm width and 1mm length). Zigzag on the wrong side around the cut design edges, centering the stitching over the straight stitching line.

Carefully trim any fabric "eyelashes" that poke out from the stitching.

Place the fleece right side down on a flat surface. Slip a piece of paper behind the cut-out areas to protect the work surface. Lightly spray adhesive around the cut-out areas. Adhere a piece of water-soluble stabilizer large enough to completely cover the cutout.

Change to decorative thread in the needle, and satin stitch the design cut edges. Set the machine for a 3mm- to 3.5mm-width zigzag stitch with a stitch length appropriate for an even fill.

For an even edge finish, keep the zigzag stitches at a right angle to the cut edge. Make sure the stitch right swing covers the stabilizing stitches, and the stitch left swing completely covers the fleece cut edge.

## Sculpturing Details

Sculpture the remaining motif details with satin stitching. The stitches will sink into the fleece loft and create a groove, imprinting the design onto the fleece. Satin stitch on the stabilized right side of the fleece, using the drawn design lines as a guide. Vary the stitch width vary from 2.5mm to 4mm, depending on the chosen design.

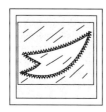

Gently tear away the water-soluble and iron-on stabilizers. To prevent stitch distortion, place the fabric right side down on a flat surface, supporting the satin stitches with your fingers; tear stabilizers at an angle to the stitches.

Position contrasting fleece behind the cutouts and tack in place through design lines.

Complete the project as desired.

See pages 68–77 for threads.
See pages 84–86 for stabilizers.
See page 202 for satin-stitched edges.
See page 203 for scalloped edges.
See page 134 for references to embroidery basics.

## Embroidered Edge Finishes

**Rebecca Kemp Brent**

*Looking for some new hems and edges? Turn to your embroidery library to make narrow or wide, lacy or filled edgings for edge appeal.*

## Getting Started

### Stabilizer

Removable stabilizers, such as water-soluble or tear-away, will not peek out from behind your edging. An outline-only design stitched on a firm, woven fabric may require only a liquid fabric stabilizer or spray starch. If your edging will show from both sides of the fabric be sure to choose a stabilizer that can be removed entirely.

### Thread

Use thread that matches or contrasts with your fabric, according to the look you want. Variegated and metallic threads often yield wonderful results. When stitching a single color, use the same color thread in the bobbin (in a lighter weight, if needed) as the needle. For a multicolor design, match the bobbin thread to the fabric or the main color in your design.

### Hoop

Smaller hoops yield more stability, which is especially important for fill-stitch designs; larger hoops can accommodate long edgings or several side-by-side designs, and work well for more open designs.

### Fabrics

Plain, woven fabrics like batiste and broadcloth have fine fabric threads that are less likely to unravel. Also try organdy and voile for lacy openwork edgings, and poplin or decorator fabrics for fill-stitch edge designs.

### Finishing

Depending on the selected design, you may need to seal and trim the edges. Draw a line of seam sealant or fray preventive along the outer edge of the embroidery. Be sure the liquid soaks into the embroidery and the fabric that will be cut away. Cover embroidery with a press cloth and press with a warm iron. Trim with small, sharp scissors.

## Selecting Designs

Many edging designs are available from machine manufacturers or independent digitizing companies. The best candidates have a satin-stitched border that finishes the edge of the fabric.

*(Continued on next page)*

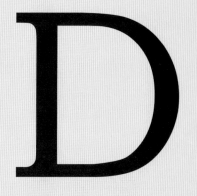

Some designs incorporate eyelets or coordinate with a fabric print.

Don't limit yourself to lace embroideries with a scalloped perimeter; other filled-in embroideries are candidates for edgings, too.

## Arranging Edging Motifs

The simplest way to arrange motifs is to line them up side by side with edges touching. Here are some strategies to best position them:

- Hoop the fabric (or attach it to hooped stabilizer). This eliminates distortion and stretching.

- Use the machine's function that positions the needle at the start point of the design, not the center point of the embroidery. The machine will finish with a placement stitch at the end of the motif so you can align the next one accurately.

- Calculate the placement of adjacent designs using the motif's measurements. A stitched sample or a printed design template are easy to measure for placement.

- Use full-size templates to position and mark placements for successive motifs.

- Use the trial or outline function on your machine to double-check alignment before embroidering.

- Use the machine's customizing software to combine and save a series of motifs into a design group. This method allows you to zoom in and check motif alignment.

- When making long edgings, the motifs within each customized design group will align, but they won't necessarily meet the adjacent group perfectly. Align separately stitched groups using one of the other methods discussed above.

## Curves & Corners

Embroideries look wonderful when they are shaped to fit into curves and corners.

- Trace the anticipated seamlines (not cutting lines) onto the fabric with a removable marker. Cut the fabric oversize.

- Hoop the stabilizer, and adhere the fabric to it with temporary spray adhesive.

- Use full-size templates to position the designs. Use the rotation function of your machine—or reposition the fabric on the stabilizer—to make designs curve to fit the shape of the pattern.

- When the embroidery is complete, remove the stabilizer and press.

- To fill a corner gap, insert a design at an angle across the corner to bridge the distance between motifs. Or, reverse the direction of a motif string to fill the space as you stitch.

 *Tip*

## Hooping Tips

- When hooping fabric at an angle to stitch a border, never stretch the fabric along the bias.

- Hooping the stabilizer allows you to place embroidery close to an edge. Using an adhesive on hooped stabilizer also allows the flexibility to reposition the fabric slightly to perfect the design placement.

## Borders

Embroidered borders often look prettier when they are placed slightly above an edge. This permits the use of open designs and outlines. Here are some ideas:

- Randomly arrange designs near the fabric edge.

- Draw a line parallel to the edge, and position the centers of all the designs along the line.

- Rotate the designs 45° and repeat them along the edge.

- Position mirror images of a design side by side to create a zigzag. (See page 177 for more on mirroring embroidery designs.)

- Flip alternating repeats top to bottom to make a wide solid border.

- Use lines of embroidery along horizontal or vertical openings and seams.

 **Tip**

## Look at All the Angles

To arrange many motifs into a single design, you may need to vary the orientation of one or more of the motifs. A single motif can be arranged in many different ways. Designs can be rotated, mirror-imaged, enlarged, and/or reduced. Experiment with a design by:

- Stitching a series of identical repeats

- Alternating a design with its mirror image

- Alternating a design with a copy flipped top to bottom

- Combining a design with a complementary design

- Combining a design with a series of designs into a repeating unit

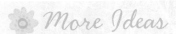 **More Ideas**

## Try Decorative Stitches

Try adding decorative machine stitches to an embroidered border—add a scallop or other built-in stitch to enhance the embroidered design.

*Embroidery designs:*
*Baby Lock, Ellageo exclusive designs*

*Brother Cards #23, #29, #54*

*Brother, ULT-2002D Mickey & Friends Designs, Disney*

# E

## EMBROIDERY

Expand your machine arts knowledge by trying some unique ways to use machine embroidery. Presented here are some ideas for using machine embroidery in ways you might not have thought about, or if you did, weren't sure how. Follow the threads below for embroidery basics and more ideas for embroidery.

### Follow this Thread

### Embroidery Basics

See pages 68–77 for threads.
See pages 162–163 for hooping.
See pages 84–88 for stabilizers and toppers.
See pages 60–62 for computerized embroidery machines.
See page 177 for mirroring designs.
See pages 238–239 for underlay stitching.

### More Ideas For Embroidery

See page 128 for cross-stitch embroidery.
See pages 128–129 for cutwork.
See pages 131–133 for decorative edges.
See pages 136–137 for hidden embroidery.
See page137 for raised embroidery.
See page138 for embroidery and appliqué.
See pages 138–139 for embroidery for the dining room.
See pages 139–140 for festive embroidery.
See pages 140–141 for embroidering on sweaters.
See pages 142–143 for embroidering on fleece.
See pages 144–145 for embroidering over seams.
See pages 167–169 for lace.
See pages 175–176 for embroidering on metal.
See pages 178–179 for mono-gramming.
See pages 193–195 for quilting and embroidery.
See pages 225–226 for shisa embroidery.
See page 228 for embroidery on smocking.
See page 237 for embroidered tucks.

## Dimensional Embroidery

**Linda McGehee**

*Add dimension to embroidery by creating freestanding motifs. Choose designs digitized specifically for this 3-D technique, or adapt your favorite design with a satin stitch or other firm outline.*

## Fabric

Dimensional designs work best when stitched on a fabric base of nylon organza. This sheer fabric supports the stitches during the embroidery process, offers a multitude of color options, and easily melts away to cleanly finish free-standing edges. Very large designs or those with dense fill stitching may require two or three layers of organza for support. Smaller, more open designs may need only one layer. For areas where curling is desired, such as the ends of flower petals, one layer will support the stitches.

When using multiple organza layers, combine colors to create shading and color variations. Use different colors in different areas of your design, combine colors or shades of a single color, or rearrange the color layers when you re-hoop.

## Stitching

Use a medium-size hoop to secure the fabric as tightly as possible, without stabilizer. Use embroidery software or on-screen editing to fill the hoop with your chosen design.

Because the designs are dimensional, both sides of the stitching will show. Match the bobbin thread to the dominant upper thread color, or change bobbin colors every time you change the top thread.

Some designs have a complete fill pattern, covering the entire motif with stitching. Depending on the desired look, bypass some or all of the fill stitching and outline or highlight areas with detail lines, shadows, and outlines. This also shortens the stitching time, offers options for blending organza colors, and creates a more flexible embroidery motif.

## Trimming

Once the desired motifs have been stitched, use 5" craft scissors to trim close to the satin stitch edges, being careful not to clip any stitches.

The organza may fray slightly after trimming. Seal the nylon edges using a 15-watt soldering iron, hot knife, or stencil knife to melt the fibers.

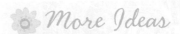

### Flower Transformations

Play with the thread or organza color to turn a programmed design into something totally different. Leaves can become flower petals, for example, or you can mix and match to create original designs.

The fuzzies melt rapidly, so avoid damaging the fabric and stitching by melting only what should be melted! One quick pass should be sufficient; practice on stitched samples to perfect the technique.

## Finishing

After the design elements are sewn, layer them onto the base fabric. Begin with the bottom elements—the leaf petals in a flower design, for example—and build up. When satisfied with the design, carefully pick up all the layers except the bottom one.

Pin the motifs in place on the base, and stitch partway down the motif center, using an open-toe foot and monofilament thread in the needle for unobtrusive stitching. Stitch each motif layer to the base before advancing to the next layer. Build up the design, using smaller parts closest to the top. If you want some edges to curl, adding more dimension to the motif, leave those edges unsewn.

When the motif is done, carefully trim the excess fabric base so none shows from the right side of the motif. Use snaps, hook-and-loop dots, or pin backs to attach the motifs to a garment or project. This allows them to be removed for laundering and also allows for several options and wardrobe versatility.

## Special Effects

Vary the thread type as you stitch for added interest. Metallic thread makes beautiful veining on red organza poinsettia petals. Variegated thread adds color interest without frequent thread changes. Glow-in-the-dark or solar-reactive threads also add variety. Make sure to match your needle size and type to the thread used.

*More Ideas*

## Design Alternatives

■ If you're stitching flowers, such as daisies, add a second (and even third!) layer of petals to make a "hybrid" variety. For raised flower centers, slip a small piece of batting or fleece under the center before stitching the layers together around the circle perimeter.

■ You can also stitch motifs onto nonraveling fabrics, rather than permanently attaching them to a garment or project. Faux suede is the perfect weight to use as a design base.

■ To finish off your design, add silk ribbon, buttons, beads, or costume jewelry parts as embellishments and to hide the stitches that attach the parts to the base.

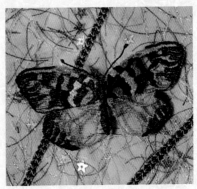

Free-standing butterfly was stitched on tulle and water-soluble stabilizer. Excess tulle and stabilizer was trimmed and remaining stabilizer dissolved in water.

*Fantasy (detail) by Lynn Koolish. See page 22 for quilt.*

*Butterfly embroidery design: Pfaff Creative Fantasy Card #1*

*Floral Embroidery Designs: Cactus Punch disk, Floral Dimensions II*

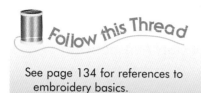

See page 134 for references to embroidery basics.

# Hidden Embroidery

***Pauline Richards***

*Embroidery doesn't always need to be front and center. Sometimes it's fun to place your favorite motifs in unusual spots visible only to the wearer or where observers catch only a quick glance. Embellishing hidden and less obvious places will allow you to practice your embroidery and placement skills while you update and personalize custom or ready-made garments.*

Simple motifs are generally best. Heavy, compact stitching can stiffen fabric and weigh down a garment.

## Positioning

Embroidery motifs should fit comfortably into the available space. Consider sizing a motif up or down slightly to create the appropriate size for the space available. Embroider small motifs onto garment pieces before garment construction. (Make sure to take seam allowances into account!).

Try one or more of these ideas:

- Position a long, narrow motif at the center back of the neckline under the collar—it will be visible only when the collar is turned up. Use a soft stabilizer: This area will always be against your neck.

- Let a little embroidery peek out from under a gently turned up cuff. This embroidery will be easy for the wearer to enjoy but create a now-you-see-it, now-you-don't effect for observers.

- Tuck a little design into a pocket or under a pocket flap. If you're working on a pre-made jacket, keep a close eye on your machine to ensure that the needle does not accidentally catch the surrounding fabric.

- Children will appreciate an embroidery label in the back of clothing. Use a 1¼"-wide satin ribbon, or make it from self-fabric. Embroider waistbands before attaching them, and consider including the name of the owner for kids of all ages.

- Add a special detail to any garment or quilt with a customized label to clearly identify the maker or owner, and to add a special, personal touch.

- Embroider labels into garment linings before or after garment construction. This example was embroidered on a scrap, trimmed to size, and hand-stitched into the garment.

## Choosing a Stabilizer

Stabilizing before stitching is always important. Stabilize knits and stretchy wovens with a cut-away stabilizer, and use a soft, non-irritating stabilizer when the embroidery will be against skin.

## Testing

Always test your design using similar fabric before embroidering a finished garment or a project. Adjust the machine tension as necessary.

A back neck facing is a good place to complete a test with the threads you've selected and embellish the inside of a garment at the same time. To simplify hooping, complete the embroidery, and then cut out the facing. Our sample facing has been lengthened to 5" to accommodate the motif and is bound in coordinating fabric.

**Pauline Richards**
*Use foam toppers to create distinctive raised embroidery designs.*

1. Use fabric that is stable enough to support foam and densely stitched designs.

2. Use 30-weight thread for better coverage of the foam, especially when using thicker foam.

3. Use a ballpoint needle to perforate the foam more completely.

4. Match the thread color to the foam color so fewer stitches will be needed to cover the foam.

5. Choose a simple design with mostly satin stitching—logos, shapes, symbols, or lettering are ideal. A filled area can be stitched with foam underneath, but the fill stitch will compress the foam with less raised effect.

6. Place your design carefully: foam adds stiffness.

7. Use a stabilizer under the embroidery design.

8. When a design has both filled and satin-stitched areas, stitch the fill parts normally, stop the machine, and place the foam on top just before satin-stitching.

9. Remove the excess foam from each completed area before straight stitching or sewing another color with foam underneath.

10. If any foam remains outside the thread after you tear away the excess, use a hair dryer to shrink the remains into the thread.

11. If the embroidery design was not digitized for foam, you may need to repeat the stitching sequence to cover the foam adequately.

12. Always make a sample before stitching on your project.

## Laundering Tips

Items made using foam can be laundered, then ironed with a medium-hot iron. Do not dry-clean items embroidered with a foam topper.

*Embroidery design: Cactus Punch Fall #1 card, stitched by Lindee Goodall.*

## More Ideas

### Use Built-in Stitches

Try the embroidery placement ideas using built-in stitches or combinations of built-in stitches.

*Sage placket & collar embroidery design: Oklahoma Embroidery Supply & Design, Sew News Collection, design SNC04*

*Black facing embroidery design: Husqvarna Viking, disk #36*

*Rust pocket embroidery design: Janome, Borders, design 3320*

*Yellow pants label embroidery design: Husqvarna Viking, Designer 1, lettering Clarendon*

*Label lettering: Husqvarna Viking, Customizing software, lettering Block*

*Brown cuff embroidery design: Janome, Borders, design 3306*

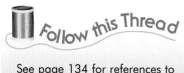

See page 134 for references to embroidery basics.

## Embroidery and Appliqué

### Barbara Weiland

*Appliquéing by hand or even by machine can be time-consuming and painstaking. With your embroidery machine, you can have beautiful appliqué in no time at all.*

### Design Selection

Select embroidery designs that are created for appliqué or that feature a satin-stitched outline. Some internal stitching is okay, but you want the appliqué fabric to be the main feature.

Stitch out potential embroidery designs to see the stitching pattern. Use designs that begin with an underlay stitch that outlines the design. (See pages 238–239 for more on underlay stitching.)

Experiment with arrangements of designs. Try grouping, mirroring, or changing the orientation of the designs. (See page 177 for more on mirror imaging.)

## Embroidering the Appliqué

Hoop the background fabric with the appropriate stabilizer.

Select your design and stitch the outline. Reset the machine to start at the beginning.

Determine the needed size of the appliqué fabric. Spray the back of the appliqué fabric with adhesive spray before placing on the background fabric, using the outline stitching as a placement guide.

Stitch the outline again to anchor the fabric.

Remove the hoop from the machine, but do not remove the fabric from the hoop. Use a pair of sharp appliqué scissors to trim the fabric as close as possible to the outline stitching.

Replace the hoop and complete the embroidery.

### Finishing

Re-hoop as needed to complete your planned appliqué designs.

The completed appliqués can be used as you would any other appliqué—for garments, quilts, or home décor projects.

*Embroidery designs:* Creative Machine Embroidery *magazine originals.*

See page 134 for references to embroidery basics.

## Embroidery for the Dining Room

### Sara Meyer-Snuggerud

*Dress up your dining room with whimsical, elegant, or color-coordinating machine embroidery. Read on for tips on design selection and placement, then try out the different embroidery ideas for yourself.*

### Design Selection

Choose embroidery designs that coordinate with the dining room décor or your china. Look for designs that work large, small, and in combinations. This will provide many creative options when putting all the pieces together.

### Design Placement

Think about where arms or hands may come into contact with the design, especially if you plan to use metallic thread. Nothing is worse than a scratchy surface that distracts guests from the atmosphere of the meal. When selecting fabric for seat covers, try the "slip" test to make sure that guests will not be slipping off their chairs all evening.

Planning where to locate the designs will take longer than the embroidery process. Test-embroider the designs under consideration before cutting out any project pieces. During testing, determine what type of stabilizer will be necessary, how many layers, and if the combination of design, thread, and fabric is what you are trying to capture.

## Preview Design Combinations

Test-stitch all possible designs. Trim the test designs close to the edges, and position them on your chosen items to see how they look. Embroider and audition mirror-image designs as well.

After you have decided on your designs and placement, use a removable fabric marker to outline each of the designs onto the fabric to be embroidered.

## Stitch

Use your test pieces to select appropriate needles, threads, and stabilizers for your chosen designs and fabrics.

If you are creating the items to be embroidered, do the embroidery first, then cut out and sew the items.

## Design Placement

Place designs carefully on seat backs: Remember that some ladies may wear low-backed dresses.

*Embroidery designs: Oklahoma Embroidery Supply & Design #CR054*

See page 134 for references to embroidery basics.

## Festive Embroidery

### Deborah Yedziniak

*Whether it's Christmas or some other special occasion, embroider festive linens to use around the house or give as gifts.*

Check out these ideas for holiday embroidery to create your own special holiday gifts.

*Sprinkle snowflakes over sheets and pillowcases for your own winter wonderland. Add other embroidered accessories to tie the room together.*

## Quick Tips to Get Started

1. Select designs according to a theme, personalized name, or special motif.

2. Combine designs, using embroidery software, on-screen customizing, or multiple hoopings.

3. Add visual interest to repeated motifs by changing thread colors, rotating designs, or altering size.

4. Consider how the embroidered item will be used, and position designs accordingly.

5. Select the appropriate stabilizer for the anticipated use, especially if the item will be laundered. Make and launder a test piece. (See pages 84–86 for information on stabilizers.)

6. When embroidering an edge or corner, hoop the stabilizer first, then adhere the item to be embroidered. Try a temporary adhesive spray or an adhesive stabilizer.

*Dress up your kitchen for the holidays. Placemats, potholders, tea towels, and more add a festive flavor.*

*(Continued on next page)*

**7.** For thick towels, embroider the design onto matching fabric, and stitch it on separately.

*Hand towels decorated for the holidays make great hostess gifts. Use metallic thread to add sparkle. Embroider the hostess's name for a personal touch.*

**8.** Purchase blank linens to embroider. Consider making:

- Placemats with a theme or personalized with names

- Hand towels for a guest bathroom

- Kitchen towels with a hobby theme

- An apron for the cook

- Personalized pillowcases for sweet dreams

*Snowflakes, holly and berry embroidery designs: Martha Pullen Disk #1023*

*Ornaments and Christmas tree embroidery designs: Martha Pullen Disk #1023*

*Pine trees and elf embroidery designs: Husqvarna Viking Disk #38*

See page 134 for references to embroidery basics.

# Embroidering on Sweaters

*Linda Griepentrog*

*Embroidering on sweaters can be a challenge, but using the proper techniques and a little ingenuity will lead to successful results.*

## Placement

Chest motifs are common on sweaters—designers use this location for their notable logos. Neckline embroidery is also popular; make sure the wearer can still get the sweater over the head. Unless you are willing to take out and re-sew a seam, placement will be determined by access to the area.

## Sweater Selection

The easiest sweaters to embroider on are those with a flat, even rib. As the size of the rib increases, the embroidery process becomes more complex. Uneven ribs add even more challenges, as does a texture of the yarns used. A sweater with moderate stretch works well, but avoid those that require over 50% stretch for fit.

## Design Selection

Simpler and smaller designs are better for sweaters. Large, densely embroidered designs limit stretchablity and can distort delicate knits. Use monograms with caution—it's hard to prevent the lettering from disappearing into the knit pattern.

## Stabilizer Selection

When embroidering on sweaters, it is imperative to stabilize the knit to avoid distortion, but hooping will also distort the knit. Instead:

- Hoop cut-away stabilizer, then use temporary spray adhesive to hold the sweater in place.

- Hoop adhesive stabilizer with the protective paper in place. Score the protective paper with a pin point around the perimeter of the inner hoop, and remove the paper. Adhere the sweater to the stabilizer. This method can result in design firmness and stiffness; the backing remains in the design.

- Hoop adhesive stabilizer with the protective paper in place. Cut an opening slightly larger than the embroidery motif. Cut a piece of cut-away stabilizer ½" larger than the opening. Peel off the stabilizer's protective paper and position the cutaway over the opening, overlapping edges to hold it in place. Adhere the sweater to the stabilizer.

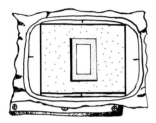

Use the pattern of the knit to line up the sweater within the hoop. The ribs of the knit (vertical patterning) and the courses (horizontal patterning) can be used to assure correct positioning within the hoop.

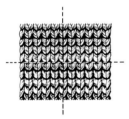

In most instances, there is no identical sweater to test-stitch the motif. Visit a thrift store and purchase a similar sweater for practicing.

Avoid using adhesive stabilizer on chenille sweaters or those with other pile texturizing, as it is easy to end up with a bald spot after removing the sweater from the stabilizer.

## Topper Selection

The bulk of sweater knits cries out for a topper to keep the embroidery stitching on top of the knit and allow better thread coverage. On washable sweaters, a clear water-soluble topper will work. On non-washable sweaters, use a clear or matching vinyl topper, organza, or fine tulle; all of these will remain under the design after stitching.

Use a colored vinyl topper when stitching a light color thread over a darker color background or print. Embroidery thread colors show up much clearer and truer with vinyl toppers. For example, white embroidered roses on a red sweater won't appear pink.

To use a topper, position it over the design area once the sweater is in position for embroidery. Baste all the layers together to secure the topper in place around the perimeter of the embroidery motif area. The needle perforates the vinyl as you sew, and you can tear away the excess, or clip close to the motif after sewing. Trim organza close to the embroidery motif using small, sharp-pointed scissors, being careful not to cut into the sweater.

### Topping, Please

Although you can embroider designs on sweaters without a topper, motifs tend to have better thread coverage and "stand above" the knit when a topper is used. The hotdog on the upper right has an organza topper, and the hotdog on the lower left has no topper.

See pages 87–88 for more on toppers.

## Embroidering Heavy Sweaters

When working on heavy sweaters, support the garment as you embroider to avoid the heaviness of the garment pulling the embroidery and distorting your stitching.

### ❀ Quick Trick

#### Creating Embroidery for Appliqué

If the motif you choose is large and/or dense, it may be better not to embroider it directly onto the sweater. Embroider it onto organza instead, then appliqué it to the sweater by hand or machine. Keep in mind that the stretchability of the sweater knit is compromised with large motifs and this could affect fit.

*Trout embroidery design: Cactus Punch, Animals 5*

*Flower embroidery design: Brother, Card #2*

*Circular embroidery design: Cactus Punch, Quilting 1*

*Hotdog embroidery designs: SewMan, Food*

*With topper*

*Without topper*

See page 134 for references to embroidery basics.
See pages 129–130 for fleece cutwork.
See page 151 for sculpturing fleece.

## Embroidering on Fleece

**Nancy Cornwell**

*Fleece provides a perfect background for many types of embroidery—float the stitches on top of the fabric, or let them sink in for textures. Use plain embroidery or use embroidery for appliqué. Take your pick and embroider away.*

### Fleece Embroidery Basics
*Fabric Choice*

Look for fleece with a dense nap and no visible base cloth.

To determine the right and wrong side of fleece, pull it along the crosswise edge (in the direction of the most stretch). Fleece will generally curl toward the wrong side.

Test the fleece's recovery. If you stretch it and it doesn't bounce back to its original dimensions, it will distort when you add embroidery stitches.

*Stabilizer*

Choose a soft, permanent cut-away stabilizer heavy enough to support the embroidery stitches, yet light enough that it doesn't interfere with the hand of the fabric.

Test-stitch the chosen design to confirm your stabilizer choice. If the stitches misalign or the fabric cups or waves, additional stabilizer is needed.

*Hooping*

Because hooping can stretch or flatten the nap of fleece, hoop the stabilizer, spray it with temporary adhesive, and press the fleece in place.

*Topper*

If you want the stitches to stay on top of the fabric, use a topper. If you want a texturized look with the stitching embedded into the fleece surface, no topper is needed.

*Stitching*

Use the fix or basting function on your machine, if available, to prevent the fleece from shifting while embroidering. This function outlines the design with basting stitches, securing the stabilizer, fleece, and topper (if used) together.

*Design Choices*

Choose simple designs without dense fill stitches to avoid heavy stabilizers, which interfere with fleece's natural soft drape. You may be able to use just the outline portion of more densely stitched designs.

## Other Embroidery Techniques
*Traditional Appliqué*

Position the appliqué fabric on top of the fleece, stitch the motif outline, trim the appliqué fabric close to the stitching, and finish the appliqué edges with the satin stitching.

When appliquéing a woven fabric onto fleece, the stitches sink into the fleece causing the satin stitches to narrow. This slight narrowing may result in the appliqué edges not being sufficiently secured to the base fabric. To ensure a secure edge finish, sandwich water-soluble stabilizer between the fleece and the appliqué fabric to flatten the fleece nap. This stabilizer also protects the fleece from accidental nicks when trimming the appliqué fabric.

*Dimensional Appliqué*

Fleece doesn't unravel, so traditional appliqué techniques can be simplified. To make a flower and leaf appliqués as shown, outline stitch the motifs onto separate pieces of fleece. Use the outline as a guide and cut out the motifs just inside the stitching.

Use matching thread matching and embroider the flower and leaf outlines onto your selected item. Lightly apply spray adhesive to the wrong side of the appliqués and adhere in place using the stitched outlines as a guide. Embroider the inner flower and leaf details to secure the appliqués. Remove the placement stitches, if desired.

## Trapunto

Embroider the flower and leaf outlines. Remove the hoop from the machine, but don't unhoop the stabilizer. Working from the wrong side, cut a 1" slit in the stabilizer layer **only** behind the flower and leaf motif centers. Insert a stylus and wiggle to release just enough adhesive to stuff with small bits of fiberfill and hand stitch the openings closed.

Be careful not to move the stabilizer in the hoop or the stitch positioning may be off. Change to a size 100/16 needle to accommodate the bulk of the stuffing and embroider the flower and leaf inner details.

## Twin-needle Embroidery

Insert a twin needle and thread both needles with contrasting embroidery thread.

Check to make sure the twin needle is compatible with your embroidery presser foot; change to a narrower twin needle, if necessary.

Stitch the flower and leaf outlines, stopping the leaf stitching as it meets the flower edge. Leave long thread tails to pull to the wrong side and secure. Change to a single needle and stitch the flower center, if desired. Secure the thread ends on the wrong side of the fleece.

## Blunt-edge Appliqué

Position a piece of fleece fabric in place for the leaf and embroider the leaf outline and veins. Trim the excess green fleece close to the outer stitching line, leaving a little extra on the upper leaf edge so it will be adequately covered by the flower appliqué.

Position another piece of fleece fabric in place for the flower. Stitch the outline and inner details. Trim excess fabric close to the stitching lines, being careful not to cut into the leaf fabric in the overlap area.

*Floral embroidery design: CD in* Embroidery Machine Essentials *by Nancy Cornwell*

*Fish embroidery design: Dakota Collectibles design # DC0066*

## Fleece Sampler Pullover

Try several embroidery techniques on a single garment to see which ones you like best. Choose a simple flower motif and explore its hidden designs.

Many designs begin with the motif outline. Use just the outline stitching for blunt-edge or dimensional appliqué, trapunto or twin-needle embroidery.

See page 134 for references to embroidery basics.
See pages 193–195 for quilting and embroidery.

## Embroidering Over Seams

*Christy Burcham*

*A smooth fabric surface is ideal for embroidery. At times, however, you may want the flexibility to embroider over seams or pre-constructed layers. By following a few rules, you can successfully embroider over seams and layers.*

Before you decide to embroider over a seam, consider these factors:

- Seam thickness: Embroidering over very bulky seams (flat fell seams in heavy fabrics, fleece, other seams in bulky fabrics) will produce a noticeable bulge in your embroidery, and your machine may have difficulty penetrating the layers. Always sew a sample to be sure. For heavier seams, choose a more open design, such as a lace, Redwork, or line-drawing design. Reserve heavier designs for less bulky seams.

- Hooping: Other "shortcuts" exist, but hooping gives you the best result.

- Placement: Use a center point template, usually available with memory cards, or print out the design, including the center cross marks. Cut out the template and poke a hole through the center, and use the hole to mark the design center placement on the fabric. Also mark the hoop alignment notches onto the fabric for perfect placement.

- Pressing: Always press the seam before you secure the stabilizer to the fabric.

### Pieced Quilt Blocks

Instead of embroidering fabric and then incorporating it into a quilt, embroider directly over the pieced seams of a quilt block before assembling the quilt.

Press the seams as usual, then apply a temporary spray adhesive to tear-away stabilizer. Place the wrong side of the pieced block over the adhesive side of the stabilizer. Smooth the quilt block onto the stabilizer from the center out. Hoop the stabilizer and quilt block together, and embroider.

### Garment Color Blocking

Color blocking can add visual interest to garments. Embroider a design that overlaps two color-blocked areas for pizzazz. For best results, press the seam open, and spray temporary adhesive onto the appropriate stabilizer. Place the wrong side of the color-blocked area on top of the stabilizer. Smooth out the fabric and hoop the layers together.

### Shoulder Seams

Embroidering over a shoulder seam can be an interesting way to dress up a garment. This designer touch adds visual impact. When possible, construct the shoulder seam first, stitch the embroidery design, and then finish the garment.

When working with ready-to-wear, hoop the garment with the stabilizer by attaching the stabilizer to the fabric with adhesive spray. For pieces that are too small to fit in a hoop, hoop the stabilizer first, then spray adhesive onto the stabilizer and attach the garment.

 *Tip*

### Avoid a Dart Disaster

You can embroider over darts as you would a shoulder seam, but remember this: Darts are usually used to remove bulk from a garment. Embroidery will add bulk, so make this choice wisely!

## Quick Trick

### Moisture-activated Stabilizers

Moisture-activated stabilizers are perfect when you can't hoop an item itself for embroidery. Hoop this stabilizer with the shiny side up. Wet it with a damp sponge or cloth, and the moistened area becomes sticky. Secure the garment to the stabilizer and allow it to dry. It has a very strong hold and will not come loose until the stabilizer is re-moistened.

## More Ideas

### Embroidery Placement

Embroider a border design on a skirt hemline, around the edge of a table cloth, on the bottom of pant legs, or on a quilt border.

*Pumpkin embroidery designs: Oklahoma Embroidery Supply & Design, Holiday 9 Pack #11437*

*Rose embroidery design: Oklahoma Embroidery Supply & Design, Roses #A1008*

# ENTREDEUX

### Follow this Thread

See pages 43–53 for a visual guide to decorative stitches.
See pages 80–82 for needles.
See pages 68–77 for threads.
See pages 84–86 for stabilizers.
See page 160 for another entredeux look.
See page 180 for wing needle techniques.

## Elegant Entredeux

### Lynn Koolish

*Entredeux means "between two." It is a narrow trim used to attach lace to lace, or lace to other fabric that is often used in heirloom sewing. Pre-made entredeux can be purchased (often in white), but it's easy to make your own in colors of your choice.*

## Making Entredeux

Often made of crisp organdy or batiste, use a firm, lightweight fabric of your choice. Starching the fabric will help keep it stable and preserve the decorative holes that are the characteristic feature.

A number of stitches can be used, including zigzag, entredeux, venetian, or other decorative stitch of your choice. Regardless of the stitch used, the trick is to use a wing needle to create the distinctive holes.

Stitch as much trim as is needed and trim excess fabric leaving ¼" to ½" from the stitches.

*Entredeux examples stitched by Elizabeth Tisinger.*

## Quick Trick

To make the edges of the entredeux more pronounced, use a multiple-hole cording foot to guide light cording (or heavy thread) down the sides of the entredeux as you stitch. Adjust the cording as you begin to stitch so that it is covered by the outside edges the stitch. (See page 55 for multiple-hole cording foot.)

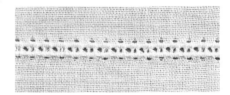

*Single row of entredeux stitching over cording*

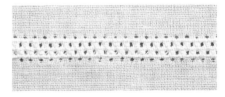

*Double row of entredeux stitching over cording*

## Using Entredeux

Use entredeux to join lace to lace, or fabric to lace.

*Eyelet lace attached to fabric with entredeux*

*Corded entredeux stitched directly on two pieces of lace*

# ERGONOMICS

## Sew Healthy
### Dr. Colleen McDonough

*End the back, neck, and shoulder pain associated with sitting at a sewing machine by making simple ergonomic adjustments to your sewing area.*

After sewing for two hours straight, you stand up and feel aches and pain in your shoulders and neck, pain in your forearms and hands, numbness and tingling in your fingers or hands, and pain in the pad of your thumb. Stitchers also commonly experience knee joint stiffness, foot cramps, headaches, and blurry vision. These symptoms are very common but can be decreased significantly and often eliminated with a few changes to your sewing work area and habits.

## Sewing Table Height
Sewing surfaces vary dramatically. Sewers use everything from the dining room table or a child's unused desk to beautiful custom-designed cabinetry. For postural wellness, adhere to a few simple guidelines in determining the height of your sewing surface.

Sit on a chair or stool that allows your feet to rest flat on the floor with your thighs parallel to the floor. With your arms close to your sides, hold your forearms parallel to the floor. Have someone measure from your forearm lower edge to the floor. This measurement (usually about 23") is the preferred height of the bed of the sewing machine (not the table height). This height allows you to sew with your elbows close to your rib cage, your head over your spine, and your shoulders back.

If you can't alter the work surface height, then change the seat height to keep your forearms parallel to the floor. If you raise your seat, provide an elevated surface so your feet can rest flat on it and your thighs remain parallel to the floor.

## Sitting Surface
The usual sewing posture has one leg extended with the knee turned outward, and the foot in a pointed position on the foot pedal, typically causing "Sewer's Hip Bursitis" or "Chronic Sewer's Knee." In the correct sitting posture, your feet rest firmly on the floor, with your knees directly in front of your hips and your feet in front of your knees. Keep the foot pedal directly under your foot.

Most chairs are too tall and deep for the average sewer's height. Many people compromise by sitting close to the chair front edge with no back support, with their feet and legs spread apart and unbalanced. This position makes your back and neck muscles work much harder, creating tension throughout your spine. Find a chair that adjusts to the proper height and provides support for your back. Use a back support or other ergonomic accessory.

## Sewing Tips
It's amazing how many sewers never change position for hours. Following are some helpful hints:

- Drink a minimum of 1 pint of water every hour you sew. It helps to re-oxygenate your muscles.

- Play pleasant background music that's easy on your ears and promotes relaxation.

- Set a timer in another room to go off in an hour. This forces you to get up every hour to turn the timer off, which helps increase movement and prevent overall stiffness.

- Diffused lighting is best. Avoid fluorescent lighting—it's too harsh on your eyes and will create muscle tension in your face and shoulders. Try to use full-spectrum lights that simulate sunlight.

## Cutting Table Height

To determine the proper height for a cutting table, stand and lift one leg up and down to find your hip socket. The table should be the same height. This allows your scissors or rotary blade to rest on the table comfortably as you cut. Keep your elbows close to your body and your head in line with your spine. (Your forearm won't be parallel to the floor in this position.)

## Hand/Shoulder Connection

Most thumb pain due to sewing is actually because of elbow position. It's essential for good hand/arm/shoulder health to keep the elbows as close to your rib cage as possible.

## Tip

### Take a Break

Incorporate as much movement as possible into your sewing time. Who says you can't sew and exercise at the same time? Here's a great one-minute exercise routine to help kick off your new sewing habits. You'll immediately feel taller, stretched, and energized!

1. Stand up.

2. Bring your head back over your shoulders, pull your stomach in and march in place, breathe, and smile.

3. Turn your head to the right, then the left. Tilt it back, then forward, bringing your chin to your chest. Return your head upright.

4. Shrug your shoulders up, then pull them straight back and squeeze your shoulder blades together. Hold and relax, then repeat.

5. March in place, then wiggle from head to toe.

6. With your arms at your sides, turn your palms forward, then backward.

7. Lift your arms up to shoulder height and extend them straight out at your sides. Pull them backward and forward.

8. Stand on your toes and rock back onto your heels.

9. Look with only your eyes to the right, to the left, up, and down.

10. Take a deep breath, hold it, inhale more air, and hold, keeping your head and shoulders back.

11. Release the breath and smile.

12. Reach your arms overhead, keeping your head over your shoulders. Breathe and reach up, up, up.

13. Shake out your hands and feet.

14. Sit down with your back supported against a backrest, keeping both feet flat on the floor.

## EYELETS

See pages 68–77 for threads.
See pages 84–86 for stabilizers.

### Eye-opening Eyelets
*Sallie J. Russell*

*There's more to the eyelet than meets the eye. Eyelet holes—not to be confused with metal grommets—have many decorative and functional uses.*

An eyelet is a small hole with stitching around the edges. Sewn eyelets have a variety of uses including fastening belts, forming an embroidery pattern, or decorating clothing, appliqué, and craft projects.

A sewing machine with built-in stitches usually includes programmed eyelets. Although these eyelets are limited to a predetermined size, you can also make eyelets using an eyelet attachment. If you have a steady hand, you can even sew them free-hand.

*(Continued on next page)*

When sewing eyelets, you may need to hoop the fabric and/or use a stabilizer. Methods using a precut or punched hole provide the cleanest edge finishes. If this method isn't available to you, consider using a fusible interfacing or a seam sealant/fray preventive, but remember to test first. For leather, suede, felt, and other nonwoven fabrics, cut the hole after the stitching is complete.

On certain machines, the programmed letter "O" or number "0" also can also be used for a straight-stitch eyelet. Cut the hole after stitching the eyelet (unless you want a decorative eyelet outline without a hole).

## Eyelet Plates and Buttonholes

If your machine doesn't have programmed eyelets, or if you want more size variety, use an eyelet plate or buttonhole attachment. For either of these methods, check with your dealer or the machine manual for instructions, feed dog and needle positions, and presser foot selection.

Snap the eyelet plate over the feed dogs. These plates are available with different size studs over which the eyelet is satin-stitched. With the fabric stabilized or in a hoop, cut or punch a small hole where the eyelet will be, and place it over the raised stud so the hole fits snugly. Lower the presser foot lever, and pull up the bobbin thread. Select the desired stitch width and rotate the fabric clockwise. Stitch slowly with the needle alternately in the hole and in the fabric. For a more filled look, stitch around a second time.

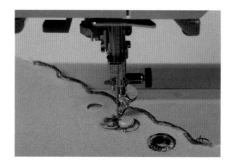

A buttonhole attachment may have a template for making eyelets. Size is limited to the available templates. Follow the instructions with the attachment.

## Freehand Eyelets

With practice and patience, you can create freehand eyelets. The hole size will determine the eyelet size. The technique is similar to appliquéing around a curve (See page 108 for satin stitch appliqué).

Mark the eyelet location and punch the desired hole size. Select the desired zigzag stitch width and use the needle-down position if available. Stitch slowly with the needle alternately in the hole and in the fabric. Take several stitches, then stop with the needle in the fabric; raise the presser foot and pivot the fabric in the direction you're stitching, then lower the foot and take the same number of stitches before stopping. Repeat these steps around the hole.

Use eyelets of different sizes to enhance machine embroidery projects. Eyelets can form a bunch of grapes, holly, or other berries, or serve as flower or snowflake centers.

(See page 108 for satin stitch appliqué).

## More Ideas

### Design Alternatives

■ When using an eyelet plate, replace the zigzag with a forward-feed compact decorative stitch like a triangle or half-circle. This is possible only on machines where the needle position is independent of the stitch selector.

■ Make an eyelet the center of larger decorative stitched circles. Depending on the method used to stitch the eyelet, it may be best to stitch the circles first.

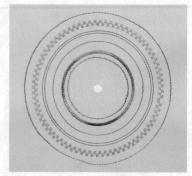

*Center hole is cut after outer circles are stitched.*

■ Combine eyelets with cutwork and heirloom sewing, or create unique eyelet trim for a special garment.

■ Use eyelets to create texture or add special details to appliqués—bubbles for a fish, exhaust from a car or train, or a connect-the-dots design.

*Eyelet examples stitched by Lynn Koolish.*

# FABRIC

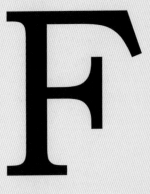

See pages 80–82 for needles.
See pages 68–77 for threads.
See pages 84–86 for stabilizers.
See pages 54–56 for presser feet.

## Make Your Own Designer Fabrics

*Pauline Richards*

*Easy embellishments transform plain fabric into customized creations.*

If you've shopped for embellished fabrics lately, you've probably noticed that many carry a hefty price tag. With a little decorative thread and trim, some standard stitching, and a few accessory presser feet, you can create your own customized fabric to incorporate into garments or home décor items. Use the fabric for an entire project, or make embellished fabric to use as an accent on cuffs, a collar, or a yoke.

## Quilted Sheer

Sandwich decorative thread between two layers of sheer fabric: Use a sheer fabric such as organza or georgette for the base fabric, and apply temporary adhesive spray. Arrange various decorative threads or cords on the base fabric in a swirl pattern.

Mark a 2" grid on a second layer of sheer fabric, and machine-quilt the layers together along the grid lines.

*Quilted sheer and pintuck diamonds*

### Other Ideas

■ Use metallic fabric and threads for added sparkle.

■ Combine several colors and weights of decorative thread and narrow ribbon.

## Pintuck Diamonds

Manipulated pintucks add fullness to your project. Draw six vertical stitching guidelines ½" apart on the fabric. To sew double-needle pintucks, tighten the upper tension, and use a 6mm twin needle and a pintuck or satin-stitch presser foot. For more pronounced tucks, cord the pintucks by stitching over perle cotton or topstitching thread. (See pages 185–186 for more information on making pintucks.)

Mark guidelines every 2" along the length of each tuck. Hand stitch the pintucks together, alternating the stitching to create a diamond pattern.

### Other Ideas

■ Complete the machine stitching and hand stitching with contrasting thread.

■ Stitch several sets of pintucks, leaving space between each set.

■ Mark hand stitching guidelines 1" apart to create smaller diamonds.

*(Continued on next page)*

## Dimensional Appliqué

To quickly make dimensional fabric without wasting a scrap, mark vertical stitching guidelines 2" apart on a base fabric. Randomly position self-fabric shapes along the marked lines. Pin the shapes in place, and machine stitch along the guidelines to secure.

### Other Ideas

- Draw the stitching guidelines random widths apart.

- Cut shapes from fabric that is a shade lighter or darker than the base fabric.

- Cut shapes from a contrasting color.

- Sew the shapes in place with metallic thread.

- Sew on the vertical lines with satin or other decorative stitching.

## Ruched Ribbon

Use a gathering foot to gather several yards of rayon seam binding or soft ribbon; adjust the fullness of the gathers by increasing the stitch length.

On the base fabric, draw vertical stitching guidelines 2" apart and straight-stitch the gathered trim into place. If you don't have a gathering attachment, gather trim by sewing narrow clear elastic down the center on the wrong side of the trim, stretching the elastic as you sew. As the elastic relaxes, it will gather the trim.

### Other Ideas

- Draw stitching guidelines 1" apart.

- Combine several colors of ribbon or seam binding.

- Cut matching or contrasting fabric into ½" bias strips, and gather the strips as you would the ribbon.

## Fringe

Create 3-D fabric with the fringe foot. Draw stitching guidelines ¾" apart on the base fabric. Thread the machine with rayon machine embroidery thread. Use a fringe foot to sew down each guideline using a medium to wide, short zigzag stitch. Press the fringed thread to one side. Use a regular presser foot and a straight stitch to secure the fringe along one edge.

### Other Ideas

- Sew two rows of fringe 1" apart, press in opposite directions, and apply a decorative stitch between the two rows.

- Create the fringe with multicolor or variegated thread.

- Sew rows of fringe just ¼" apart to create more texture.

## Basketweave

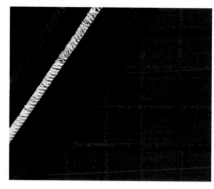

*Fringe and basketweave*

Create the look of basketweaving with vertical and horizontal rows of satin stitching. Back the base fabric with tear-away stabilizer. Mark a 1" stitching grid on the fabric, aligning the guidelines with the fabric grain. Straight-stitch along each horizontal and vertical guideline

To form the basketweave, sew a 4mm- to 6mm-wide satin stitch along the horizontal stitched guidelines. The vertical guidelines will create the appearance of weaving. On the first vertical stitching line, stitch over the first horizontal row, then stop and tie off the stitches when you reach the next horizontal row. Lift the presser foot over the horizontal row of stitching and begin stitching again just on the other side. Continue this over-one/under-one pattern for the row, then reverse the pattern in the next vertical row to create the faux weaving. Remove the remaining tear-away stabilizer.

(See page 201 for more on satin stitching.)

### Other Ideas

- Use one color of stitching for the horizontal rows and another for the vertical rows.

- Sew rows of straight stitching beside each satin-stitched row.

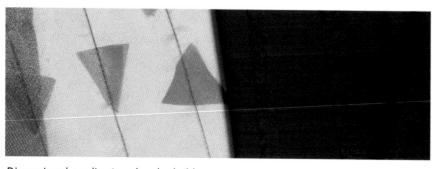

*Dimensional appliqué and ruched ribbon*

# FLEECE

## Follow this Thread

See pages 80–82 for needles.
See pages 68–77 for threads.
See pages 84–86 for stabilizers.
See page 201 for satin stitching.
See pages 129–130 for cutwork on fleece.
See pages 142–143 for embroidery on fleece.

## Sculpturing Fleece

**Nancy Cornwell**

*Satin stitching on fleece sinks into the fleece loft and creates an imprint of designs and patterns that texturize the fleece.*

## Needles and Thread

Choose a thread that complements the fleece. Rayon offers a wide color selection and adds shine and interest to the design. Metallic thread adds a hint of glitter. Clear thread is a good choice when outline sculpturing a print that doesn't have a dominant color to accent. Regular sewing thread gives a shadowed imprint. Use regular or lightweight thread in the bobbin.

Choose a needle type and size appropriate for the thread choice.

## Stabilizer

Use a dry iron and fusible tear-away stabilizer to eliminate the stretch factor of knit fleece.

Stabilize the wrong side of the fabric.

## Sewing

Simple sculpturing doesn't alter the finished size of the project piece, so embellish the cut piece before constructing the project.

The same techniques used for fleece can be used on other fabrics such as wool melton. *Fling Thing* Coat by Linda MacPhee.

Set the sewing machine for a 3mm to 4mm stitch width (wider for thicker fleeces or a more noticeable imprint) and a stitch length that allows a hint of fleece to show between the stitches.

Always stitch a test sample to adjust the stitch width and length to achieve the desired look.

## Try These Ideas

- Sculpturing works on Berber, too. Thick, rich Berber requires a 4mm stitch width for the design to be noticeable.

- Accent a plaid fabric with sculpting: Choose a few lines to follow, and satin stitch along them. If you can't find a thread color to match your project, twist two colors together for a heather look, and thread both through a single needle.

- Accent a motif in your fabric by satin stitching around its perimeter. It's the perfect way to add interest and texture to a yoke, pocket, inset, or garment back.

- To dress up a solid color, sculpt a grid onto the garment's yoke. Use a fabric marker or the quilting guide on your sewing machine to sew intersecting bias lines, 2" apart.

- Instead of using a simple satin stitch, choose a decorative satin stitch, such as a scallop, wave, dot, or rectangle.

- Use pintucks to sculpt raised lines. They don't need a stabilizer, and they won't affect the size of the pre-cut piece if you use them only as an accent. (See pages 185–186 for more on pintucks.)

## More Ideas

### Fleece Ribbing

Use pintucking to create matching fleece ribbing. Closely pintucking the fleece will give it a ribbed look but won't increase the stretch. Before making fleece ribbing, be sure your fleece has enough crosswise stretch to work as a self-fabric band, collar, or cuff.

Cut a fleece band the desired width (usually 6"- to 7"-wide) and 25% longer than the desired finished ribbed band measurement.

Using a 3mm twin needle and a 5-groove pintuck presser foot, sew pintuck rows across the band width, spacing the rows every other groove.

Cut and sew the band or cuffs as though you're making self-fabric band and cuffs.

## Quick Trick

### Temporary Spray Adhesive

As an alternative to fusible stabilizer, spray your favorite tear-away or cut-away stabilizer with a temporary adhesive, then smooth the fleece onto it. This prevents residue from accumulating on your garment, and ensures your sculpturing won't pucker or ripple during stitching.

## Follow the Lines
### Carol Zentgraf

*It's fun and easy to sculpt fleece when you use heavyweight thread in the bobbin and stitch along the design lines of a print facing or lining fabric.*

Choose a lining or facing fabric with a print large enough to outline stitch. Avoid small all-over prints and prints without any continuous lines. Geometric designs or large floral designs are easiest to stitch and look best from the sculpted side.

When cutting the facing or lining fabric, pay attention to the placement of the design elements you're going to stitch. Make certain any vertical lines in the print fabric are aligned as needed.

Pin or baste the lining or facing fabric to the fleece.

Stitch a test piece to make sure the tensions are adjusted so that the bobbin thread shows as desired on the fleece side.

Use heavyweight thread in the bobbin and all-purpose thread in the needle. Stitch with the lining or facing fabric face up and follow the desired print design lines.

(See page 191 for quilting from the back.)

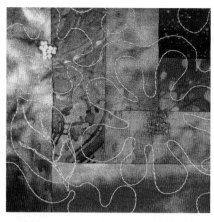

# FREE-MOTION STITCHING

*Presented here are a variety of techniques that require the feed dogs of the sewing machine to be dropped or covered. There are a number of similarities in techniques whether you are stitching on one layer of fabric, a quilt, or even just on stabilizer. Be sure to follow the threads for more information.*

### Free-motion Basics
See pages 80–82 for needles.
See pages 68–77 for threads.
See pages 84–86 for stabilizers.
See pages 162–163 for hooping.
See pages 54–56 for presser feet.
See pages 57–59 for adjusting tension.
See page 154–155 for free-motion embroidery.
See pages 156–158 for free-motion quilting.

## Free-motion Thread Painting
### Linda Griepentrog

*Create an outline, embroider, or quilt with free-motion stitching. Try any of these techniques—most of them lend themselves to more than one use!*

### Getting Started
To work most comfortably, position the sewing machine so your elbows rest on the table and your body is directly in front of the needle. If that isn't comfortable, place your forearm against the table edge, or put one elbow on the table and tuck the other against your body to anchor your arms for complete control. A flat surface works best for free-motion embroidery. If your machine isn't mounted in a cabinet, use a table cut to fit the

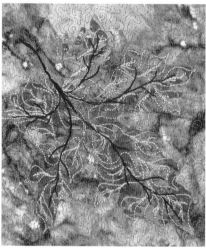

machine bed so the hoop will lie flat and level.

Follow these guidelines for successful free-motion sewing:

- Use a spring hoop or a thin wooden hoop with a screw adjustment.

- Hoop an appropriate stabilizer under the fabric.

- Drop the machine feed dogs. If that isn't possible set the stitch length to 0—feed dog covers sometimes interfere with free-motion stitching by creating a raised surface that may catch on the hoop.

- Use a darning foot, open-toed embroidery foot, or be brave and go footless. If working without a hoop, use a darning foot or spring needle to prevent the fabric from riding up on the needle during stitching.

- Use 40- to 50-weight cotton or rayon embroidery thread. After you've mastered free-motion embroidery, try polyester, metallic, silk, and acrylic threads.

- Use a fine bobbin thread to prevent a buildup of thread on the under side.

- Choose an embroidery needle in a size compatible with the thread and fabric.

- If bobbin thread shows on the right side, decrease the top tension.

- Loosen the upper thread tension until the top thread is about ⅔ of the thread visible on the underside.

## Stitching

The goal is to draw with the needle and create texture with thread. Simple exercises will develop your comfort level with free-motion work and allow you to go on to more complex projects.

Hoop your fabric, making sure it's taut, smooth, and lies flat against the machine bed. With embroidery thread in the needle and lightweight thread in the bobbin, place the hoop under the needle. Lower the presser foot lever to engage the upper tension.

Bring the bobbin thread to the top and set the machine for a straight stitch. Hold onto the threads as the stitching begins.

Hand position is important for control. Form two sides of an imaginary triangle with the index, middle, and ring fingers of each hand, and the needle is the center of the third side. This position gives the most control and is the safest for fingers. Rest your pinkies and thumbs on the edge of, and occasionally nudge, the hoop; the further your fingers are from the needle, the less control you have.

## Try This

As you sew, remember that the feed dogs are inactive, so all movement is up to you! Move the hoop smoothly and evenly. Try writing your name as a first step, then try these leaves.

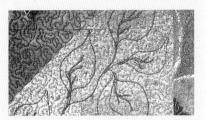

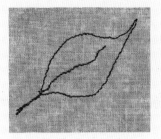

*Stitch a basic leaf shape.*

*Stitch a basic leaf. Stitch a center vein, then fill with lines that echo the center vein.*

*Trace around the shape again. Don't worry if your lines don't line up.*

*Stitch a basic leaf. Switch to a zigzag stitch and go around a second time. Return to a straight stitch for veins.*

*Stitch another leaf. When stitching around the second time, move the fabric back-and-forth to create a jagged edge. Add more veins.*

## Add a Kick to Your Stitch

For a different look, after mastering the straight stitch, begin working with a zigzag.

Remember, your movement controls the fabric and resulting stitch appearance.

*Enlarge and use these designs for more free-motion practice.*

See page 152 for references to free-motion basics.

## Free-motion Embroidery

### Joyce Becker

*Free-motion machine embroidery enhances quilts by adding depth and texture. But don't limit this technique to just quilt tops. Think of all the other machine arts projects you can machine embroider: garments, pillows, home décor items . . .*

For quilts, it is best to machine-embroider the quilt top before it is sandwiched with the batting and backing. It is easier to stitch extensively through one stabilized layer instead of three layers, and you don't have to worry about how the back of your quilt top looks.

To help with proper fabric tension, roll the edges of the quilt top toward the center of the sewing machine, then hold the rolled edges to manipulate and control the tension while embroidering. Maintain enough tension with your hands so the quilt doesn't pucker as you stitch.

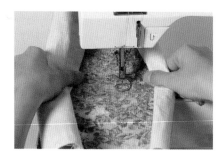

## Preparation

Use an appropriate stabilizer under all your machine embroidery.

Be sure the top and bottom tensions are adjusted correctly for your thread choices.

Pull the bobbin thread to the surface, take a few stitches in place to lock the threads, trim the threads, and you're ready to stitch.

## Stitching

Avoid pesky thread changes: Once you've finished a color in one section, "jump" to another section that will be stitched with the same color thread. Secure the stitches at the beginning and end of each section, and cut the adjoining thread later.

Free-motion machine embroidery can be purely decorative or can be used to secure appliqué pieces, but it should always enhance your design. Accentuate patterns that are already in your fabric, or add your own design elements.

## Selecting Thread

Twisted thread works well in landscape quilts because two colors are twisted together into one thread, adding texture. In general, shiny and metallic threads don't look realistic, but there are a few exceptions. Metallic and silver threads are perfect for water, icy scenes, or the sun's reflection. Cotton 12- and 30- weight threads are wonderful for machine embroidery and easily go through the needle.

*Here Chickee, Chickee, Chickee* from *Lucsious Landscapes* by Joyce Becker. Quilt by Joyce Becker.

## *Tip*

### Holding the Fabric

Some quilters use a small wooden or plastic hoop to control the quilt top as they sew, but this means constantly repositioning the hoop. In most cases, the amount of machine embroidery will be evenly spread across the entire quilt top, so try to use your hands to control fabric tension instead.

Check your favorite mail-order source or your local quilt or sewing shop for special finger cots or gripping gloves. These tools help you hold the fabric without slipping. Or, buy a big box of latex surgical gloves, and wear them as you work to help control the fabric

Free-motion trees

# *Free-motion Thread Scribble Appliqué*
### *Ricky Tims*

I use a technique I call "thread scribbling" to create texture, shadows, and depth on small pictorial quilts.

I start with the sky and build the scene from back to front, cutting out shapes from fabric to represent elements of the quilt. The shapes are raw edge and are tacked to the quilt using a glue stick. Until they are stitched down, the edges of the shapes can be temporarily moved so that areas underneath can be stitched. The quilt top is built directly on top of batting and all stitching is done through the fabric and the batting so the batting acts as a stabilizer. The backing is added when all the stitching is complete.

Once the scribble-stitched project is ready for quilting, I square the edges and add borders if desired. A typical quilt sandwich is made with the top, batting and backing. Quilting adds dimension to the scribble appliquéd elements, but I don't do a lot of quilting in those areas—just enough to add dimension and attach all the layers.

Before scribble stitching an area of the scene, I stitch around each piece about 1⁄16" from the outside edge to secure it in place.

The scribble stitching can be random texture or more representational such as twigs, leaves, or tree bark. By using scribble stitching in the background, I can add detail with thread, rather then with individual pieces of fabric. The resulting quilts are rich in texture and detail. The process is really a combination of both appliqué and embroidery.

*South Cheyenne Canyon* by Ricky Tims.

# FREE-MOTION QUILTING

Presented here are quilting techniques specific to free-motion quilting. Be sure to follow the threads below for quilting basics and other quilting techniques.

 Follow this Thread

See page 152 for references to free-motion basics.
See pages 187–191 for quilting basics.
See pages 94–98 for helpful tools.
See pages 54–56 for presser feet.

## Free-motion Quilting Basics
### Kathy Sandbach

*Free-motion stitching and embroidery have many of the same characteristics as free-motion quilting, so be sure to read those sections (pages 152–155) to add to your free-motion know-how.*

## Presser Feet

For free-motion quilting, you must have a darning foot for your machine. They come in many sizes and shapes.

If you're quilting easy curves or straight lines, use the walking foot with the feed dogs up, and the machine will automatically take the correct number of stitches per inch.

*Poppin' Poppies* (detail) from *Show Me How to Machine Quilt* by Kathy Sandbach. Quilt by Kathy Sandbach.

## Fingers or Gloves

When free-motion quilting, your hands act as a hoop. Use the same hand position for all free-motion work. Your hands need to hold the fabric sandwich taut but not stretched. Rubber fingers from a stationery store or quilter's gloves will help hold the fabric taut and help you guide it smoothly. This will eliminate pleats or tucks on both the back and the top. It's very important to remember that your hands are guiding the fabric and keeping it taut at the same time—just as a hoop would.

## Hand Position

By using the "U" position for hands, you can maintain both the tautness and control of the quilt. Keep your thumb tips together and only quilt within this 5" to 6" space. When the needle comes too close to your fingers, stop the machine and reposition your hands. This is a bit tricky to get used to, but when mastered it will give your quilting lines smooth continuity.

 *Tip*

## Bigger Sewing Surface

If your sewing machine isn't set into a sewing table where the bed of the machine is at the same height as the table, an extension table can make quilting much easier by providing more surface to support the quilt.

## Using Needle-down

If you have the needle-down feature on your machine, use it. This helps secure the piece when you reposition your hands. Otherwise, you need to move one hand at a time so the piece doesn't move on its own.

## Stitch Length

Your goal is approximately 10 to 12 stitches per inch. When you are first using the darning foot, you will probably need some practice to get even stitches. If you move the piece too fast, you'll have only four stitches per inch; too slow and you'll have 60 or so stitches per inch. With just a little practice, you can get even-length stitches.

## Practice, Practice, Practice

Unless you are experienced and very comfortable with free-motion quilting, you need to practice your designs before beginning to quilt on the quilt top or garment that you've spent months piecing or appliquéing.

Make a practice quilt sandwich with cotton fabric, batting, and backing. Pin the layers securely, thread your machine with a thread color you can see on your fabric, and just begin to "draw" with the needle. Make mistakes, start, stop, stitch however you want. Start with an easy design, and work you way up to more complicated designs.

Don't try to make all your stitching perfect. Small variations or imperfections won't be noticeable, they will look like they are part of the plan. After a bit of practice, you will find that small errors will become part of the charm and personality of the quilt. Also remember that quilting on printed fabrics hides your irregularities.

# 7 Tips for Free-motion Quilting
### Katie Pasquini Masopust

1. Try leaving the feed dogs up; some quilters find the friction helps move the fabric along.

2. Set your machine to zigzag with a stitch width of 0—when you move the quilt quickly, you produce a straight stitch; slowly, a satin stitch. Use the width of the satin stitch to create texture and to add accents.

3. Use a darning foot or Big Foot to hold the quilt on the bed of the machine.

4. Bring the bobbin thread up to the top before you start to sew to avoid messy threads underneath.

5. Follow the print of the fabric, or create your own textures by doodling with the needle.

6. For a good satin stitch, gradually increase the stitch width as you sew, press hard on the foot pedal, but move the fabric slowly.

7. Be patient and learn your rhythm and your machine's.

## Stippling

Stippling is tight, random stitching. The "rule" for stippling has always been never to cross over the stitching line. Keep this in mind, though: While crossing the line once or twice is a "mistake," crossing ten or twelve times is a "pattern."

*Colored Village* from *Ghost Layers and Color Washes* by Katie Pasquini Masopust. Quilt by Katie Pasquini Masopust.

# Quilting the Contours

**Hollis Chatelaine**

My quilting must do more than just hold the three layers together; it needs to be an integral part of the overall design. By quilting in lines that follow the contours of an object or shape, I add dimension and texture to my quilts.

When trying to decide how to place my quilting lines, I think of an ant that is walking across the object with dye on his feet. He leaves a trail of dye as he walks down into the crevices and up over the humps of the object. That ant trail is my quilting line. By quilting with threads in colors that enhance the shadows and highlights, I achieve an even greater sense of depth and texture.

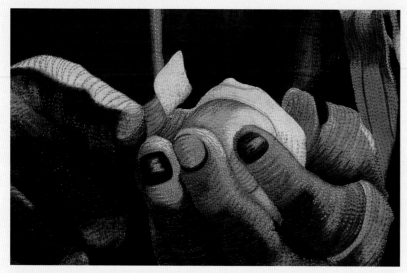

*The Grandfather* (detail) by Hollis Chatelaine. See page 19 for quilt.

## Transferring Quilting Design Lines

**Laura Lee Fritz**

If you aren't ready to make the leap into no-mark free-motion quilting, here are some easy ways to transfer quilting designs onto your quilt top.

- Draw or trace the design on paper with a black permanent pen, and resize the image on a copy machine. Make different sizes for blocks and borders. Trace the photocopy onto template plastic, cut it out, then trace the template onto your quilt. Or, trace the design onto tulle and draw over the tulle, leaving a dashed line on the fabric. Both of these methods are a means to draw directly onto your quilt top with chalk, washout pencil, clean-erase pencil, or a water- or air-soluble pen.

- Use a wash-out pencil or pen to trace the pattern onto a piece of water-soluble stabilizer. Pin the drawing in place on your quilt. Use the transparent drawing to place the drawing where you won't need to sew over bulky seams. Sew through the drawn lines, then pull away the large chunks of the stabilizer, and mop up the remaining fragments with a wet cloth or a damp scrap of batting.

If you leave large pieces of stabilizer on the quilt after wetting, they will turn to slime, which dries on the quilt, and the quilt will need a thorough washing.

- Draw directly onto your quilt top with a washable marker. Use a good, bright light source to see exactly what and where you're drawing.

- Support a glass panel on a quilt frame or set of sawhorses, and place a light source such as a 4-foot fluorescent shop light below the "table."

- Spread your quilt top on the glass, turn the light on, slide your drawing under the quilt, and trace onto the quilt with temporary markers. Clean white paper and bold black drawing lines will project best through the cloth.

## Tip

### Starting or Ending a Line of Quilting

When you start or end a line of quilting, or when your top thread or bobbin is depleted, knot the end(s) of your stitching line and thread a needle with the thread tails. Use a long-eye sharp embroidery needle so both threads will fit through at once.

To thread the needle try wrapping the pair of threads around the eye tightly, pinch the thread to hold the tiny loops as you withdraw the needle, then slip the eye over these tight little loops. Sew these ends by sliding the needle back along your quilting line, pull the needle out, bury the knot into the batting, and cut the tail.

# GATHERING

**Follow this Thread**

See pages 54–56 for presser feet.
See page 226–227 for gathering
for smocking.

## Gathering by Machine

**Lynn Koolish**

*Gathering is used to produce fullness in
fabric. The gathered fabric is then used in
smocking, shirring (numerous rows of
gathering), ruffles, and other surface
effects.*

Gathering can be accomplished using
several techniques.

- Use a long stitch length and pull
  one end of the bobbin thread to
  gather the fabric. Several rows of
  stitching can be used to alleviate
  thread breakage. This technique
  works best for lightweight fabrics
  and relatively short lengths of fabric.

- Use a zigzag stitch over a heavy
  thread and pull the heavy thread to
  gather the fabric. This technique
  works best for heavier fabrics and
  relatively short lengths of fabric.

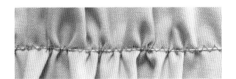

- Multiple rows of straight stitching
  can be used for shirring. With a
  contrasting thread, the stitching
  becomes a decorative element
  in itself.

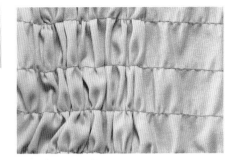

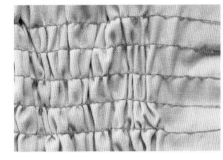

- Use a gathering or ruffling foot
  when longer lengths of fabric need
  to be gathered.

  With a gathering foot, the amount
  of fabric gathered is determined by
  the weight of the fabric, the stitch
  length, and the needle tension.
  With a ruffling foot, there is an
  adjustment that controls the
  amount of fabric that is gathered.
  With either foot, a single layer of
  fabric can be gathered, or fabric can
  be gathered and stitched onto
  another piece of fabric.

# H

# HEMSTITCHING

Follow this Thread

See pages 80–82 for needles. See pages 181–182 for more on using wing needles.

## Heavenly Hemstitches

**Ann Price Gosch**

*The delicate, airy effect of hemstitching has captivated sewing enthusiasts for centuries. Once a tedious process, hemstitching today is much easier because of our modern machines. The key is a hemstitch or wing needle.*

## The Basic Stitch

Set your machine for a medium-width, close zigzag, and insert a wing needle. Sew the first row, ending with the needle in the fabric on the left swing of the zigzag.

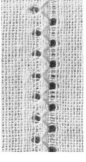

Turn the fabric 180°. Sew the second row so each left swing of the zigzag pierces a hole of the previous row; end with the needle in the fabric on the right swing of the zigzag.

Turn the fabric 180° and sew the third row so each right swing of the zigzag pierces a hole of the previous row. Continue in the same manner for as many rows as desired.

## Hemstitch Appliqué

To make textured appliqués, hemstitch an entire area of fabric on the bias. Cut out shapes from the fabric and satin-stitch appliqué onto the base fabric or garment.

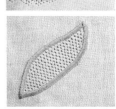

For a see-through effect, cut the base fabric from behind the appliqué

## Attaching Lace

Twin-needle hemstitching is ideal for attaching lace edging to simulate the look of entredeux. (Look for a twin needle with one wing needle and one standard needle.)

Mark the fabric with placement lines for the lace. Baste the lace in place, or secure it with water-soluble glue.

Position the work under the presser foot so the wing needle is just to the left of the lace and the standard needle attaches the lace to the fabric close to the lace edge; stitch.

Wing needle

Standard needle

Raise the needles and presser foot, turn the fabric and lace 180°, and position the wing needle in the first hole of the previous row. Stitch a second row, piercing the holes of the previous row.

## Hemstitch Topstitching

If you're looking for an attractive alternative to conventional topstitching, consider using the twin hemstitching needle.

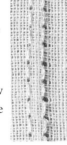

Use a straight stitch to sew the first row, then raise the needles and presser foot.

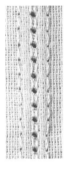

Turn the fabric 180° and position the wing needle in the first hole of the previous row; sew the second row so the wing needle pierces each hole of the first row.

## For Another Look

Try using utility or decorative stitches on your machine. The blind hemstitch, for example creates an attractive hemstitching with both single and double hemstitch needles. Many machines have other stitches specifically designed for hemstitching. (See pages 43–53 for a visual guide to decorative stitches.)

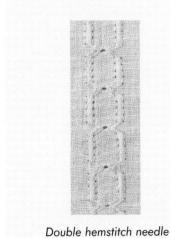

*Double hemstitch needle*

*Hemstitching examples stitched by Elizabeth Tisinger.*

# HONEYCOMB STITCH

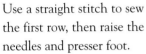 Follow this Thread

See pages 226–228 for more smocking techniques. See pages 113–115 for bobbinwork.

## Honey of a Stitch

*Sallie J. Russell*

*Use the honeycomb stitch to create smocking and other decorative details.*

The honeycomb stitch—created by a combination of needle swing and feed dog action—forms stitches often referred to as stretch, tri-motion, or super-automatic. The honeycomb is formed as the feed dogs move the fabric forward and back and the needle bar moves to multiple positions across the stitching area.

## Reverse Embroidery

Use the honeycomb stitch for bobbinwork. This technique can be used to fill in or layer on color for a three-dimensional look, or to create textured embellishments.

Bypass the bobbin tension, loosen it completely, or use a second bobbin case (see page 114). Use a bobbin wound with perle cotton or another decorative cord or thread, and match the needle thread color to the bobbin or use monofilament thread.

Transfer the reversed design to tearaway stabilizer. Place the stabilizer on the wrong side of the fabric. Use an embroidery hoop for additional stability if needed.

With the wrong side up, begin at the outside edge and sew a row of stitches. Continue stitching around, working from the outside toward the center, with the stitching rows right next to each other for a lacy design. For an easy first project, match the bobbin thread to the fabric to create a tone-on-tone design.

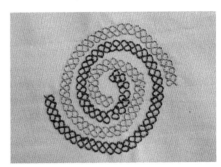

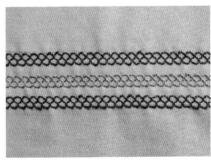

## Smocking

Use elastic thread in the bobbin, and a matching or contrasting color needle thread. Or you can use a decorative thread in the needle for a special look.

Hand-wind the elastic thread onto the bobbin, being careful not to stretch it as you wind. Insert the bobbin in the usual manner.

Draw guidelines at least ½" apart on the right side of the fabric using chalk or a water-soluble marker.

Place water-soluble stabilizer under the fabric to keep it flat, help prevent tension problems, and maintain uniform feeding.

*Honeycomb examples stitched by Elizabeth Tisinger.*

*(Continued on next page)*

Stitch the first row slowly and check the stitch tension. The elastic thread should form a straight line on the wrong side of the fabric.

Carefully remove the stabilizer after the stitching is complete. Pull on the elastic threads if more smocking is needed.

## Using in Garments

Place the pattern pieces on a single layer of the pre-smocked fabric, following the usual grainline placement. Smooth out the fabric when pinning the neck, shoulder, and armhole edges; pin the remaining pattern edges to relaxed fabric.

Before cutting, trace around the pattern pieces; zigzag on the traced outlines to secure the elastic thread ends. Cut the pattern pieces out with 1" seam allowances.

Baste the garment together, fit, and adjust if necessary. Stitch the seams permanently and double-stitch 1/8" inside the seamline to secure the elastic threads. Pink or serge raw edges to trim off the excess seam allowances. Press the seams to one side.

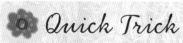

### *Quick Trick*

### Smocking Sample

Make a smocking sample using the thread, needle, and settings you'll use on your project. Start with a 12" fabric square, smock the entire width, and then measure it. Use this sample as a guide for purchasing fabric for your smocked project.

# HOOPING

**Follow this Thread**

See pages 84–86 for stabilizers.
See pages 94–95 for hooping aids.

## Hooping Techniques

### Deborah Jones

*Next to the design itself, hooping is perhaps the single most important key to achieving successful embroidery results. Don't forget stabilizer, though—hooping and stabilizing work together for embroidery you'll be proud of.*

## Selecting and Preparing the Hoop

Always choose the smallest hoop that will accommodate the size of the design. Jumbo hoops and multi-position hoops have been introduced to allow for the stitching of larger embroidery designs, but their long sides often do not grip the fabric securely, allowing it to slip, which results in puckering and drifting outlines.

After matching the stabilizer to your fabric type, cut a piece of stabilizer that is 1" larger in all directions than your hoop. This helps make it easier to completely cover your hoop.

Before hooping, mark the item to be embroidered with an air- or water-soluble marking pen, masking tape, basting tape, or other means so you know where to place the item in the hoop. Mark the center with short horizontal and vertical line. You will be able to line these up with the center notches in the hoop.

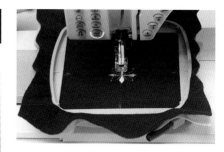

## Hooping the Fabric

Tension is the key to proper hooping. It may take more than one try to get the fabric in the hoop with the proper tension. Here are some pointers to help you get your hoop adjusted properly:

- The fabric should be taut, rather than the hoop being tight.

- When inserting the inner ring into the outer hoop, your goal is moderate resistance. Too much resistance can mar the fabric. Loosen the screw on the outer hoop ring slightly to loosen the tension, and try again.

- Apply the inner hoop to the fabric at the hoop upper edge. Continue moving toward the hoop lower edge until the inner hoop snaps into place. (This technique is especially helpful when hooping knits.)

- Be careful not to pull on the fabric during the hooping process. Pulling on a knit fabric can stretch or distort the fibers, which creates puckering when the fabric is unhooped. The embroidery needle can also cut knit fibers that stretched during the hooping process.

- While hooping, keep the fabric markings in alignment with the hoop. Be sure that the cross marks on the fabric align with the hoop notches.

## Checking the Hoop

Once the fabric is in the hoop, inspect the fabric surface and the stabilizer underside. Push the inner ring slightly past the outer ring to remove any surface ripples. The inner ring should be slightly lower than the outer ring so the fabric is closer to the machine bed and to hold proper tension.

Place the hoop in the machine, and embroider the design. After embroidery is complete remove and use a damp cloth to remove any hoop ring that shows. Test on an inconspicuous spot for suitability to your fabric. Your hoop may have been adjusted too tightly if this remedy fails to remove the hoop ring. Use a press cloth, and press or steam the design on the wrong side of the fabric.

 *Tips*

### Using Large Hoops

If you need to use a larger hoop (for very large designs, for example), get a better grip on your fabrics by wrapping the long side of the inner ring with removable tape. Try florist tape, athletic gauze, or twill tape to allow for a snug fit. As you wrap the hoop, do not cover the hoop notches so you can align the hoops. Some larger hoops provide clips to hold the fabric between the inner and outer hoop. Binder clips can also help hold the long sides secure.

### Hooping First-aid

To treat wrinkles in the fabric or stabilizer: Unhoop the item, loosen the hoop tension screw, and begin again.

To treat severe rippling: The result of a too-tight hoop, ripples can't be corrected by tugging on the fabric. Remove and re-hoop.

# I

## INTERNET

### Information on the Internet

*C&T Publishing Staff*

*The Internet is one of your most valuable tools when it comes to machine arts. Hundreds of websites have "Links" lists to other, related websites, so if you find one good one, you're assured a continuous supply of information on whatever topic you're interested in.*

Check the ideas below for ways you can use the Internet to begin, add to, or share your own stitching expertise.

### Books and Magazines

■ Many sewing magazines (such as *Sew News* and *Creative Machine Embroidery*) have additional information and articles on their websites that's not in the print versions.

■ Book publishers also maintain websites with information, links, and online sales.

■ Bookstores and online-only "book stores" stock hundreds of machine arts-related titles.

### Embroidery

■ Search for embroidery designs that you can download free or purchase online.

■ A few embroidery machines can connect directly to websites and download stitches, embroidery designs, and more.

### Individual Websites

■ Sewing personalities, artists, authors, teachers, and hobbyists often maintain websites that display their work, share ideas and techniques, offer products and patterns for sale, and have workshop schedules.

### Information

■ Product information is readily available from most manufacturers. Check out "FAQs" (frequently asked questions) for answers to many questions you may or may not have known you had! They can also help you locate an authorized dealer or retail store near you.

■ Check for websites maintained by sewing-related organizations, such as the American Sewing Guild, Home Sewing Association, Embroidery Software Protection Coalition, and University Cooperative Extension Programs (those with textile programs are especially good sources of information).

■ If you don't have a peer group of sewers in your neighborhood or town (or even if you do), log on and join an online discussion group, newsgroup, or community bulletin board.

■ Check out the programs and activities at your local quilt guild.

■ If you have a specific question or are looking for a specific product, try a search engine. You'll generally get hits for both.

### Shopping

■ Mail-order catalog companies generally sell online as well—it's a great way to shop for everything you need for machine arts. Frequently, you can also find other customers' comments about products offered for sale.

■ Many fabric, quilting, and crafts shops also have websites and sell online.

■ Comparison shopping for a large (or small) item? Check pricing on the Internet. Some search engines will do this automatically.

## KIDS

### For Kids

*Whether you make something special and give to a child or want something for children to do themselves, there's plenty of machine arts for kids.*

Use solar-reactive or glow-in-the-dark threads (see page 72) for a delightful surprise for your favorite child.

For a really unique gift for a newborn, make a christening quilt using vintage stitching techniques, or use heirloom stitches to make a blouse or dress for the special little girl in your life. (See page 240.)

Appliquéd and embroidered button-holes can dress up a kid's shirt or dress. (See page 120.)

 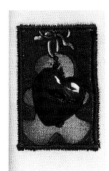

Many built-in stitches feature kid-oriented designs. (See pages 48–49.)

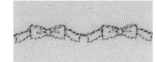

*(Continued on next page)*

Embroider names, labels and other designs in your kid's clothes. (See page 136.)

Embroidered edge finishes (see pages 131–133) and lettuce edges (see page 202) are perfect for kids' clothes.

Smocking is perfect for little girl's dresses. (See pages 226–228.)

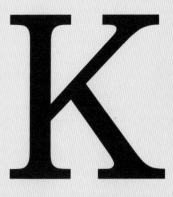

Use pictorial chenille for a quilt or appliqué using a favorite image or motif. (See page 124.)

Embroider decorative appliqués for clothes or school packs. (See page 134 for references to embroidery basics.)

Embellish clothing with embroidery for a unique look. (See pages 144–145, 177, and 228.)

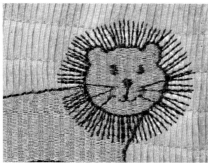

*Mickey and Minnie embroidery designs: Brother, ULT-2002D Mickey & Friends Designs, Disney*

*R and S embroidery designs: Brother, ULT-2002D built-in alphabet*

*Car and skateboard embroidery designs: Dakota Collectibles, Fun Times Collection*

*Pumpkin embroidery designs: Oklahoma Embroidery Supply & Design, Holiday 9 Pack #11437*

*Lion embroidery design: Husqvarna Viking, Disk #44*

*Sun embroidery design: Oklahoma Embroidery Supply & Design, #CR119*

*Floral embroidery designs: Creative Machine Embroidery magazine originals*

Make a quilt using machine embroidery for easy appliqué. (See page 138.)

Stitching on paper (see pages 183–184) and stitching greeting cards (see pages 184–185) are great kids' projects.

Decorative stitches on bindings are great for kids. (See page 113.)

## LACE

### Follow this Thread

See pages 80–82 for needles.
See pages 68–77 for threads.
See pages 84–86 for stabilizers.
See pages 162–163 for hooping.
See pages 238–239 for underlay stitching.

## Machine-embroidered Lace

*Rebecca Kemp Brent*

*Create delicate works of embroidered art with professionally digitized lace designs. Choose white for breezy summer days, or an explosion of color—you're sure to fall in love with the handmade look of machine-embroidered lace. Stitch an open, airy design onto fabric to create the illusion of appliquéd lace, or stitch on soluble stabilizer to create true, stand-alone lace.*

## Lace-look Designs

When choosing designs for lace embroidery on fabric, look for motifs that simulate the appearance of purchased lace. Areas of light fill stitches mimic the netting background of purchased lace, and shaped satin stitch outlines define the motif's border.

### Threads

Select thread as you would for any embroidery. Finer threads (40- to 60-weight) are great for delicate embroidered motifs. Ordinary sewing thread can be used for lace and may provide a convenient match to a handmade garment, but often produces stiffer, heavier laces. And don't forget variegated thread to blend in with tone-on-tone fabrics or to stand out on a contrasting color.

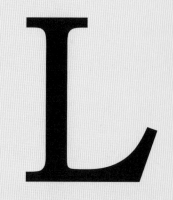

Experiment with slightly heavier, 30-weight embroidery threads, especially cotton, to approximate the appearance of crocheted laces. When using heavier thread, increase the size of the motif slightly (10% to 20%) to allow for the extra thread weight.

Metallic threads look wonderful when stitched into lace, but the high stitch count of lacy motifs may result in the shredding of these coarsely textured threads.

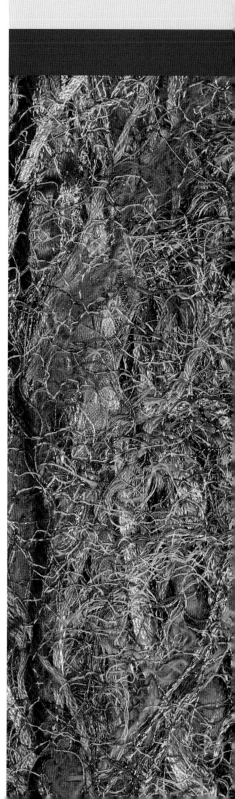

Mimic the appearance of metallic embroidery with shiny rayon thread in metallic colors instead (for example, golden-colored rayon to mimic the patina of brushed gold). Always stitch a test sample to gauge the particular combination of thread and motif you have chosen.

*(Continued on next page)*

### Needles

Select a needle based on the thread, fabric, and stabilizer you will be using. Generally, a finer needle yields better results with lace designs. Size 75/11 embroidery needles work with most threads. If you experiment with heavier threads, choose a larger needle or one designed for topstitching. Most knit fabrics require a ballpoint needle to avoid tearing holes in the fabric.

### Fabrics

When selecting the fabric for a lacy motif, stay away from highly textured fabrics such as terry and fleece. The fine details of the lace will be lost in the fabric's texture. Flat fabrics such as broadcloth, denim, satin, tulle, or sheer organdy are all possible bases for lace embroidery. Cotton netting (available from heirloom sewing suppliers) works well for the embroidery of fine lace motifs.

### Stabilizers

Less stabilizer is required for open, airy lace than for dense designs of similar size. The open texture of the lacy designs makes removing stabilizer difficult, so use a water- or heat-soluble product, or consider a lightweight cutaway if the wrong side of the finished project will not be visible.

## Freestanding Lace Designs

Lace designs suitable for freestanding stitching include underlay stitches to provide support for the embroidery once the heat- or water-soluble stabilizer foundation is removed. When in doubt, stitch a test sample; if there are no underlay stitches, the design will fall apart when the foundation is removed. Designs without appropriate underlay stitching should be stitched on fabric or on tulle.

*Designs with underlay stitching stay intact when stabilizer is removed.*

### Threads

The thread is both the visible design and its underlying support. Too fine a thread results in limp lace with gaps between stitches; too heavy a thread creates stiff lace and leads to broken needles and frustration. Follow the specific thread recommendations for your chosen design, and use the same thread in both the needle and bobbin.

### Needles

Size 75/11 embroidery needles are appropriate for most threads. Needles for freestanding lace should be small enough to place stitches side by side without tearing the stabilizer foundation.

### Stabilizer

Use heat- or water-soluble stabilizer as a foundation. Freestanding lace designs typically contain a large number of stitches, so use a heavyweight (or several layers of a lighter-weight) stabilizer. Hoop up to six layers of lightweight water-soluble stabilizer, several layers of a medium weight, or just one layer of the heaviest weight.

Try cut-away water-soluble stabilizer; It's less prone to tearing, and one layer is enough for most freestanding designs.

### Machine Tension

Freestanding lace designs look best when the needle and bobbin threads meet in the middle. Stitch a test sample, and adjust the tension as needed.

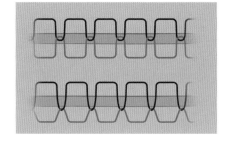

### Embroidering Freestanding Lace

Hoop the stabilizer of your choice. Use the editing capabilities of your machine or software to fill the hoop with embroidered lace motifs. After stitching, remove the embroidered stabilizer from the hoop and carefully cut away the excess close to the edge of the motif.

When embroidering connected motifs, sew them together before removing the stabilizer. Place the edges to be joined side by side and use a zigzag or multistep zigzag stitch and matching thread to stitch the motifs together. The stitch will swing back and forth between the motifs to join without overlapping.

Remove the stabilizer by soaking the lace pieces in water, following the manufacturer's instructions. Repeated periods of soaking in fresh water may be necessary. When the lace is free of stabilizer, roll it in a towel and squeeze gently to remove excess water.

Lay the lace pieces flat to air-dry, or carefully iron them dry, using a clean press cloth. Any residual stiffness in the lace is an indication that there is still stabilizer in the embroidery. Soak stiff motifs again until they are soft and supple.

## Lace Appliqués

To stitch freestanding lace appliqués in place, set your machine for an open zigzag stitch (not a satin zigzag) approximately the same width as the lace motif outline. Use matching thread or an invisible monofilament in the needle. Or, stitch the motif in place by hand.

*Gold motif embroidery design: Criswell Embroidery and Designs, K-Lace for Christmas*

*Gold on black embroidery design: Amazing Designs, Nancy Zieman collection VIII Lace Vignettes*

*White blouse embroidery designs: Brother card #29*

*Daisy embroidery designs: Criswell Embroidery and Designs, Bouquets of K-Lace*

*Blue flower embroidery design: Brother card #29*

*Floral scallop embroidery design: Zundt Design Ltd, design 202025*

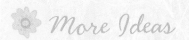

*More Ideas*

- Use a single lace motif, especially a large one, as a dramatic focal point on a garment or home décor project.

- Make lace in a contrasting color to stand out, or match the thread to the fabric for a more subtle appearance.

- Arrange motifs side by side or interlocked to create borders or larger pattern areas.

- Use tulle or sheer fabric as a foundation for lace. If you match the tulle color to the fabric where the lace will be appliquéd, it virtually disappears.

- Add a layer of tulle or fabric to the foundation of freestanding lace to add strength and durability. For a sheer look, match the foundation color to the lace thread, or for clothing match it to your skin tone for a daring, bare appearance.

See page 152 for references to free-motion basics.
See pages 68–77 for threads.
See pages 84–86 for stabilizers.

## Free-motion Lacemaking

### Carola Russell

*Straight stitching is all you need to make beautiful free-motion lace. The lace can be used to make inserts, appliqués, patches, collars, or edging. Experiment with different thread types and weights to explore the potential of this technique.*

### Choosing Stabilizer

Choose an extra-heavy, water-soluble stabilizer that doesn't require hooping. With extra-heavy stabilizer, only one layer of stabilizer is required for lacemaking. With a regular-weight, water-soluble stabilizer, you will need at least two layers and will need to hoop the stabilizer.

### Machine Setup

Set the machine for free-motion stitching, and use a darning or free-motion presser foot. Insert a size 80/12 topstitch or metallic needle. The large eye accommodates thicker thread and eliminates fraying. Loosen the upper tension, and thread the needle with cotton or rayon machine-embroidery thread. Wind several bobbins with cotton thread to match the upper thread.

### Stitching

Begin stitching in a continuous circular motion at a slow to medium speed at one end of the stabilizer, ½" from the edge. Stitch one circle on the stabilizer then stitch over it a second time, directly over the first stitching. Make bubble-like circles, continuously

*(Continued on next page)*

moving the stabilizer. Vary the circle sizes from ⅛" to ⅝" diameter, overlapping some stitches.

Continue to build on the circle clusters until the stabilizer is covered with circular stitching. By overlapping the circle edges, the lacy stitching will have at least four thread strands for stability.

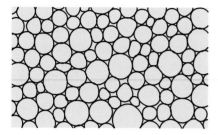

To remove the stabilizer, place the lace in a bowl of cool water, let it soak, and gently rinse. Roll the lace in a towel to blot the excess water. Lay flat to dry or press dry, using a press cloth to avoid scorching. Gently reshape the lace into its original shape.

To maintain the lace shape, use one or two applications of spray starch, then press the lace dry, again using a press cloth for protection. Trim the lace to the desired size and shape. Apply seam sealant or fray preventive to the cut edges to prevent fraying. Use as you would any other lace.

### 🌸 More Ideas
**Try Decorative Threads**
Try using metallic, variegated, and other decorative threads. For heavier lace, wind the bobbin with a heavier decorative thread. See pages 113–115 for bobbinwork.

### 🌸 Quick Trick
**Quick and Easy Lace**
For another lace look, stitch on tulle using a variety of built-in decorative stitches for quick and easy lace. Use a heavyweight water-soluble stabilizer underneath for support.

### Follow this Thread
See pages 68–77 for thread.
See pages 84–86 for stabilizers.

## Machine-spun Lace
### Sharee Dawn Roberts
*Lace is one of the most intriguing textiles available. Make your own spun lace to showcase in a fabulous quilt or garment.*

### Stabilizer
Use a disappearing stabilizer such as heat-away or water-soluble.

### Threads
Always use machine embroidery thread in the needle. In the bobbin, use either machine embroidery thread or, to add dimension, strength, and texture, one of the heavier decorative threads. When using a heavier decorative thread in the bobbin, be sure to stitch so the heavier threads are consistently on one side of the stabilizer; this makes the stabilizer much easier to remove later.

After you've emptied your bobbin, replace it with another bobbin holding a different decorative thread and continue stitching. Periodically change the needle thread for additional interest.

Apply fragile metallic threads before the stabilizer starts becoming filled with other stitching lines. Add the heavier threads last.

### Setup
Loosen the needle tension setting approximately 1½ numbers. Insert a metallic thread sewing machine needle. Use an all-purpose sewing foot or, if you have one, a straight-stitch sewing foot. Use a straight-stitch throat plate if available. The smaller size opening in both the foot and throat plate helps to reduce puckering.

Set your machine for a normal-length straight stitch, approximately 8 to 10 stitches per inch. Fill bobbins with each specialty thread.

Adjust the tension on your bobbin case to accommodate heavier threads. On some sewing machines with built-in bobbin cases, you won't be able to adjust the bobbin tension, but must bypass it entirely. Refer to your sewing machine manual for these instructions.

## Stitching

The trick to creating beautiful lace with your sewing machine lies in understanding your threads, the stabilizer, and your machine's tension settings (both needle and bobbin). Be prepared to test several thread types and adjust your tensions to achieve the stitch you desire.

Begin sewing and gradually turn the stabilizer in wide curves as you approach an edge so it won't be necessary to stop, turn, and pivot. Instead, sew long continuous lines, gradually turning at the edges in wide curves to change direction, until the bobbin runs out. Cut the thread close to the stabilizer. Don't turn the stabilizer in fast, tight curves because that causes puckering. Keep the stabilizer flat and stitch from end to end and side to side.

Gradually "close in" the curves until the spaces between the lines become narrower and narrower, graduating from ½" to ⅛".

If you like, use free-motion embroidery as needed to fill in the remaining spaces more quickly.

The threads must intersect closely enough to form a network of lace that will hold together once the stabilizer is removed. However, if your lines are too close, the stabilizer is difficult to remove; it's better to have too little stitching than too much. Remove a little stabilizer from a corner to test the results; it's easy to add more stitching if necessary.

## Finishing

Once you're satisfied with the stitching pattern, remove the stabilizer following the manufacturer's instructions.

Most methods of removing stabilizer require some rinsing. Lay the lace flat on a towel until it's dry, then carefully press it with a steam iron. Treat the lace like any other purchased lace yardage.

*Garments modeled by Patti Lee.*

### Winding Bobbins with Decorative Thread

There's no need to wind the thicker threads by hand; use your sewing machine's bobbin winder. Place the spool on the spool holder and pull the thread through the first thread guide only. Pinch the thread between your left thumb and forefinger to provide manual tension as you bypass the thread guide. Slowly press the foot control; the bobbin will fill as long as you keep pinching the thread to give it slight tension. Don't go past the edge of the bobbin.

# Thread and Ribbon Scarves

*These aren't lace, but they're made with a similar technique using water-soluble stabilizer. You can make scarves, shawls, or other accessories and use up your odds and ends of thread, trims, yarns, and more in the process.*

## Basic Technique

It's easiest to use extra heavy water-soluble stabilizer. If you use regular weight, use double or triple layers.

1. Start with a piece of water-soluble stabilizer the size of your finished item.

2. Layer thread, ribbon, yard, trims, et cetera.

3. Cover with another piece of water-soluble stabilizer.

4. Pin to hold everything together.

5. Stitch (as described below).

7. Soak and rinse in water.

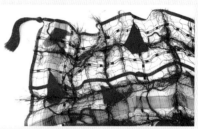

If you prefer, you can use temporary spray adhesive instead of pins. Just be sure the adhesive can be removed with water.

## Zigzag Scarf
### Sally Houk

Start with a long, narrow piece of water-soluble stabilizer. Lay ribbon, yarn, and threads lengthwise, allowing the ends to go past the stabilizer to form fringe. For extra stability, use some of the ribbon or yarn in a zigzag pattern. Lay another piece of stabilizer on top. Stitch in a grid pattern across the length and width of the stabilizer. Soak and rinse in water to remove stabilizer.

## Free-motion Scarf
### Lynn Koolish

In a variation, use thread, ribbon, and yarn sparingly. Add loose pieces of thread. Lay another piece of stabilizer on top. Pin. Free-motion stitch heavily to hold it all together. Change needle and bobbin thread often for more color variation. Soak and rinse in water to remove stabilizer.

## Grid Shawl
### Marinda Stewart

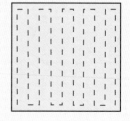

For this variation, carefully place ribbon, trims, and scraps on the water-soluble stabilizer in a grid. Use a continuous piece of ribbon to outline the perimeter. Place another piece of stabilizer on top. Pin. Stitch around the perimeter, then stitch in a ladder pattern every ½" to ⅝". Soak and rinse in water to remove stabilizer.

# LETTERING

## Follow this Thread

See pages 80–82 for needles.
See pages 68–77 for threads.
See pages 84–86 for stabilizers.

## The Write Stuff

*Peggy Bendel*

*Whether embroidered or programmed into your machine's memory, putting words to fabric (or paper) has never been easier. If you've never used your machine's lettering function, take a look at the manual to see how to set up your machine for lettering.*

Match the needle size and type to the base fabric and the thread type you're using. The thinner the fabric and finer the thread, the smaller the needle size should be.

Stabilize fabrics to prevent tunneling or puckering on the base fabric. Tear-away stabilizer is fine for small-scale lettering. If you're creating a lot of lettering, removing stabilizer may become tedious; instead, use a liquid or water-soluble stabilizer.

Use an air-soluble marker to mark a straight guideline onto the fabric.

Proofread before you stitch.

## Using Lettering

Try one or more of these ideas to make the most of your machine's lettering function:

- Write your name. It's fun to see your name in stitchery, and it's a good way to get acquainted with your sewing machine's alphabet system.

- Sign your quilts with machine lettering.

- Repeat a name in rows on a length of plain fabric, using the mirror-image feature for alternate rows if desired. Use the new decorative fabric for detail areas of a garment, on accessories such as a belt or purse, or cut into strips and use as a ruffled trim for a quilt or pillow.

- Record dinner guests' names on a special tablecloth or table runner instead of place cards.

- Sew a special birthday tablecloth for each child to keep track of guests through the years, or make a holiday tablecloth to document celebrations and to keep as a family treasure.

- Offer a personalizing service for a fee at a fundraising event. Sell personalized dishtowels, fabric ornaments, children's jackets, and more.

- Create memorial items, such as family trees or anniversary banners.

- Help children make a handprint banner for a special friend or relative by stamping their hands in fabric paint, then sewing their names beneath.

- Embellish a ring-bearer's pillow with the bride's and groom's names and their wedding date.

- Write a favorite girl's name over and over on grosgrain ribbon and tie it into a pretty hair bow for special occasions.

- Create wall hangings adorned with inspirational, educational, or sassy sayings; a list of rules and regulations; or a collection of your favorite quotations on a subject.

- Reproduce the text from an antique nursery rhyme book on squares for a quilt, or make a soft fabric story book for a special child.

- Use script lettering for making greeting cards and formal invitations that will become mementos. Look in a card store for card blanks designed for photo inserts, and fuse or glue your stitched message behind the opening. Or purchase firm stationery stock and stitch directly onto the paper; then fold it into a card.

# LONGARM QUILTING

A longarm quilting machine can quilt through several layers of fabric at any angle making chenille quick and easy. See Pages 122–123 for making chenille.

## Follow this Thread

See pages 68–77 for threads.
See pages 78–79 for thread lubricants.

## Decorative Longarm Quilting

### *Linda V. Taylor*

*Decorative thread can add color, shine, and sparkle to quilting done on a longarm machine.*

Because of the variety of needle sizes, there are many different types and sizes of thread that can be used on a longarm quilting machine. Quilting machines are designed to hold very large cones of thread, as well as smaller spools. While the most convenient and generally the best value are the 6,000 yard cones, many specialty threads are not put up on such a large cone. They can, however, often be purchased in 1,000–3,000 yard cones.

Polyester-wrapped polyester, or cotton-wrapped polyester thread is usually easier to use because it has more tensile strength and will not break as easily as 100% cotton thread. However, if the top tension is backed off slightly, cotton thread sews beautifully on quilting machines.

Occasionally, with cotton or specialty threads like metallic and rayon, it may be necessary to sew at slower speeds to avoid thread breakage. Use a slightly larger needle (or a ballpoint needle) and give the top thread more slack when pulling the needle away from one area to another.

It also helps to use a similar weight and kind of thread in the bobbin as on the top of the machine.

If the top thread is breaking often, thread lubricant applied to the thread should help it slide smoothly through the needle eye more easily. Apply the lubricant to the spool of thread in several places before beginning the quilting process. If in doubt, check with your machine manufacturer for their recommendation regarding thread lubricants.

Heavy jeans stitch thread used for the quilting adds bold color. *Little Kats* from the *Ultimate Guide to Longarm Quilting* by Linda V. Taylor. Quilt pieced by Cheri Meineke-Johnson and quilted by Linda V. Taylor.

## METALWORK

 Follow this Thread

See page 134 for references to embroidery basics.

### Embroidery on Metal

**Linda Griepentrog**

*Pioneers used folk-art tin punching on wood cabinet fronts for ventilation and decoration in rustic kitchens. While true tin punching requires a selection of metal-work tools, you can duplicate the look on your embroidery machine.*

Check with your embroidery machine dealer before using this technique (verify warranty issues, maximum needle size, and mechanical compatibility). This technique creates sharp edges, so protect your hands and eyes.

### Supplies

Use lightweight metal flashing from your local home improvement or roofing center, or tooling foil from your hobby center. The metal must be flexible, you should be able to bend it with little effort. Look for brass, copper, and silver finishes.

Cutting metal is not good for dressmaker shears, so use old ones, or designate the pair you use for this task to an area other than your sewing room.

### Machine Settings

Use a large needle (100/16)—it doesn't have to be new, it is being used only to pierce the metal. The larger the needle, the larger the holes. Adjust the machine speed to the slowest setting.

### Quick Trick

**Tricking Your Machine**
Outsmart the thread sensor feature by threading the upper machine but not the needle. Tape the thread end to the machine just above the last thread guide.

### Hooping

Cut the metal to fit within the inner hoop (overhanging metal is difficult to hold in place during embroidery). Use a hoop large enough to hold the entire metal piece.

Hoop adhesive stabilizer, and coat the back side of the stabilizer with temporary spray adhesive. Adhere felt to the **back** side; this will prevent damage to the machine throat plate from the sharp metal edges.

Peel the protective paper from the stabilizer, and firmly adhere the metal to the exposed adhesive.

If the metal tends to separate from the stabilizer, tape the edges to the embroidery hoop. It is very important to keep the metal in place to avoid breaking needles.

*(Continued on next page)*

## Design Choices

The easiest designs to work with are those made specifically for appliqué, where there is a row of straight stitching sewn to initially hold down the fabric. Straight stitching is the only stitch used for this technique—any satin, fill, or other stitch configurations will over-perforate the metal and destroy the design. Follow these guidelines:

- For maximum impact, enlarge the embroidery design so the stitches (needle holes) will be spaced more openly.

- Avoid designs with duplicate needle penetration in the same hole, as this can rip the metal and distort the design. If you choose a design with multiple hole penetration, try using a slightly smaller needle.

- Try using only the straight-stitch outline of the design, advancing forward to skip the filled sections.

- Digitize your own designs using only straight stitching.

## Embroidery

Test the design with hooped stabilizer, and then a piece of scrap metal before beginning an actual project.

As you begin, hold the metal against the stabilizer, as it has a tendency to ride up on the needle. Embroidering on metal is a noisy process, but holding the metal with both hands near the presser foot helps to eliminate some of the racket.

Use a fix or baste option to add a border to your motif, if your machine has this capability.

To perfect the motif, it may be necessary to skip (or advance) beyond some stitching. For example, if your machine makes a single stitch in the design center at the beginning and end of the stitching process, advance to eliminate this puncture. Metal holes stay forever!

## Finishing

The underside of the metal is very sharp, so handle carefully.

After the "embroidery" is complete, peel the metal from the stabilizer and recycle the felt to stitch other metal designs. Soft metal foiling will mar and scratch with handling, so protect pieces from abrasion.

## Design Ideas

- Leave an extension of metal at the design upper edge to use as an ornament hanger, if desired. Or punch a hole in the metal with an awl, nail, or paper punch and add a ribbon or thread hanger.

- For a decorative look, thread heavy thread in and out of border holes, or color sections of your design with permanent markers.

- Frame punched pieces as you would a photograph, use them on wooden boxes, baskets, gift bags, papier-mâché shapes, or as gift tags. A visit to your local hobby/craft store will offer a multitude of options.

- If you're making a holiday ornament or gift tag, cut around the motif, leaving a ¼" border. Use scissors with decorative blades, such as pinking or scallop patterns.

*Reindeer, star, and heart embroidery designs: Husqvarna Viking, disk #27*

*Candle sun embroidery design:* Creative Machine Embroidery *magazine original*

## Follow this Thread

See page 134 for references to embroidery basics.

## Mirror-image Embroidery

**Christy Burcham**

*Looking for a new way to expand your designs? Try mirror imaging. With a little imagination and a simple "flip" you can change a basic design into something unique.*

## Mirroring

Mirror imaging is the process of transforming an embroidery design into the exact opposite of the original motif. To get a good idea of what mirror imaging will do to a design, sew a design on sample fabric and draw a square around it. Label the sides top, bottom, left, and right. Place a mirror along the right side of your square: This is the horizontal mirror image. Place the mirror edge along the top, and you see the vertical mirror image.

### Quick Trick

**Audition Images**

Use two mirrors—one on the left and one on the right, or one at the top and one at the bottom of the design. You'll be able to see what a chain of mirror-image designs would look like.

See page 25 for dress with mirror-image design.

## How to Mirror

Check you sewing machine manual for the specific method you must use to create a mirror image of a design. (Many have a "mirror" or "flip" function). To create a vertical mirror image, you may have to rotate your design 180° (turn it upside down) before you create the mirror image.

Original design

Original and horizontal mirror

Original and vertical mirror

Original and horizontal and vertical mirror; this is the same as rotating the design 180°.

Use these techniques when you sew to ensure success:

- Draw a guideline on your fabric so you can line up your design. Draw a horizontal line if you want to line the designs up side-by-side, or a vertical line if you wish to line them up on top of each other.

- Use your hoop's grid to line up the design center with the drawn guideline.

- Re-hoop the fabric after each design is embroidered to place the next design in the center of the hoop.

- Stitch the designs onto the garment fabric before you cut and sew, then press out any pulls or puckers that have developed.

- Group your mirror-image design parts together as one piece before you begin any stitching. (Consult your software help menu or manual for details.)

## Design Selection

It's possible to mirror most designs, but choosing an appropriate design takes a little thought. Many designs are already symmetrical either vertically or horizontally and will not change if mirrored—in the same way some letters, like H or I, look the same forward and backward. Look for designs with a strong directional point of interest. In other words, does the design appear to be "looking" or "pointing" in a particular direction? Often, as many as four mirrored designs can be combined together to create a whole new design.

# MONOGRAMS

Follow this Thread

See page 134 for references to embroidery basics.

## Monogramming

**Peggy Bendel**

*You can create marvelous monograms for customized projects with your sewing machine. Here's some ideas of what you can monogram and where to place monograms so they show to their best advantage.*

There are few limits on what you can monogram, but the fabric does influence the quality of this decorative detail. Monograms show up best on finely textured fabrics such as percale, linen, broadcloth, batiste, lawn, and muslin, and they look especially rich against the background of textured fabrics such as damask and other jacquard weaves, moiré, raw silk, piqué, plissé, terry cloth, velvet, velour, corduroy, and baby cord.

Unfortunately, monograms blend into the background of many prints. To show off beautifully stitched lettering, select household items made from plain, solid colors or subtle, tone-on-tone prints and weaves, although you may also find understated miniprints, small checks, and tailored stripes suitable.

Try monogramming with metallic or variegated thread. And don't forget to use to appropriate stabilizers and toppers (see pages 84–88).

*Evening Clutch* monogrammed with metallic thread by Tom Kohl.

## Home Décor

Household linens for bed, bath, and dining are among the most popular items to monogram. By custom, household items are monogrammed in standard locations.

### Flat Sheets

Monogram flat sheets in the upper center hem, with the base of the letters toward the hem. When the hem is turned back over the blankets, the full monogram shows and appears right side up to a person standing at the foot of the bed.

### Pillowcases

Monogram pillowcases on or slightly above the hem, halfway between the horizontal case edges. The idea is to show off the monogram, but not place it where you might actually have to sleep on it.

### Decorative Pillow Covers

Shams, tosses, and neck roll cases are monogrammed in the center.

### Bedspreads

Monogram bedspreads in the center, so when the bed is made with sheets and blankets turned back over the spread, the monogram appears right side up to a person standing at the foot of the bed.

### Towels

Monogram towels in the center, above any hems and woven bands, so the monogram is centered when the towel is folded and hung on a rack.

### Tub Mats

Tub mats are monogrammed in the center or across one corner.

### Napkins

Fold the napkin as it will be folded in use. A large napkin may be folded in half, then in thirds, and monogrammed in the center of one side, while small napkins may be monogrammed across one corner.

### Tablecloths

Square or rectangular tablecloths are usually monogrammed across one corner so the monogram shows gracefully when the cloth is draped over the table.

For an oval or round tablecloth, the placement depends on where you'd like to position the monogram on the dressed table. One suggestion is to monogram these cloth shapes near the hem and dress the table so the monogram graces the host's or hostess' place.

## Garments

Clothing for all sizes, ages, and genders can be monogrammed. Favorite clothing types to monogram include sportswear and sleepwear, but you can add a monogram to virtually anything in anybody's wardrobe, including accessories.

### Pajamas and Robes

Monogram pajamas and robes on the left breast pocket or in the left breast area if there is no pocket.

### Baby Bibs and Other Layette Items

Monogram blankets, buntings, and hooded towels are monogrammed at a corner or other appropriate position.

### Coat Linings

Monogram coat linings at the lower right edge about thigh level—especially on a fabulous fake fur you've sewn yourself!

### Jacket Linings

Monogram jacket linings at the upper center back, as if the monogram were a custom label.

### Classics

The left breast or center front chest of shetland sweaters; the foldover portion of turtleneck shirts; various positions on sweatshirts, sweatpants, polo shirts, and rugby shirts.

### Handkerchiefs

Monogram handkerchiefs across one corner of both men's and women's; the same is true for scarves.

### Men's dress shirts

Monogram dress shirts on the cuff, breast pocket, or front left tail.

## Gift Items

Monograms on gift items are especially thoughtful, as they add a personal, luxurious touch. Gifts you might monogram include the household linens and wardrobe items already mentioned, plus bedroom accessories such as jewelry rolls, fabric-covered boxes, sachets, and lingerie bags; elaborately dressed dolls used as room-decorating accents; lap robes, stadium blankets, and quilts; or an armchair pillow for the bed—perfect for the college student.

## Luggage

Ideally golf club covers, duffle bags, stuff sacks, soft-sided luggage, fabric purses, and purse accessories should be monogrammed before construction.

*More Ideas*

*Towel embroidery design: Embroidery Arts, Gothic Monogram Set 5 stitched by Elizabeth Tisinger.*

*Shirt lettering: Husqvarna Viking VIP Software stitched by Elizabeth Tisinger.*

*Napkin lettering: Pfaff 7570 built-in lettering stitched by Lynn Koolish.*

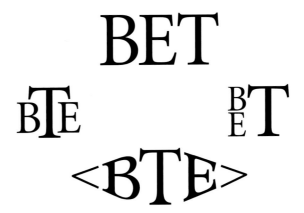

Classic arrangements of initials for monograms

# N

**Follow this Thread**

See pages 80–82 for basic information on needles.
See page 145 for entredeux.
See page 160 for hemstitching.
See pages 185–186 for pintucks.

## Novelty Needles

**Ann Price Gosch**

*Use twin and triple needles for a variety of easy decorative stitching effects.*

### Twin Needles

*Twin needles require a zigzag sewing machine that threads from front to back.*

Twin needles, featuring two needles on a crossbar mounted to a single shank, stitch two parallel rows of stitching; the bobbin thread produces a single zigzag on the underside.

The twin needle can create sensational decorative effects, but it's also a functional tool for hemming and topstitching. Twin-needle topstitching is ideal for knits because the bobbin-produced zigzag offers stretch that a single straight stitch can't provide.

Utility stitches take on a decorative quality when sewn with the twin needle. These "new" stitches will vary in appearance, depending on fabric type and stitch length and width. Try one as an alternative to straight-stitched channel quilting. Two thread colors add even more interest.

Remember to allow for the distance between the needles when setting the machine's stitch width. For example, if the machine's maximum stitch width is 5mm and you're using a 2.0 twin needle, the maximum stitch width is 3mm. Before sewing, manually turn the handwheel to make sure the needles clear the presser foot and throatplate.

Some computerized sewing machines have a twin-needle limitation feature, but it may be preprogrammed only for a 2.0 or smaller twin needle. To use a wider twin needle, manually reset the stitch width to a narrower setting.

### Embossing

Lofty fabrics, such as boiled wool and outerwear fleece, naturally lend themselves to an embossed surface embellishment. Sew curves and geometric schemes using a twin needle and an open-toe embroidery foot. The stitches create the impressions in the fabric's loft without actually tucking the fabric. See pages 143 and 151 for details on using twin needles on fleece.

## Tip

### Threading for Twin Needles

When threading the machine for twin-needle work, place the spools so they unwind in opposite directions—the left thread from behind the spool, and the right thread from the front. Thread the two threads separately to prevent twisting, placing the threads on opposite sides of the tension disc, if possible.

## Pintucks

Traditional pintucks are formed by stitching next to a folded edge, but an easier method is to use the twin needle and a pintuck foot. With a little help from increased tension or cording, a pintuck forms between the stitching rows because of the single bobbin thread underneath. The pintuck foot helps because its underside grooves travel easily over the pintucks as they form. The special foot also simplifies stitching multiple parallel rows because you can guide a groove in the foot down a previous tuck as you stitch the next row.

Pintucks most often are associated with fine fabrics, but you can make them on bulkier fabrics using a larger twin needle and corresponding pintuck foot. For example, the 4.0/75 twin stretch needle makes lovely pintucks in plush velour, an accent that would be impossible to create with the traditional folded-tuck method. Consult your dealer about pintuck feet available for your machine and, if you have a choice, use the one that corresponds to the twin needle size you're using.

## Triple Needle

*As with twin needles, triple needles require a zigzag sewing machine that threads from front to back.*

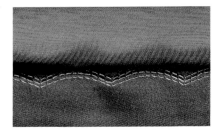

Triple needles come in just one variety—three size-80 universal needles on one shank. The triple needle stitches three parallel rows for a 3mm-wide stitch.

This can add an attractive, unexpected detail to hems and other topstitched areas. Also experiment with stitches other than the straight stitch, but be sure to limit the stitch width to allow for the triple needle's 3mm width.

For an attractive hem on sheers, fold up the hem to triple thickness and topstitch with the triple needle and the serpentine stitch. Then trim away the surplus fabric along the stitching line on the wrong side; the inner hem edge will disappear.

## Tip

### Threading for Triple Needles

Thread the machine with two spools as for a twin needle. Wind an extra bobbin to be used as the third spool. Place it under the left spool, releasing the thread from the front, and thread it through the center needle.

## Wing Needles

*Wing needles require a throat plate with an oval slot.*

Wing needles, so named because they appear to have "wings" mirroring each other from opposite sides of the needle, produce the characteristic holes in hemstitched fabric. Also called hemstitch needles, they're available in sizes 100, and 120, with the 120 size producing the largest holes. Another choice is the twin wing needle, featuring a wing needle and a standard needle on one shank.

A wing needle traditionally is used for heirloom effects on delicate, crisp fabrics, such as handkerchief linen. As the needle pierces the fabric, the large needle shaft and the wings create the characteristic holes. The effect is enhanced when the needle enters a hole more than once. Use a wing needle with the fabric on the bias or crosswise grain for a more open look than along the lengthwise grain. For the best visibility during stitching, use the open-toe embroidery foot.

You can hemstitch directly on a garment section or project—it's often seen as a border—or on fabric strips or blocks to use as insertions or appliqués.

*(Continued on next page)*

Entredeux effects are easy to create with the twin wing needle and the straight stitch:

Sew the first row, then raise the presser foot. Turn the fabric 180° and position the wing needle in the first hole of the previous row; sew the second row so the wing needle pierces each hole of the first row.

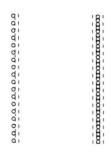

To apply lace trim at the same time, position the work under the presser foot so the wing needle is just to the left of the lace and the standard needle attaches the lace to the fabric close to the lace edge. Stitch two rows as described above.

## Hemstitching Effects

Many computerized machines feature stitches intended for hemstitching. The star stitch is ideal because the wing needle goes in and out of the same hole several times. In addition to delicate heirloom effects, it can be used to create the look of hand-tooling on faux suede.

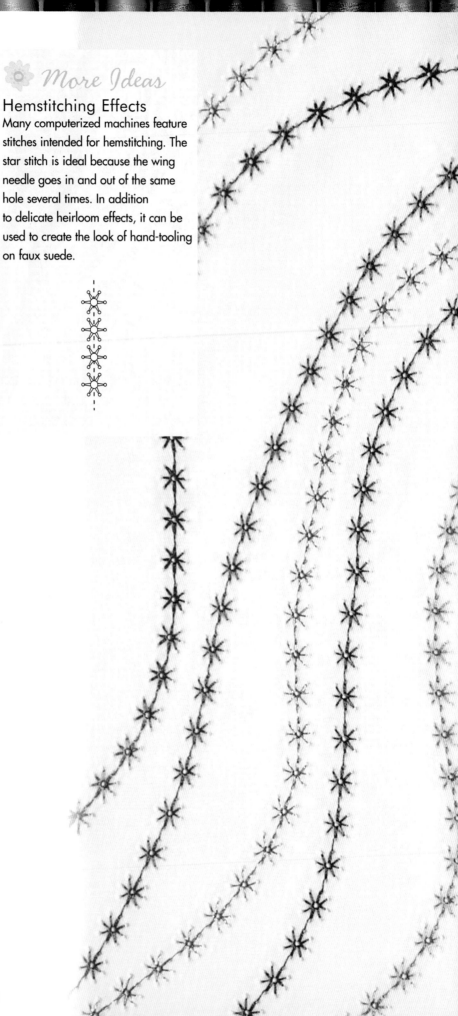

## PAPER

### Follow this Thread

See pages 43–53 for a visual
guide to decorative stitches.
See pages 80–82 for needles.
See pages 68–77 for threads.
See page 173 for lettering.

## Stitching on Paper

### Mary Griffin

*Many of us made our first attempts at
machine stitching on paper, learning to
follow lines and curves with precision.
Today, using the decorative stitches in
your sewing machine and exciting embroidery threads, you can transform sewing
on paper into an art form. This is a fun
technique for adults, and it makes a great
first project for children.*

## Choosing Papers

Use a medium-weight paper that provides stability but won't be too heavy
to stitch through, such as 70-pound
smooth text and 24-pound smooth
writing paper. Paper with a special finish or texture, such as a linen-finish,
will give your project a unique look.

### Tip

### Paper Sources

Your local office-supply and art stores
are good places to find paper suitable
for stitching. Stationery shops and
copy/printing services are good
sources, too, but it can be expensive
to purchase boxed stationery. To
save on costs, consider purchasing
8½" x 11" sheets and having the store
cut them in half with a paper cutter.
Also ask about matching envelopes.

## Needles and Thread

Used or dull needles are perfect for
sewing on paper because paper will
dull a new needle quickly. Sizes 80/12
and 90/14 work well on most papers
and with most decorative threads. If
you get skipped stitches, try a ballpoint
needle. Experiment with twin needles
for interesting double stitching effects.

Decorative threads are a great choice
for stitching paper. Choose from 40-
weight rayons, shiny metallics, or
reflective lamé thread. Use variegated
thread for extra stitching excitement.
Most monofilament threads are too
strong and may tear the paper.

If your paper tears when stitching, try
a lighter-weight thread.

Use the same thread in both the bobbin and the needle, or use a fine-
weight bobbin thread.

## Stitching

Even if your sewing machine has only
a few decorative stitches, enjoy the
effects of varying zigzag widths or the
surprising beauty of the simple honeycomb stitch. Most basic machines can
do twin-needle sewing—what a risk-
free place to try it out!

If you have a computerized machine,
experiment with new and exciting
stitch combinations, size variations,
and alphabets. To prevent paper from
tearing and shredding, choose stitches
with minimal satin stitching and ones
where the needle doesn't go into the
same hole more than twice. After
stitching, pull your needle thread to
the wrong side; it's not usually necessary to tie off the threads unless your
creation will be used more than once.

*(Continued on next page)*

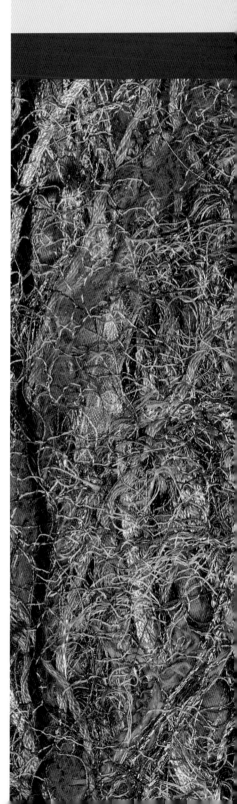

P

## Ideas for Projects

- Jazz up your paper with pinked or scalloped edges.

- Make personalized book covers by stitching on heavyweight wrapping paper.

- Use metallic thread and a narrow zigzag to stitch beautiful garlands, and a tiny star stitch to top a straight-stitched tree on this year's holiday greeting card.

- If your sewing machine has an alphabet, sew your own greeting cards; if it doesn't, add hand lettering after stitching a decorative design.

- Transform a paper lunch bag into an elegant gift bag. Place the gift inside, and stitch it closed with decorative designs, laces, and ribbons.

- Stitch a bookmark from wrapping paper, and include it with a book for a special occasion.

- Make name cards for your next party; your guests can take them home as favors.

- Add stitched design accents to heavyweight wrapping paper for a special gift.

 *Tip*

### When Sewing on Paper

- Practice by sewing the paper without thread first, allowing the needle holes to form the design. Then thread the machine and sew.

- When stitching words or involved designs, start with a larger piece of paper than your final project so you can trim away any mistakes.

- Avoid stitching into envelope glue.

## Stitch a Holiday Greeting
*Marla Stefanelli*

*Use these ideas to create a greeting card for the holidays, or create your own designs to use any other time of the year.*

Make a variety of greeting cards by drawing simple designs and then stitching them with your sewing machine. Make up the designs, or look at Christmas wrapping paper or coloring books for inspiration. Keep the designs simple so stitching around them is easier. Once you get started, experiment with a variety of techniques.

Draw the designs ½" smaller than the outside card dimensions. For cards sewn with thread, use a bobbin thread to match either the card or the needle thread. Test the stitches on scrap paper and adjust the stitch tension, length, and width if necessary.

To hide the underside of the stitching when you're done, cut a paper rectangle slightly smaller than the card, and glue it inside the card front.

### Reverse Appliqué Tree

Lightly draw a simple tree shape on the card front. Carefully cut out the shape with scissors, creating a hole in the card front. Cut a piece of print fabric larger than the hole, and place it right side up on a flat surface. On the card inside front, apply a light coat of glue around the shape edges, and then place the card front over the fabric and press in place.

Set the machine for a medium-length, wide zigzag stitch. Sew around the opening—don't backstitch at the beginning or end, but do leave long thread tails. Thread a hand-sewing needle with the tails, and pull them through to the card inside. Tie square knots with the tails and bobbin threads; clip close to the knots. From the back, trim the excess fabric close to the stitching.

Sew small beads to the tree for ornaments.

### Needlepunched Bow

Lightly draw a bow on the inside front of the card. The resulting design on the card front will be the reverse of what's drawn, so avoid numbers and letters.

Use a leather needle with no thread. Set the machine for a medium-length straight stitch. Sew along the design lines from inside the card, then erase the lines.

Sometimes the presser foot pushes the holes closed as it passes over a punched portion of the design. If this happens, repoke the holes with a hand sewing needle.

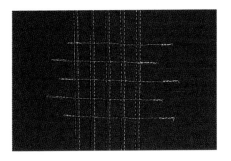

**Follow this Thread**

See pages 68–77 for threads.
See page 55 for presser feet.
See pages 57–59 for adjusting tension.
See page 181 for more on pintucks.
See page 221 for serger pintucks.

## Quick Trick

Electronic machines will need to be fooled to think they're threaded, or the machine won't operate. Thread the machine, except for the needle, and tape the thread to the side of the machine. Leave the threaded bobbin in the bobbin case.

## Stitch-filled Star

Lightly draw a simple star shape on the card front. Set the machine for a medium-length, wide zigzag stitch. Starting at the outside edge of the star, stitch around the design. Continue stitching around the design just inside the previous stitching until the shape is filled.

Pull the thread tails to the back and tie them together; clip. Erase any visible lines.

*More Ideas*

Have fun creating cards for all the holidays.

# PINTUCKS

## Making Pintucks

**Elizabeth Tisinger**

*Twin-needle pintucks and topstitching in a contrasting thread liven up any quilt or garment.*

## Supplies

*Needles*

Use a 1.6mm to 2mm twin needle for lightweight fabrics, and a 2.5mm to 3mm twin needle for medium-weight fabrics.

*Fabric and Thread*

Light- to medium-weight wovens work best for machine pintucking.

*Presser Foot*

Use a pintuck foot if available; if not, use a zigzag, satin stitch, or embroidery foot. The pintuck foot has grooves on the underside that help form the raised tucks and keep them equally spaced. Use a foot with narrower grooves on light-weight fabrics, and one with wider grooves on medium-weight fabrics.

## Setup

*Tension*

Follow the sewing machine manual to thread the machine for twin-needle stitching. Make sure the two thread spools don't rub together and the threads aren't twisted together (see page 181 for tips on threading for twin needles.) Make test samples with different tensions to create the desired look.

Increase needle tension to raise pintucks. If the pintucks still aren't pronounced, try tightening the bobbin tension as well.

If the fabric puckers, loosen the needle tension a bit. For the most raised and pronounced pintucks, use a pintuck foot, tight needle tension, and thin fabric.

## Spacing

Mark the first pintuck with an air-soluble marker or a pressed crease, and stitch along the fabric grain. To keep the remaining tucks straight and consistently spaced, guide the first pintuck into one of the presser foot grooves or along the presser foot edge, or line it up with a quilting guide. If you have trouble keeping the pintuck in the groove, lift the fabric in front of the presser foot as you sew.

## Plan Ahead

Pintucks take up a little yardage, so when you determine the yardage needed for the garment area or block that will be pintucked, you'll need to allow for extra. Rough-cut fabric to size, allowing extra for the pintucks. The more pintucks you plan to make, the more fabric you need to allow. Trim to size after the pintucks are sewn.

*(Continued on next page)*

## Corded Pintucking

Cording pintucks helps eliminate puckers and raises the pintucks on heavier fabrics. Slightly tighten the upper tension, and feed perle cotton or topstitching thread through the throat plate cording hole from the bottom to the top, then back under the foot.

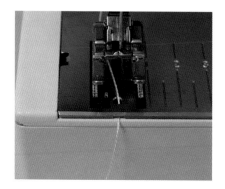

If the machine doesn't have a cording hole, use a 2" length of drinking or cocktail straw taped to the machine in front of the needle, and thread the cording through the straw and under the needle. Place the fabric over the cording, hold the cord, and begin to stitch; corded pintucks will automatically form.

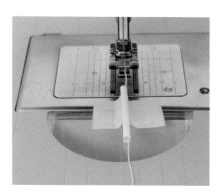

## Pressing

Don't press the pintucks themselves, as this will flatten them. Press the fabric between pintucks or, if they're spaced very closely together, press the fabric on either side of the set of pintucks.

## Tip

### Using Decorative Thread

If you're having trouble making pin tucks with metallic or other decorative thread, use a twin needle specifically designed for metallic or embroidery threads.

## Eliminating Puckers

Pintucks on the lengthwise fabric grain tend to pucker more than those on the cross grain. When making vertical pintucks on craft or home décor items, use fabric cut on the cross grain. For garment sewing, where pattern pieces are usually cut on the lengthwise grain, try one or more of the following:

- Sew at a slow to medium speed.
- Spray-starch and press the fabric before pintucking.
- Loosen the upper tension slightly.
- Cord the pintucks.

If the fabric still puckers, block the fabric before cutting it. Pin the tucks to the ironing board in the desired shape, and steam or spray-starch; allow the fabric to dry and cool completely before handling.

*Fantasy* (detail) by Lynn Koolish. See page 22 for quilt.

## More Ideas

Pintucks don't just have to be stitched in rows or with a straight stitch. Try a grid of pintucks, or pintucks made with a long zigzag or serpentine stitch.

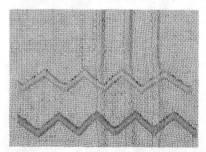

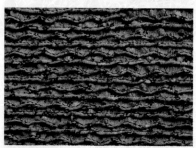

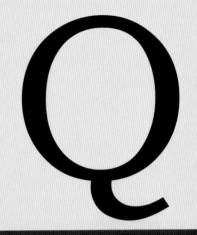

# QUILTING

*Presented here are quilting basics and techniques for "straight line" or quilting with the feed dogs up. Follow the threads below for more information on related topics including free-motion quilting.*

Follow this Thread

## Quilting Basics

See pages 80–82 for needles.
See pages 68–77 threads.
See pages 94–99 for helpful tools.
See pages 57–59 for adjusting machine tension.

## More Ideas for Quilting

See pages 156–158 for free-motion quilting.
See page 158 for transferring quilting designs.
See page 189 for quilting templates.
See page 190 for quilting tips.
See page 191 for back-to-front quilting.
See pages 191–192 for quilting garments.
See pages 193–195 for quilting and embroidery.

## Quilting Basics

### Kathy Sandbach

*Whether you're doing straight-line quilting with the feed dogs up or free-motion quilting with the feed dogs down, get off to a good start with the proper tools, supplies, and machine setup.*

## Sewing Machine

Success in machine quilting starts with a sewing machine in excellent working order. Have your machine freshly serviced and the timing adjusted to produce quilting stitches that look good on both the top and back of your quilt.

## Presser Feet

For straight-line quilting, use a walking or even-feed foot for your machine. This foot pushes the top layer of fabric through the presser foot at the same rate that the feed dogs push the bottom layer. Some machines have a built-in even-feed or dual-feed feature. Be sure to engage it when quilting.

## Needles

A very sharp needle, the correct size, is a must for successful machine quilting. The needle size depends on the thread that you are using. Most of the decorative and metallic threads will require a larger needle than the one used for piecing. A topstitch needle will work very well in most machines, as will a jeans (denim) and a quilting needle. These sharp, strong needles have a pointed end, not a ball or rounded tip like a universal needle.

Experiment with different needles to find the right one for the project. Keep a small notebook next to your machine and keep track of which needle works with which thread. This will eliminate needing to experiment and test each time you use a particular thread.

*(Continued on next page)*

*Walking (even-feed) feet*

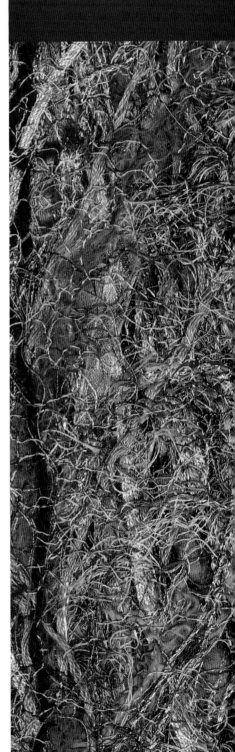

## Work Surface

To help you manipulate the quilt under the machine needle, use a large work surface. This means space for the quilt to lie without being pulled in any direction while you are quilting. Optimal features include a backstop to keep the quilt from falling off the back of the table, and a breadboard or pull-out on your left to support the quilt bulk. A card table or other small surface can also be used to help support the quilt.

A large acrylic table surround (or portable extension table) provides excellent additional support for free-arm-style platforms.

## Threads

Machines prefer the same thread in the top and the bobbin, but if you are using a rayon or metallic in the top, you probably don't want that in the bobbin. Use a thread of equal strength in the bobbin and, if possible, the same color. By using the same color in the top and bobbin, the thread from the bobbin won't show on the top, and the top thread won't show on the back.

Don't be afraid to experiment with different threads on the same piece. Sometimes the whole piece won't look good with metallic, but some metallic will look great with other parts quilted in cotton thread.

With the wonderful array of threads available to quilters now, it's sometimes hard to pick the perfect one for your project. Try a variegated thread, if possible, when the fabric colors allow, as it's so much more interesting and eye-catching than a solid. A word of caution about the variegated threads: If your quilting design must be completely visible to look great, use a slightly contrasting color. "Matching" colors can disappear for sections at a time as they blend with the fabric. If you are uncertain about the effect a certain thread will create, be sure to test it on a scrap of fabric. Of course, if you want your design to really show, use a very high-contrast thread.

## Thread Tension

You may have to adjust the tension on your machine if you are using unusual threads on your quilt. Most of the time you can adjust just the top tension. The lower the number on the tension dial, the looser the tension; the higher the number, the tighter the tension. Quilt a sample using the decorative threads to make sure the tension is correct. You don't want to see the top thread on the underside of the quilt, or the bobbin thread on the top of the quilt.

Bobbin tension is a bit trickier to adjust. For machines with a removable bobbin case, loosen or tighten the large screw. Hold the bobbin case with the closed side of the case facing right. Turn the screw right and it will be tighter, turn it left and it will be looser. Because a little goes a long way with bobbin tension, turn it only a quarter-turn, and then it's easy to reset to its original position.

If your bobbin case is not removable, refer to your machine instructions or local dealer to see how to adjust the bobbin tension. You want the loosest tension possible while still getting a good stitch.

## Fabric

Virtually any fabric can be quilted by machine. Silk, polyester, rayon, cotton, linen, and other specialty fabrics machine-quilt beautifully. Feel free to use any fabric you want in a piece you will machine quilt.

Backing fabric choices impact the total look of the quilt. To help the felting of the layers, it's best if the back is 100% cotton. With the choices available, and especially the many decorator fabrics that are 100% cotton, you have hundreds from which to choose. A large, busy print with many colors will allow you to change the thread and bobbin colors many times and still have a wonderful-looking quilt back.

## Batting

Batting choice is very important for a machine-quilted piece. The easiest batting to use is cotton. Cotton batting felts the layers of the quilt, almost eliminating shifting, and helps to avoid pleats or tucks in the quilting on both front and back.

The larger your piece, the more bulk you must deal with. Rolling your quilt up and pushing it through the machine becomes more difficult with a high-loft or thick batting. Experiment with different battings on smaller pieces before trying to quilt a really large (queen-size or larger) quilt. Even small amounts of loft multiply quickly when a large piece is rolled.

All-cotton and cotton/polyester battings give a flat, old-fashioned appearance to your quilt that many quilters want today, especially if the quilt is going to hang on a wall. Cotton battings also block very well. Polyester battings often allow quilt layers to shift, and the bulk of their loft can become a real problem when machine quilting. Polyester battings do not block at all.

## Basting

The most important part of the preparation for quilting is the basting. Good basting will eliminate pleats on both the top and the back. Follow these guidelines carefully for consistently good results:

- Make sure that the backing is freshly pressed.

- Spread the backing right side down on a large, flat surface. Use masking tape to tape the entire perimeter of the backing, starting in the middle of opposite sides and working out to the corners. Make sure that the sur-face is taut and smooth but not stretched.

- Lay the batting on top of the backing, smoothing it flat. Place the quilt top on the batting, smoothing it flat and gently patting down any fullness that may have occurred in the piecing.

- Baste the entire surface with safety pins or quilt basting spray. Basting for machine quilting cannot be done with thread because removal of thread basting will break the machine quilting stitches. Place pins 4" to 6" apart in each direction.

- Remove the tape, and trim the edges of the batting and backing down to about an inch outside the edge of the quilt top. This will eliminate as much of the bulk as possible and make pushing the quilt through the machine easier.

## Grid Quilting

Grid-quilt before doing any decorative quilting: That means stitch all the ditches (seams) that need quilting first. While quilting, be careful that the top does not move and create pleats. Carefully push any accumulating bulk toward the needle as you stitch, working in bits of fullness if there are any. If there is fullness in a block, make sure it stays in that block—don't let it get pushed to another area and distort the whole quilt.

Quilting compresses the layers, shrinks the entire project, and allows you to work in fullness without creating pleats. Because of this shrinkage, however, it's important that you evenly quilt your pieces. If you combine light and heavy quilting on the same project, it will distort. Evenly quilting your quilt will improve the overall appearance and help the quilt hang nicely.

## Starts and Stops

This is a very important detail to make the quilting durable and secure through washing and handling.

Begin quilting by taking one complete stitch about ¼" away from where you actually want the quilting to start. Stop and pull the bobbin thread up to the top. Stitch back to the start spot using regular-length stitches, then stitch over those stitches. After stitching, stitch back over the final ¼" of stitches.

Begin and end stitching where the thread matches the fabric, if possible, to camouflage the stitches.

## Quilting Templates

*Jane Sassaman*

I often use an all-over pattern of wavy quilting. Over the years I have made many sizes of wiggly templates, each made with template plastic and cut with a sharp knife. The curve on each side is the same, like a wavy ruler. This allows the template to fit perfectly beside the previously drawn lines and repeat at regular intervals. I use soft colored pencils, such as Prismacolor, to faintly trace the quilting pattern. Over time this pencil line simply disappears.

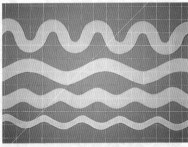

# 10 Tips for Better Straight-line Quilting

**Mary Mashuta**

1. A slow-to-moderate, even sewing speed produces the best results. If your machine has a slow or half-speed setting, use it.

2. If your stitching line weaves back and forth, slow down. Sewing more slowly helps you be more accurate.

3. The longer the stitch length, the easier the quilt will move through the machine. Try 8 to 10 stitches per inch. A longer stitch also shows off decorative threads more.

4. Remember to reset your machine to the longer stitch length when you turn it on to quilt.

5. Always pull the bobbin thread up before you begin stitching. This prevents thread snarls on the bottom side. Hold both threads when you begin stitching.

6. Figure out a secure but nonvisible way to secure your stopping and starting so that you don't have to tediously bring the ends to the back, tie them off, and work them in. (However, you will need to tie when you use heavier threads and in places where stops and starts would really be obvious, such as a circle design.)

7. Some machines will stitch two or three stitches in place as a securing stitch, but this isn't strong enough for machine quilting. If you machine will zigzag a very small stitch with a width less than .5mm, try this for about 1/16"; otherwise, stitch very small stitches for 1/8"–1/4" and then immediately switch to the longer stitch length.

8. Always test your anchoring stitch by tugging on the thread ends to see if you can pull it out easily.

9. When you pivot or make slight adjustments on curves, make sure your needle is in the down position. Lift the presser foot, leave the needle down, turn the quilt, then lower the presser foot. Use the needle-down feature if your machine has it.

10. Take only one stitch after you pivot. Sometimes the needle doesn't go down where you think it will after you turn. You can always remove the last stitch and reposition it, but if you have stitched two stitches it is too late.

Bold orange stitching is size 8 perle cotton used with a 120/19 topstitching needle.

*Out-of-Sight Circles* from *Cotton Candy Quilts* by Mary Mashuta. Quilt by Mary Mashuta.

## Quilting Back to Front

*Larraine Scouler*

Quilting from the back of the quilt is a great way to save yourself the trouble of marking your quilt top. Use the design printed on the backing fabric as your quilting pattern. The thread showing on the front of the quilt will be from the bobbin, so take advantage of the opportunity to use specialty and decorative threads in the bobbin (including metallic thread, which rarely breaks or frays in bobbins). Use regular sewing thread and needles in the machine.

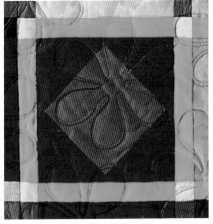

*Square in a Square* (detail) from *Quilting Back to Front* by Larraine Scouler. Quilt by Larraine Scouler.

*Rail Fence* (detail of back)

*Square in a Square* (detail of back)

*Rail Fence* from *Quilting Back to Front* by Larraine Scouler. Quilt by Larraine Scouler.

**Follow this Thread**

See pages 187–190 for quilting basics.

## Quilting Garments

*Barbara Weiland*

*Quilting isn't just for quilts—it can add a new dimension to garments, too.*

### Ideas for Quilted Garments

Try one of these techniques to jazz up your next jacket, vest, or bag:

- Quilt an all-over visual design on the surface of an entire garment.

- Emphasize or elaborate on a shape by echo-quilting rows of parallel outlines.

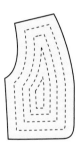

- Follow the lines in the fabric in a contrasting color.

- Accentuate seams and edges or add the illusion of detail by quilting only in certain areas, such as creating a faux "yoke" with lines of quilting.

- Quilt only part of the project, or only the body of a short jacket.

*(Continued on next page)*

- Add partial crisscross quilting to an otherwise unquilted project

- Quilt a project, then embellish the quilted pattern with buttons, baubles, or other trims.

- Quilt fabric to create enough fabric for an entire garment.

## Making Quilted Yardage

When creating yardage for garments keep in mind that simple designs (without darts) are easier to quilt and sew than more complex ones.

### Fabrics

Choose soft, lightweight fabrics for less bulk and easier sewing. Heavy or stiff fabrics are difficult to machine-quilt and add bulk.

### Needles

Some decorative machine stitches are quite effective stitched in either widely or closely spaced rows.

Twin-needle stitching is also an effective and easy way to add more visual interest to simple channel quilting.

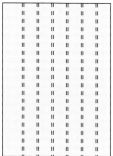

### Thread

Consider thread color, too. For the illusion of pinstripes, channel quilt in white thread on a dark background. If you want stitches that won't be seen, experiment with clear or gray monofilament nylon thread, or simply match the thread to the fabric.

### Marking

Mark the quilting lines on the right side of the quilt top, using your choice of marking tools, and a yardstick or ruler to draw straight lines. Baste as you would for a quilt.

### Tension and Settings

Set the sewing machine for a stitch slightly longer than that used for standard sewing. Too-short or too-tight stitches will make the quilted fabric less flexible and stiffer-looking. If you have stitching problems, loosen the upper tension slightly or change to a straight-stitch throat plate, which will lessen the tendency for the lowermost fabric layer to be pushed into the needle hole. If the machine doesn't have a straight stitch plate, use masking tape over the larger zigzag hole for the same effect.

### Making the Garment

Pin and cut the garment pieces from the quilted yardage. If the quilting was done in vertical rows, use a line of quilting as the grainline to keep the rows in line on your body. Cut garment pieces from a single layer of quilted fabric, being sure to cut a right and left side as needed. Because the garment will fit differently when cut from quilted fabric, cut at least 1" seam allowances all around to allow yourself some fitting flexibility.

## Quick Tricks

### No-mark Quilting

Many fabrics have an obvious directional component that you can follow for quilting—a woven stripe or plaid, or a print motif that follows a straight line, for example. Straight lines or gently curving lines are the easiest to quilt. This is called channel quilting and works best when the parallel lines are spaced 1" to 1½" apart.

### Plan Ahead

Before you start quilting on your garment, make a 12"-square test sandwich of the layers you plan to machine quilt, using the quilting pattern you've chosen.

# QUILTING AND EMBROIDERY

## Follow this Thread

See pages 80–82 for needles.
See pages 68–77 for threads.
See pages 84–86 for stabilizers.
See pages 162–163 for hooping.
See page 138 for appliqué
    and embroidery.

## Quilted Blocks

*Linda Griepentrog*

*The marriage of an embroidery machine and quilting is a match made in heaven. You can embellish quilt blocks for a quilt-as-you-go approach, or create an entire quilt from start to finish.*

## Blocks

Pieced projects are most attractive when they combine embellished blocks with "connector" blocks, which may feature a quilted pattern, but no embellishment. When every square is embellished, the designs tend to blend together, and the project looks overdone.

Use a single embroidery design (A), multiple motifs (B), or appliqué designs (C) to embellish a block. Embroider the fabric block only, or add a lightweight batting and/or backing to help stabilize.

## Batting

Batting comes in various weights, thicknesses, and densities. When using your embroidery machine for the quilting process, it is best to use a lightweight batting, no more than ¼" thick. Fusible bats work well to keep layers in place, or use temporary spray adhesive or quilt basting spray.

## Embroidery-quilting

When using an embroidery design with heavy fill stitches, it's best to embroider only the block. However, when using outline motifs (D, E, F), the underside is generally visually acceptable, and you can stitch through the batting and backing as well.

*(Continued on next page)*

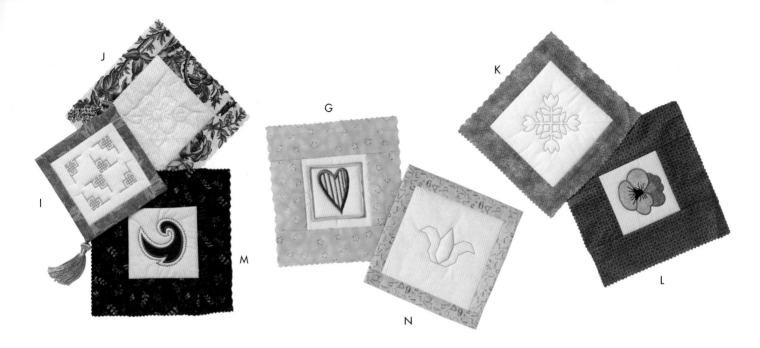

Some machine embroidered quilt motifs actually become your block (G) and need only framing to complete. Allover designs can be used as the decorator blocks (H) when sewn in a contrasting thread, or as connectors when stitched in a tone-on-tone combo. Be innovative when creating block designs—six corner designs were combined in a software program to make the oriental hanging block sample (I).

Layer the quilt block, batting, and backing. If using a nonfusible batting, pin or baste the layers together, depending on the size of the piece. No stabilizer is needed when stitching through these multiple layers. Hoop the quilt layers, or adhere them to a hooped water-soluble stabilizer with temporary spray adhesive.

Position the center of your block in the hoop center, and use the machine's baste function to secure the layers together. The stitching will show on the project underside, so use a bobbin thread that matches the backing or the top thread.

Variegated quilting thread (D) works well for outline designs, as does 30-weight embroidery thread (E) or heavier 12-weight thread. The latter can be used to stitch prominent Redwork designs (F). Consider tone-on-tone single motifs for subtle quilting highlights (J).

Outline quilting motifs may actually stitch out using a straight stitch, a chain stitch or a blanket stitch (K). Some embroideries outline the design only once, others multiple times, so test-stitching will ensure the effect you like best.

## Borders

Use embroidery software to combine designs for quilting borders. Individual motifs can be repeated, combined with other motifs, or combined with the machine's decorative stitches. Use matching or contrasting threads, depending on the desired look.

If turning border corners makes you a bit stitch shy, consider adding a contrasting square at each corner, then quilting a single motif in the corner. No corner turning needed.

## Other Ideas

If you stitched a motif on only the block, now is the time to use that motif as your quilting guideline, holding the project layers together. Use your non-embroidery machine settings, monofilament thread in the needle, and bobbin thread that matches your quilt backing.

### Outlining

Following the outer edge of your embroidery motif, stitch close to the edges through all layers. This gives the motif a slightly raised effect (L).

### Echoing

Stitch ¼" outside the embroidery motif and then repeat the process, stitching parallel rows, until you reach the block edge (A).

### Decorative stitching

Use a decorative machine stitch to outline or echo quilt. Our sample design (M) had the decorative stitch programmed with the embroidery motif.

## Trapunto

Add additional stuffing to a block motif, or portion of it. (See pages 234–235 for trapunto techniques.)

Embroider an outline motif through two layers of fabric—your block face fabric, and a lightweight backing.

After completing the embroidery, make a small slash through only the backing layer in the area where you want additional dimension. Stuff small bits of polyester fiberfill into the motif area until the desired dimension is achieved (N).

Whipstitch the opening closed, then continue the layering and quilting process.

### Tip

**Keep a Notebook**

Save your test blocks in a notebook. List the batting, design, needle, thread, and other techniques used to create each sample. This gives you a head start on the next project!

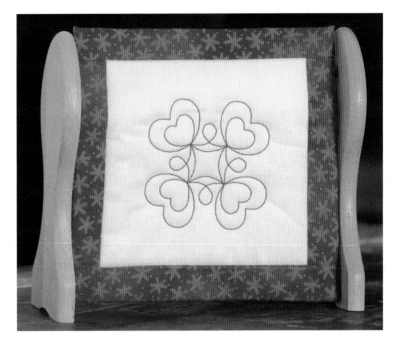

*Watermelon embroidery design (A): Wimpole Street, Taste of the Seasons*

*Corner embroidery designs (B,I): Oklahoma Embroidery Supply & Design #Cr004*

*Frog embroidery design (C): Oklahoma Embroidery Supply & Design #NW559*

*Leaves embroidery design (D): Cactus Punch, Quilting Vol. 1, QCh011*

*Four-heart block embroidery design (E): Quilting Vol. 1, QBN003*

*Apple embroidery design (F): Cactus Punch, SIG 12, single apple*

*Single heart embroidery design (G): Oklahoma Embroidery Supply & Design #NW470*

*Fireworks embroidery design (H): Embroidery Resource, Allover & Everywhere, design ER0107*

*Dogwood embroidery design (J): Cactus Punch, SIG 27, SCL100*

*Blanket stitch tulips embroidery design (K): Cactus Punch, Quilting Vol. 1, QBL008*

*Pansy embroidery design (L): Amazing Designs, #3012*

*Paisley embroidery design (M): Amazing Designs, #3005*

*Tulip embroidery design (N): Husqvarna Viking #14, design 17*

*Wooden block stand from Nancy's Notions*

## Quilted Evening Bag

**Linda Griepentrog**

Fusible batting is used between the top fabric and backing of this enchanting evening purse. The fused quilt sandwich is hooped and embroidered before finishing with a zipper, cording, and tassels.

*Medallion embroidery design: Husqvarna Viking #111*

# R

**Follow this Thread**

See pages 84–86 for stabilizers.
See pages 113–115 for bobbinwork.

## Ribbon Embroidery

**Rochelle Jay**

*The look of time-consuming hand ribbon embroidery can be duplicated in a fraction of the time by machine. Here's how to make flowers that look complex but are really quick and easy.*

### Bobbinwork for the Stem

Fuse tear-away stabilizer to the wrong side of the fabric. Draw the flower stems onto the stabilizer (the designs will be reversed on the right side). Wind narrow (2- to 4mm-wide) green silk ribbon onto the bobbin by hand or machine. If winding by machine, wind the bobbin slowly, guiding the ribbon onto the bobbin by hand.

Insert the bobbin into the bobbin case. Don't put the ribbon through the tension slots. For oscillating bobbins, thread the ribbon through the large hole in the bobbin case. Thread the needle with monofilament thread.

Work from the fabric wrong side, and straight-stitch the stems, following the drawn lines. At the stem ends, pull the ribbon ends to the fabric wrong side and tie off. Carefully remove the stabilizer.

## Flower Embroidery

Set the machine for free-motion embroidery by lowering or covering the feed dogs. Remove the presser foot and shank. Thread the needle and wind the bobbin with all-purpose thread.

Cut colored ribbon into 12" to 18" lengths and press out any creases. Hoop the fabric with the stitched stems in a spring-action embroidery hoop.

### Loop Flower

Pinch the ribbon end at the stem end, and take a few stitches over it. End with the needle in the down position.

Form a small loop with the ribbon by folding it back on itself, use tweezers to pinch the ribbon, and secure it to the flower center with two or three stitches, being careful not to hit the tweezers with the needle.

Fold a second loop in thte opposite direction as the first, securing as before. Continue making loops and securing them at the flower center until a pleasing flower is created.

Leave a 1"-long ribbon tail, pull it to the fabric wrong side with a hand sewing needle, and secure the tail to the wrong side.

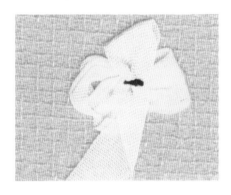

## French Knots

Secure the ribbon end at the flower center with a few stitches. With the needle down at the flower center, loosely wrap the ribbon around the needle three to five times. Take one stitch out of the wrapped ribbon and slightly left or right to secure the loops in place.

Wrap the ribbon around the needle again. Take a stitch or two, then move to a new spot. Continue making knots to form complex flower heads, like chrysanthemums.

*Note: Contrasting threads used for visibility only.*

## Lazy Daisy Flowers

Secure the ribbon end as above.

Stitch about ¼" out from the flower center for the first flower petal.

With the needle down, pinch the ribbon up against the needle and secure with two or three stitches.

Make a loosely wrapped French knot over the securing stitches.

Holding the ribbon out of the way, stitch back to the flower center, pinch the ribbon, and secure it with a few stitches. This completes one petal.

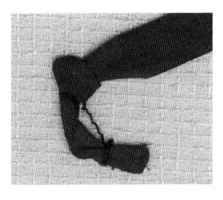

Create five or six petals to complete a flower. Leave a 1"-long tail, pull to the fabric wrong side, and secure.

### Roses

With an air- or water-soluble pen, mark three dots approximately ¼" apart at the stem end. Anchor the thread in the center of the dots and trim the ends.

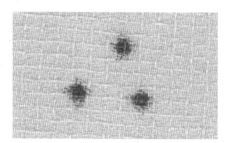

Using the machine's needle-down function, if available, stitch to the first dot. Pinch and secure the midpoint of a 12" to 18" ribbon length with a few stitches. Keeping the ribbon free, stitch to the next dot.

Pull the ribbon ends around, crossing them in front of the needle. Take a stitch over the intersecting ribbons.

Keeping the ribbon free, stitch to the third dot. Again, cross the ribbon ends around the needle and stitch over the intersection. Stitch to the first dot again, just outside the first stitching, cross the ends, and secure.

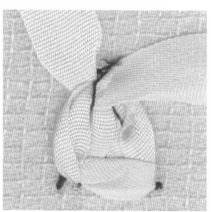

Continue around the circle, securing the crossed ends at the dots. When the rose is the desired size, pull the ribbon tails to the wrong side and secure.

Stitch crystal beads to flower centers for seeds, if desired.

# SASHIKO

Follow this Thread

See pages 68–77 for threads.
See page 50 for hand-look
quilting stitch.

## Sashiko by Machine

**Alice Allen**

*Traditional Japanese sashiko uses repeated designs stitched in heavy white thread on indigo blue fabric. Choose your own colors for beautiful designs on garments, accessories, and quilts.*

## Sashiko Designs

To create designs, choose geometrics and outlines that can be stitched continuously or with as few breaks as possible. Practice drawing a few on paper, following these guidelines:

- Motifs that incorporate straight lines are good bets—variations on squares, diamonds, hexagons, and long zigzagging or broken lines. Use a ruler, triangle, and/or compass to draw straight line sashiko motifs.

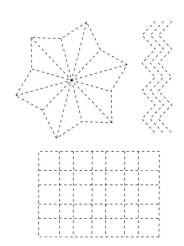

- Nonlinear motifs that aren't too intricate, like simple foliage or flowers, take a little more work but are a good place to add small hand or machine-stitched embellishments.

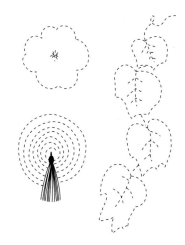

- Create groups of motifs that vary in angle and shape. Try combining a diamond grid, horizontal wavy lines, and vertical ivy-like foliage.

## Transferring Motifs to Fabric
### Linear Motifs

Mark straight line designs directly onto fabric with a removable marker or chalk. You may want to draw a grid to help with placement.

### Non-linear Motifs

Draw the sashiko patterns on plain paper or very lightweight cardboard.

Use a sewing machine, a large unthreaded needle, and a medium-length straight stitch to create perforated patterns. Stitch around the designs and punch the outlines through the paper.

*(Continued on next page)*

Make a pouncer by sprinkling a small amount of talc, baking powder, or cream of tartar in the center of an 8" broadcloth square. Pull up the corners and tie or rubberband them together.

Position the perforated pattern over the desired fabric area and tap (pounce) the pouncer on the pattern. The powder will sift through the needle holes, leaving the motif outline on the garment. If necessary, trace the pounced lines to better retain the design.

## Stitching

Insert a large needle in the machine. Thread the machine with heavy thread in the needle and matching or contrasting thread in the bobbin. Set the stitch length to between four and eight stitches per inch. If you use a thread in the bobbin that contrasts with the top thread, and adjust the tension, the contrasting thread will cause slight visual breaks in the stitching. While not as pronounced as a hand-look stitch, these breaks can provide an interesting visual texture.

Test the straight stitch and any stitch variations you plan to use on a scrap of the project fabric until you're satisfied with the results. The heavier thread may require a tension adjustment.

Sew each motif following the pounced or drawn design. Begin at an outside edge, leaving 3" to 4" thread tails; following the motif outline, and sew continuously (pivoting as needed) as far as possible. End the stitching, and leave 3"- to 4"-long thread tails.

Use a large-eyed hand needle to pull the thread tails to the wrong side, tie them off, and trim the excess tails. Repeat to complete the motif. Remove any remaining chalk residue.

### More Ideas

### Stitch Ideas

Use decorative stitches to accent the motifs. If the machine has a hand-look quilting stitch, try it for sashiko designs.

*Sashiko example stitched by Lynn Koolish.*

# SATIN STITCHING

## Follow this Thread

See pages 57–59 for adjusting tension.
See pages 68–77 for threads.
See pages 84–86 for stabilizers.
See pages 106–110 for satin stitch appliqué.
See pages 147–148 for eyelets.
See page 150 for satin-stitched embellished fabric.

Satin stitching is used to define whiskers, inner ear, facial features, and leaf veins in addition to finishing the edges of the appliqué in *Carlotta in the Secret Garden* from *Laurel Burch Quilts* by Laurel Burch. Quilt by Barbara Baker and Jeri Boe.

## Decorative Satin Stitching

*Lynn Koolish*

*Satin stitching is often synonymous with appliqué, but it can be used in many decorative ways.*

From extra-wide to super skinny, straight edge to curvy, satin stitching finds its way into many decorative techniques. Here are some tips for great satin stitching:

- Be sure to use the correct presser foot. It may be called a satin stitch foot, or an appliqué foot—the key is that the bottom of the foot is grooved to allow the raised satin stitch to pass easily under the foot. An open-toe appliqué foot makes it especially easy to see where you're stitching.

- Use stabilizer under the fabric to prevent tunneling. The wider the satin stitch, the more likely it will cause the fabric to buckle or tunnel. Select a stabilizer that provides enough support for the fabric and density of stitching.

- For curves and corners, pivoting is essential. (See Satin Stitch Appliqué on pages 106–110 for tips on pivoting.)

- Adjust the stitch density (controlled by the stitch length) for the type of thread you're using. A heavy thread will require a different stitch length than a fine thread to get the same density of stitches.

- To avoid holes at the edges of the stitching, use the smallest needle that will work properly with the thread. For specialty threads, use appropriate needles.

- Loosen the top tension to make sure that the bobbin thread doesn't show on the top.

- Use a fine bobbin thread to avoid bulk on the underside of the stitching.

*(Continued on next page)*

Satin stitching used for bold definition of lines in *Six of One* (detail) by Libby Lehman. See page 18 for another quilt by Libby.

## Finishing Edges with Satin Stitching

Satin stitching provides an easy and interesting edge finish.

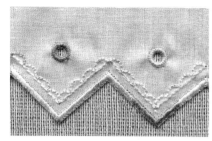

Variegated thread adds interest to this satin-stitched edge. By Rebecca Brent Kemp.

*Embroidery design: Brother Card #23*

## Finishing Quilted Edges

Stitch the edges to be finished with a narrow, open zigzag stitch to hold the quilted layers together. Repeat several times, increasing the stitch width and decreasing the stitch length each time.

Satin stitching used to finish edges of fabric bowl by Linda Johansen.

Choose a thread color that blends or contrasts, depending on the desired look. Metallic or variegated thread provides another element of color and contrast.

For shaped edges, drop the feed dogs, and free-motion stitch around curves and points.

Shaped satin stitching is used to finish edges of vest by Rosemary Eichorn. See page 15 for vest.

Shaped satin stitching is used to finish edges of vest by Lynn Koolish (made in class with Rosemary Eichorn).

## Lettuce Edging

Another use of satin stitching is lettuce edging, a ruffled edge that looks like the edge of a lettuce leaf. Most often seen as an edge finish for knits, it can also be used on cottons—if you know how.

To create lettuce edges you need to stretch the fabric as it is going through the sewing machine. Use one hand in front of the presser foot, and one hand behind. The more you stretch, the curlier the edge. You can stitch on either a raw or folded edge.

Use a tightly spaced satin stitch of any width you like. If the edge is not completely covered, stitch over it again. You can use either a regular zigzag or a decorative satin stitch.

It will never be as curly as on a knit, but the trick to a lettuce edge on cotton is stitching on the bias. Woven cotton fabric may ripple just a bit if you stitch on the straight of grain, but for maximum lettuce edges, cut and stitch on the true bias.

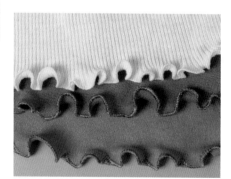

Lettuce edging on knit cotton

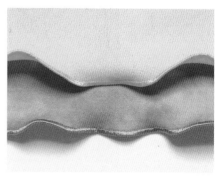

Lettuce edging on woven cotton

See pages 43–53 for a visual guide to decorative stitches.
See pages 57–59 for adjusting tension.
See pages 80-82 for needles.
See pages 68–77 for threads.

## Scallop Stitch Embellishments

**Sallie J. Russell**

*The scallop stitch can turn ho-hum ribbon into a festive embellishment, give fabric the look of eyelet or cutwork, and decorate hems on sheer and knit fabrics.*

The scallop is a decorative stitch and requires an embroidery or appliqué foot; decorative thread in the needle is especially nice with this stitch. Begin with the preprogrammed stitch settings, or set the machine for a wide stitch width and a short stitch length. Like other embroidery stitches, the tensions may need to be adjusted. Shortening the stitch length will shorten the stitch pattern; narrowing the stitch width produces a less-defined stitch pattern.

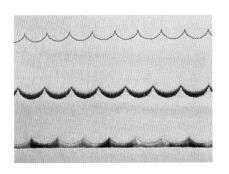

### Tracery Scallops

The tracery scallop is a line of straight stitches in a scallop pattern. You can create a shadow effect on sheer fabrics with tracery scallops, using a twin needle and bobbin thread in a contrasting color or several shades darker than the fabric.

The contrasting thread will show through the fabric between the two rows of scallops. For knits or heavier fabrics, use matching or contrasting needle thread with a single or twin needle.

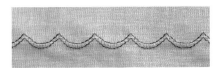

Dress up hems and edges with tracery scallops. Turn up the hem allowance and press. With the right side of the garment up, stitch a double row ½" from the hem cut edge; on the wrong side, trim the excess hem allowance above the scallops. Add a decorative border or eyelets above the scallop-stitched hem.

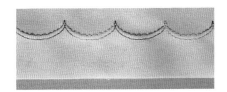

Use a twin needle and stitch one row of scallops. Stop stitching at the end of a scallop and leave the needles up. Lift the presser foot and pivot the fabric. Lower the needles into the fabric so the left needle is in the last hole made by the right needle. Stitch a second row of scallops, creating a mirror image of the first row.

### Closed Scallops

The closed or satin-stitched scallop is a series of contoured zigzag scallop stitches.

The closed scallop can be used with a twin needle for stitching hems and decorative edgings. For added interest, use variegated thread.

### Cutwork Scallops

Create "cutwork" by stitching two rows of closed scallops with the points touching. Stabilize the fabric for stitching, then remove the stabilizer and carefully cut out the area between the stitched rows.

### Off-the-edge Scallops

Off-the-edge scalloping creates a lacy edge finish or a unique insert between two pieces. Adjust the stitch length for a closely spaced satin stitch. Use a heavy thread like No. 5 perle cotton, 12-weight rayon, or gimp cord through a cording or rolled hem foot. Leave at least 2" of cord extending behind the foot. With the fabric right side up, place stabilizer under the fabric folded edge. Begin stitching so the scallop point catches the folded edge and the remaining scallop forms only on the stabilizer and over the cord. Carefully remove the stabilizer.

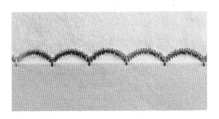

*(Continued on next page)*

## Insert Scallop

A scallop insert is easy to make: Scallop two folded edges, butt the scallops together, and join the centers of two scallops with a machine bartack; repeat until all sets are joined.

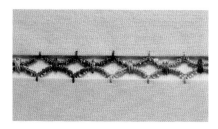

## Straight-edge Scallop

The straight-edge scallop is a scallop stitch with one straight edge.

Use the straight-edge scallop as a replacement for traditional satin-stitch appliqué. Stitch with the points in either direction and the straight edge along the appliqué outline.

Apply ribbons and lace with the straight-edge scallop: Use matching, contrasting, or metallic thread to stitch the straight edge onto the trim edge or fabric, and allow the points to catch the trim. For a picot effect, stitch with the points over the trim edge.

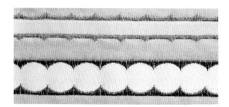

*Scallop stitch examples stitched by Elizabeth Tisinger.*

# SEQUINS

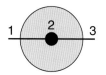

*Follow this Thread*

See pages 80–82 for needles.
See pages 68–77 for threads.
See pages 54–56 for presser feet.
See page 126 for couching.

## Sequin Sewing Basics

### Sallie J. Russell

*Sequins bring glitter and sparkle to any project. Sequin strands are flexible, so they adapt well to many shapes and easily follow the design lines of fabric.*

Sequins are available in flat—the easiest to sew by machine—and cup shapes. Most flat sequins are 6mm wide; cup sequins are 5mm wide. Individual sequins also are available in other shapes and sizes. Keep in mind when working with sequins that while they aren't as heavy as beads, large sequined areas on sheer fabric may require the support of interfacing or underlining.

For machine stitching, use matching thread or monofilament in the needle and bobbin. Adjust the tensions as needed.

## Individual Sequins

Use free-motion machine stitching, and hoop the fabric. Lower the feed dogs, and insert a 60/8 needle. Use a darning foot, or remove the presser foot from the machine and use a spring needle.

Take the first stitch beside the sequin edge; manually move the fabric so the second stitch is in the sequin center; move the fabric so the next stitch is off the sequin outer edge.

## Sequin Strands

Sequins—available by the yard—are held together with a chainstitch. When the strand is cut, the chainstitch will unravel, so apply seam sealant or fray preventive to the cut edges.

Instead of using seam sealant or fray preventive, you can leave several inches of the sequin strand unattached at the beginning and end of the design, then unravel the chainstitch to remove the sequins not used in the design. Use a hand-sewing needle to pull the unraveled threads to the wrong side of the fabric, and secure.

Couching with a machine zigzag is the easiest way to attach sequin strands. These strands have a nap similar to fish scales, so run the presser foot down the smooth side of the sequins to keep the edges from catching on the foot. Use a sequin foot if there's one available for your machine. If not, use an open-toe foot.

Use the appropriate needle size and type for the project fabric, and set the zigzag width wide enough (usually 6mm or wider) to clear both the right and left sequin edges. The stitch length should be identical to the strand width. For the most inconspicuous stitching, use monofilament thread.

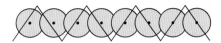

After applying the sequins, slide your finger over them, hiding the thread in the sequin overlap.

## Care and Handling

Most sequins are heat-sensitive, so test-press on scraps first. Use a low iron temperature and press the wrong side of the project. Don't use steam when working with metallic sequins because it will dull the shine.

To clean a sequin-embellished garment, turn the wrong side of the garment out, hand wash it in cold water, and allow it to air-dry.

 Quick Trick

### No Zigzag?

If your machine doesn't have a 6mm-wide zigzag stitch, sew the strand on with a straight stitch. Carefully stitch along the strand, letting the needle pierce the sequins.

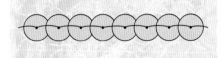

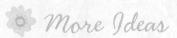 More Ideas

### More Uses for Sequins

Cover appliqué edges with sequin strands instead of satin stitching, or highlight design areas with individual sequins or sequin strands.

Create your own plaid or striped sequin fabric with sequin strands by following the fabric design lines or using quilting patterns to create a unique look.

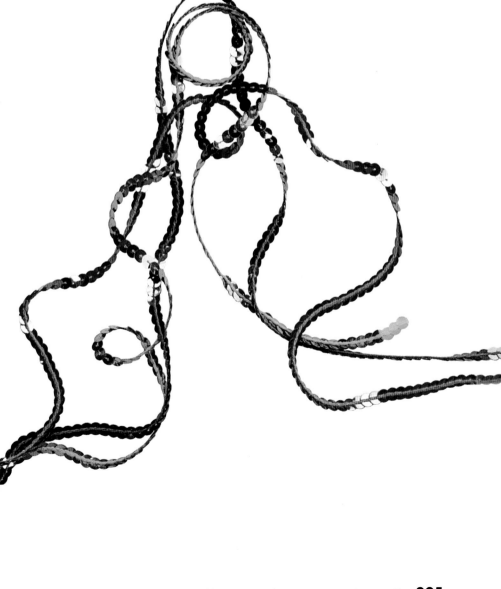

# SERGING

Sergers can do so much more than finish seams and hems of garments. Presented here are some ideas for using your serger for decorative stitching. Follow the threads below for serger basics and more on decorative serger techniques.

## Follow this Thread

### Serger Basics
See page 63 for serger features and terminology.
See pages 64–65 for common serger stitches and presser feet.
See pages 65–66 for understanding differential feed.
See pages 68–77 for thread.

### More Ideas For Serging
See pages 208–209 for braids and cording.
See pages 210–211 for chain.
See pages 211-212 for coverstitches.
See pages 212-214 for double sided serging.
See pages 215–216 for flatlocking.
See pages 216–218 for embellished fleece.
See pages 218–219 for flatlocked patchwork.
See pages 220–221 for textures.
See pages 222–223 for yarn-serged edges.
See page 244 for serger appliqué.
See page 242 for embellishing fabric.
See pages 243–244 for serger tips.

## Serger Blanket Stitches

**Naomi Baker**

*Serge a decorative-edge finish on heavyweight fabric with the blanket stitch.*

The blanket stitch is best used on heavyweight knit or tightly woven fabrics, such as fleece, woolens, felts, and quilted fabrics. Blanket-, mock blanket- or wrap-stitch techniques are appropriate for finishing garments, throws, placemats, pillows, scarves, and more.

## Threads

Heavy decorative threads provide stitch durability as well as a more dramatic look.

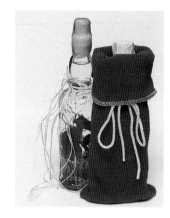

However, lightweight thread requires fewer tension adjustments.

A tightly twisted thread such as buttonhole twist, heavy rayon, or lightweight, yarn-type threads are easiest for serging.

When using heavy, decorative thread in the needle, test the threading first. A needle threader and/or a larger needle size may be necessary.

Variegated threads won't color-block evenly when used in both the upper and lower looper in a balanced stitch but the effect can be achieved by using the decorative thread in one looper or the needle and a blanket or wrap stitch.

## Tip

### Self-adjusting Tension
Some self-adjusting tension machines have built-in blanket and wrap stitches, but additional tension adjustments may be needed for different thread weights. Check the manual for your machine's capability and adjustments.

## Needles

Heavy decorative threads require the use of a larger needle. Use a 90/14 for less thread breakage and fewer stitch challenges. Large-eye needles including jeans, topstitching, metallic, or machine embroidery types are helpful, if appropriate for your serger model.

For easier threading, use a needle threader or thread cradle.

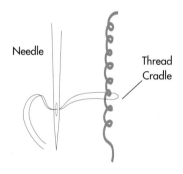

Needle — Thread Cradle

## Blanket Stitch
*Stitch Length*

Adjust for the longest and widest stitch, with the needle in the left needle position. When serging on the crosswise grain or bias, a longer stitch length will help prevent stretching. It also may be necessary to adjust to a plus differential feed.

*Tension*

Loosen the needle tension almost completely. Test by removing the thread from the guides or tension so it's visible on both sides. Tighten the looper tensions almost completely.

Hold the beginning thread chain to prevent catching it while serging. If the fabric edge puckers, loosen the looper tensions slightly, adjusting only one at a time.

When serging the 3-thread blanket stitch, the tensions are adjusted to allow the needle thread to be pulled to the fabric edge by both looper threads. The looper threads should be tightened enough to form a straight line at the fabric edge. Serge with the fabric right side up.

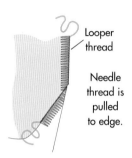

Use decorative thread in the needle and matching texturized nylon thread in the loopers.

If the decorative thread needs a looser tension, remove it from one or more thread guides.

Depending on the thread, you may have to completely remove it from the tension guide.

If the threads don't pull completely over the edge, try texturized nylon thread at the tightest tension setting. If more tension is needed, place a thread net over the thread spool.

## Helpful Hints

*Helpful Hints*
If the stitch rolls to the fabric top, gently use your fingernail or tweezers to pull it to the edge.

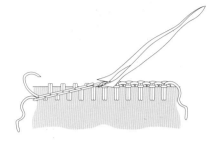

Or, serge over a 1½"-wide, water-soluble stabilizer strip, folded in half lengthwise, and use it to pull the stitch to the edge. Carefully remove the stabilizer from the stitches after stitching.

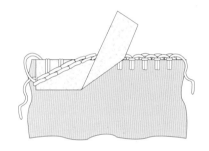

## Mock Blanket Stitch

This 2-thread stitch uses decorative threads in the needle and lower looper.

Loosen the needle tension so all threads interlock on the fabric edge. The lower looper thread forms loops on the fabric top while the needle thread forms Vs on the underside.

Serge with the fabric right side face down to form the mock blanket stitch on the right side.

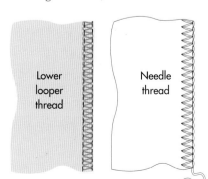

Lower looper thread

Needle thread

 *Tip*

## For Easier Serging

Round the project corners, eliminating sharp angles, for easier serging.

## Wrap Stitch

If your serger doesn't do a clean blanket stitch, a wrap stitch is another option.

When using a 3-thread edge finish, either the upper or lower looper wraps the fabric edge. The needle and the other looper thread are tightened and are inconspicuous. Test, using the decorative thread in the upper looper first (it's the easiest to thread) and matching threads in the needle and lower looper.

Loosen the upper looper thread tension and tighten the lower looper thread tension. It also may be necessary to tighten the needle thread tension.

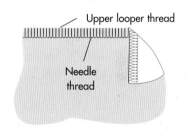

Upper looper thread

Needle thread

In a variation of the wrap stitch, the needle thread wraps the edge. Tighten both looper tensions and loosen the needle tension so it wraps completely around the edge. If the thread doesn't completely wrap the edge, try a narrower stitch.

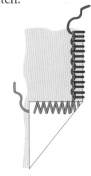

See page 206 for references to
serger basics.
See page 126 for couching.

# Serger Braids & Cording

*Naomi Baker*

*Save time and money searching for a perfectly matched trim by making your own serger cords and braids. Then use them for couching or other decorative applications.*

## Creating Serged Trims

Use decorative thread in the upper looper for the most visibility.

Thread the needle and lower looper with lightweight matching serger or all-purpose thread, or use monofilament thread.

Most decorative trims are made with a 3-thread, balanced stitch or roll-hem stitch.

Heavier threads require a longer stitch length than lighter threads. Adjust the stitch length and tensions accordingly. To avoid jamming, begin serging with a medium stitch length, then shorten the stitch and hold the thread chain taut. Test various threads, stitch widths, and lengths to achieve the desired effect.

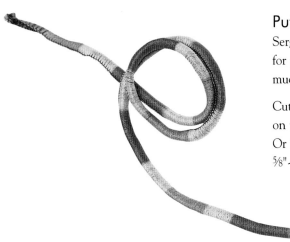

## Serger Cording

Serger cording is made by serging over a filler with a narrow stitch.

Adjust for a roll-hem setting and a short stitch length, tightening the lower looper tension.

For a more uniform chain, hold the thread chain taut while serging. Serge chain to test the stitch length and tension.

Serging over a filler produces a thicker, more durable cording. Serge over two or more heavy thread strands, string or yarn. Increase the stitch width if serging over several heavy filler strands. Place the filler under the foot back and over the foot front between the needle and knife. Hold the filler threads taut while serging.

When serging over a filler, the upper looper tension may need to be loosened to cover the filler completely. If full coverage isn't attainable, try clear monofilament thread or texturized nylon in the lower looper.

## Puffed Cording

Serge over thick yarn or a fabric tube for puffed cording. This produces a much thicker cording.

Cut a strip of 1"-wide jersey or tricot on the crosswise grain so it will curl. Or for a lighter weight cording, use ⅝"-wide, bias-cut tricot.

Use decorative thread in both the upper and lower loopers. For a heavier braid, a beading foot may be needed.

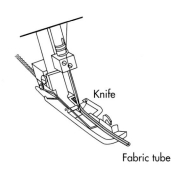

Knife

Fabric tube

Adjust for a wide serger stitch and tighten the lower looper tension so the tube is completely covered. The lower looper thread will show because of the tube thickness. The stitches should cover the tube—not stitch through it. Pull the fabric so it rolls into a tube and position it between the needle and knife.

## Serger Braids
### Basic Braid

A basic serged braid is made by finishing the edge or edges of a bias-cut fabric strip such as sheer tricot binding (for a lightweight, invisible base) commercial bias tape, narrow ribbon or elastic, braids or stabilizers.

Thread the serger with decorative thread in the upper looper and lightweight matching serger or all-purpose thread in the needle and lower looper. Adjust for a balanced 3-thread stitch. Begin testing with a medium-length stitch, loosening the upper looper tension and tightening the lower looper tension slightly until good coverage is obtained.

For narrower trims with maximum thread coverage, adjust for a narrow or roll-hem stitch and use texturized nylon in both loopers.

Shorten the stitch gradually to achieve a satin stitch with the upper looper thread pulled completely to the fabric edge or wrapped slightly to the stitch underside.

For the braid base, select a fabric that blends or color coordinates with the decorative thread.

Serge onto the fabric strip length, adjusting the stitch width and length until the desired stitch is achieved. With scissors, carefully trim the excess base strip.

For a wider braid, serge both long edges of the fabric strip. Serge one long edge, reverse the strip and serge the opposite edge with the needle lines overlapping each other. Use the needle marking on the front of the presser foot for the needle guideline. If the marking isn't available on the serger foot, mark the needle line on the front of the presser foot with a marking pen.

If desired, let the fabric show through the serging for contrast, or vary the stitch width from one side to the other. Serge the first row with one color and rethread a different color in the upper looper for the second row.

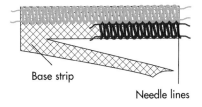

Base strip

Needle lines

## Braid Using Tear-away Stabilizer

This technique produces a wide, stable braid and is made by joining several serged strips together using a conventional sewing machine.

Adjust for a wide, short stitch with heavyweight, decorative thread in the upper and lower loopers and matching lightweight serger- or all-purpose thread in the needle. Serge over a strip of tear-away stabilizer.

On the sewing machine, straight stitch over both long edges of the serging and carefully tear away the extra stabilizer.

Thread the sewing machine with clear monofilament thread and adjust for a narrow zigzag. Join the widths together by placing the braids side-by-side and zigzagging over the straight stitching on each braid.

## Braid Using Water-soluble Stabilizer

A water-soluble stabilizer base gives a lightweight, but stable, braid. The threads used must be colorfast since the stabilizer is soaked away.

Thread the serger as for the tear-away stabilizer braid, except use clear monofilament thread in the lower looper. For a lightweight lacy trim, adjust for the longest, widest, balanced 3-thread stitch.

Serge over a water-soluble stabilizer strip. On the sewing machine, use a narrow stitch and zigzag over the needle line with matching thread to secure the stitches. Stitch several strips together for a wider braid.

Trim the stabilizer ⅛" from the serged stitches. Moisten the braid with water to remove stabilizer residue, then block it on a paper towel and allow it to air dry. The stabilizer adds a starched effect to the braid.

A shaped trim can be made with decorative thread in both loopers. Adjust the serger for a wide, short stitch. Serge over water-soluble stabilizer and trim the stabilizer after serging.

Stretch the chain gently—it will lengthen and narrow.

Moisten the braid and shape it as desired before drying.

## Applying Serged Trim

Mark the desired design on the fabric with a water- or air-soluble pen.

Dab the wrong side of the trim with a glue stick and position the trim over the traced design.

Use clear monofilament thread in the needle and matching thread in the bobbin of a conventional sewing machine, and straight stitch through wider braid.

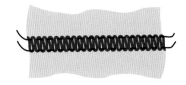

You can also zigzag over narrower trims to secure.

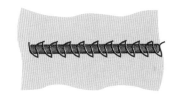

See page 206 for references to
serger basics.
See page 126 for couching.
See pages 233–234 for tassels.

## Serger Chain
*Naomi Baker*

*Think of serger chain as you would any
other decorative thread or yarn type and
you'll be on your way to dozens of
creative ideas.*

## Making the Best Chain
If it's difficult to begin chaining, serge
onto fabric first, then serge off.

Hold the chain taut behind the presser
foot without pulling.

If the chain is irregular or has skipped
stitches, make sure the needle is in the
correct position. If the stitches are still
irregular, try a larger size needle or
slightly loosen the tightest tension.
When the machine is set up for a rolled
edge, the tightest tension setting
usually is the lower looper.

When serging a long chain length, wrap
the thread chain around a spool or
cone for storage and to avoid tangling.

If a heavier chain is desired, serge over
one or more strands of a filler, such as
buttonhole twist, perle or crochet
cotton, metallic, yarn, fine wire, or
nylon fishline.

## Threads
Create a variety of thread chain looks
simply by changing the thread type.
Just remember when determining the
thread chain color and texture, the
upper looper thread is the most visible
and the needle thread is the least visible.

All-purpose thread forms a matte-look
chain, usually is the lightest weight
and is used most for practical purposes.

Texturized nylon thread forms the
densest rolled edge and provides the
most coverage. It's the least likely
thread chain to unravel after cutting.

Rayon threads make a delicate chain

ideal for fine tas-
sels. You may need
to tighten tensions
for this slick
thread.

Heavier acrylic
thread gives the
effect of wool yarn.

Metallics make a
sparkly, elegant
chain. Combine
metallics with
other threads to add sparkle.

Perle or crochet cotton, as well as
heavier rayon threads, make a durable,
more visible chain that's especially
good for couching. When serging with
heavier threads, begin with a 3mm
stitch length, then shorten the length
to prevent jamming.

## Chain Cording
Make twisted cord for a decorative treat.

Use Ribbon Floss, perle cotton, or
heavy rayon thread in both loopers
and all-purpose thread in the needle,
and serge off chain. You'll need two
strands, each three times the desired
cord length.

Place a bobbin on the bobbin winder;
attach the strands to the bobbin top.
Hold the free ends and wind until the
strands are tightly twisted.

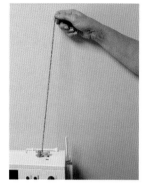

Hold the twisted strand at the halfway
point and allow the cording to twist
back on its self.

Pull on the cording for uniform twisting. Remove the ends from the
bobbin top.

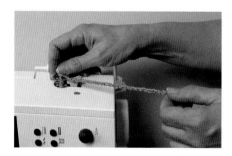

## Uses
Use as you would any other decorative
cording: couching, making tassels,
piping, ornament ties, garland bows,
et cetera.

## Finishing Chain Ends
### Sallie J. Russell

Knowing a few tricks to begin and end serging can help to neaten your projects by locking and hiding the chain ends.

**1.** Leave a thread chain at the end of the seam. Apply seam sealant to the chain; clip off the excess thread chain when dry.

**2.** Weave the excess thread chain back under the stitching using a large-eye needle or small loop turner.

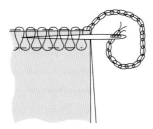

**3.** Serge one stitch off of the fabric; raise the presser foot and carefully pull the threads off the stitch finger (if necessary pull a slight amount of slack in the needle thread above the eye).

Turn the fabric over and re-stitch the seam for 1", raise the presser foot and fold the fabric back to the left of the needle. Lower the presser foot and chain off the fabric; trim off the excess chain.

**4.** When serging circular shapes like garment hems, clean-finish at the seam beginning and end. Before beginning to serge, carefully pull the thread chain off the stitch finger; begin serging. At the seam end take a few stitches over the first stitches, cutting off the original thread chain. Raise the presser foot and again pull the thread off the stitch finger, angling the fabric back to the left. Lower the presser foot and chain off the fabric; apply seam sealant and trim off the excess chain.

Follow this Thread

See page 206 for references to serger basics.

## Serger Coverstitches
### Naomi Baker

*The coverstitch is both a decorative and utility stitch available on select sergers. Although it's usually used on knits because it allows for stretch in a seam, it also can be used on wovens.*

The coverstitch is functional, as well as durable, but it can also be decorative. It's used most often for hemming and topstitching but also is used to apply elastic, laces, ribbons, and ribbing.

The coverstitch showcases two or three parallel straight stitch rows on the fabric upper side. It is usually formed by two or three needles and a chainstitch looper. If only one needle is used, a single chainstitch is formed. Needle placement determines the stitch width. Either side of the stitch may be used on the right side of the garment.

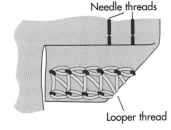

Needle threads

Looper thread

*(Continued on next page)*

The stitch lies flat on the fabric, so the knives and upper looper are disengaged and a special throatplate is inserted to form a flatbed. (See the machine manual for instructions on adjusting the serger for a coverstitch and for threading.) This allows the coverstitch to be used anywhere since the fabric isn't trimmed during serging.

For easier coverstitch serging, accessories and additional feet are available for some machines; check with your dealer. Accessories include elastic applicators and guides for hemming, topstitching, fagoting, flat-fell seaming, pintucking, belt loops, tape, and ribbon and lace application.

## Stitching

Always begin stitching on fabric and serge off the fabric no more than 1".

Adjust for a longer stitch length, usually 3mm to 4mm.

For ease, serge as much as possible in flat construction. Keep in mind space is limited to the right of the needle so little fabric bulk can be moved through the machine. If necessary, and if possible, serge decoratively on smaller pieces, then add them to your project.

If the coverstitch tunnels the fabric, the needle tensions are most likely too tight and need to be loosened.

If fabric is thick or jams when beginning, serge on a fabric scrap, serge off for approximately ½" and serge onto the project, without clipping the threads. The scrap helps to guide the project fabric.

When serging in the round, overlap the original stitching approximately ½". Turn the handwheel towards you until the needles are in the lowest position. Slowly reverse the handwheel until the needles are in the highest position. Release the tension by raising

the presser foot or pressing the tension release lever. Carefully pull the fabric to the left of the foot and cut the threads, leaving tails. Pull the thread tails to the fabric underside and knot.

Coverstitch hemming can be done in one step by turning the hem allowance to the wrong side of the garment and topstitching on the right side of the garment. The hem is straight stitched on the right side and the underside is serge finished and secured. For a decorative hem, serge-finish the hem raw edge, turn the hem to the wrong side of the garment and coverstitch from the wrong side of the garment.

When coverstitching knit hems, adjust the differential feed to a slightly positive setting to prevent stretching and steam the hem carefully after serging.

### Tip

## Securing the Ends

The coverstitch unravels easily so it's important to secure the ends. Securing is easier on flat construction as opposed to serging in the round.

To secure the coverstitching, turn the handwheel towards you and remove the fabric from under the presser foot. Pull the needle threads to the fabric underside by pulling the looper thread to the left until the needle thread comes through. Tug on the needle threads to lock them with looper thread. Knot the threads and clip the tails.

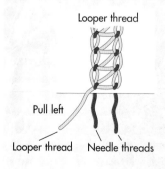

Looper thread

Pull left

Looper thread    Needle threads

Follow this Thread

See page 206 for references to serger basics.
See pages 68–77 for threads.

## Double-sided Serging

**Naomi Baker**

*Create decorative edge finishes that look great from both sides.*

If the edges will be visible from both sides, serged stitches need to be perfect on both the top and underside. To get the best stitches, test a variety of threads and stitches using the actual fabric.

### Before you begin

For a balanced stitch, the upper and lower looper threads should interlock exactly on the fabric edge.

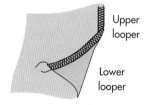

Upper looper

Lower looper

If stitches skip, make sure the needle is completely up in the needle clamp, loosen the tightest tension, or change to a larger size needle.

To ensure uniform stitches, be sure the thread feeds smoothly from the spools or cones. Use the spool caps in the machine's accessory box to prevent the thread catching on the spool edges. If the thread tends to slide off the spool or cone, place it on the table behind the thread stand, use a thread net, or a specially designed thread stand.

To prevent stretching when using heavier thread or serging around curved areas, adjust the differential feed. Using too short a stitch length also can cause stretching.

To perfect decorative serging on curves, shorten and/or narrow the stitch. Trim the seam allowance before serging and just overcast the edge.

Begin stitching at an inconspicuous place, such as a side seam lower edge.

For most stitches, decorative thread will be used in both the upper and lower loopers with matching serger or all-purpose thread in the needle(s).

Be sure to purchase enough decorative thread to allow for adequate testing. Allow 10 times the finished stitched length for each looper. For testing, you'll need an additional 7 yards for each looper and 2 yards for the needle. It's always advisable to purchase an extra spool or cone if serging long edges.

Experiment with stitch length and width, as well as tension.

For variety, use contrasting threads in the upper and lower looper or blend threads.

## Thread Choices

Coordinate thread with the fabric, using heavier threads for heavy- and mediumweight fabric. For outerwear fleece, sweater knits, and medium-weight suitings, the following threads are appropriate:

Texturized nylon provides the most coverage. It can be used in the lower looper to tighten rolled or binding stitches. The tension must be loosened slightly for fluffy coverage. Shorten the stitch length for the most coverage.

Buttonhole twist is easy to use with few tension adjustments. It is available on larger spools for ease of use.

Acrylic yarns are easy to use with good coverage. Loosen the tensions slightly when using these yarns.

Perle cottons are more challenging to use. Loosen the tension and lengthen the stitch slightly when using.

Crochet thread requires the same adjustments as perle cotton, but is most available wound on balls. For ease of use, rewind this thread onto cones.

Metallic threads are available in many weights. Loosen the tensions moderately and narrow the stitch when using lightweight metallic threads. Loosen the tensions slightly and widen the stitch when using heavier threads.

Heavy rayon threads are easy to use. Tighten the tensions and lengthen the stitch when using.

RibbonFloss is easy to use by loosening the tension and lengthening the stitch.

## The Stitches

Experiment with these simple and easy, serged-edge, decorative stitches:

### Balanced Stitch

Choose either a narrow or wide stitch width by using either the left or right needle. In most cases, the 3-thread stitch is the most attractive finish. A short stitch provides the most coverage, but lengthen the stitch slightly to prevent bunching or jamming.

Use decorative thread in the upper and lower loopers. The stitch will look the same on the top and underside.

### Corded-edge Stitch

Matching or contrasting cording applied with the serger finishes and stabilizes the edge. The cording or trim must be narrow enough to fit between the needle and knives and the upper looper must be able to go over the trim without catching. Serge-finish the edge with a narrow balanced stitch or a narrow bound stitch. Use thread that matches the trim and a beading foot; tighten the lower looper tension. With a medium to long 2- or 3-thread stitch, serge over the trim, just catching it to the edge. The stitch with the cording will look the same from the upper and underside.

### Decorative Balanced Stitch

Use heavy rayon thread in the upper and lower loopers. Adjust for a short, balanced narrow or wide stitch. Tighten the tensions slightly so the stitch hugs the edge. Serge-finish the edge. With matching thread in the sewing machine, adjust to a blindhem stitch with the same or slightly narrower stitch than the serge-finished

*(Continued on next page)*

edge. Blindhem the edge, allowing the needle stitch to go off the edge to form a scallop. (The fabric must be fed through to the right of the needle.) Adjust the blindhem stitch length to vary the stitch. The scalloped stitch looks the same on the top and underside of the fabric.

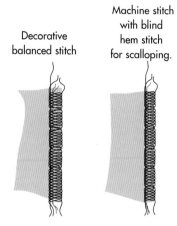

Decorative balanced stitch

Machine stitch with blind hem stitch for scalloping.

## Double Stitch

For a more stable edge, serge the edge with a narrow balanced stitch, using all-purpose or serger thread in the needle and loopers. Adjust the serger for a wider, short stitch with decorative thread in the upper and lower loopers and serge over the original stitching, being careful not to cut the threads in the previous stitching.

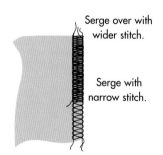

Serge over with wider stitch.

Serge with narrow stitch.

## Reversible-edge Binding Stitch

Use heavy decorative thread in the upper looper and adjust for a narrow stitch. Loosen the upper looper tension and tighten the lower looper tension so the upper looper thread completely wraps the edge.

Use matching texturized nylon in the lower looper to assist the stitch to completely wrap the edge. This binding is similar to a rolled edge but the fabric doesn't roll in the stitch. Correctly adjusting the tension allows the stitch to be identical on the top and underside.

## Reversible Needle-wrap Stitch

Also called blanket stitch. Use either the 2-thread overedge or 3-thread overlock stitch with decorative thread in the needle. Thread choices may be limited since the decorative thread must be able to be threaded through the needle. Loosen the needle tension and tighten the looper tension so the finished stitch has the upper and lower looper threads of a 3-thread stitch interlocking on the edge. If the needle thread can't be loosened enough, narrow the stitch and remove the thread from one of the needle thread guides. Using texturized nylon in the loopers may help perfect the stitch. This crochet-like stitch allows the needle thread to wrap to the edge on the top and underside.

## Self-braid Stitch

For an even more stable edge, serge-finish as previously described for the double stitch, fold the width of the narrow stitch to the right side. With a wide balanced stitch, serge over the folded edge.

## Tuck and Roll Stitch

Check your serger's manual to determine if the left needle position can be used for a rolled hem. If so, use both needles and adjust for a rolled edge stitch and use decorative thread in the upper and lower loopers. Shorten the stitch and tighten both the upper and lower looper tensions. A tuck is formed on both sides of the needle on the right side of the fabric and a cord-like finish appears on the underside. You may need to use matching texturized nylon in the lower looper to pull the thread completely to the wrong side. As an option, adjust for a wider stitch using the same adjustments.

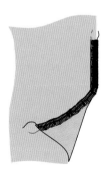

See page 206 for references to serger basics.
See page 218 for flatlocking on fleece.
See pages 218–219 for flatlocked patchwork embroidery.

## Serger Flatlocking

*Naomi Baker*

*Give your next fleece or knit garment a professional touch with flatlocking—a technique that's practical as well as decorative.*

Flatlocking is a serger stitch where the needle tension is loosened and the stitch is flattened on the fabric surface. It forms decorative loops on top side of the fabric and a ladder of evenly spaced stitches on the underside when the stitched seam is pulled flat.

Either side of the flatlocking stitch may be used on the right side of the project.

- To place the loops on the right side of the fabric, flatlock the fabric with wrong sides together.

- For the ladder stitch on the right side of the fabric, serge with right sides together.

Flatlocking may be done with a 2-or 3- thread stitch. Check your machine manual to determine if your serger is capable of 2-thread serging.

The 2-thread stitch needs very little tension adjustment for flatlocking. Because it's not a locking stitch and uses less thread, it automatically pulls flatter and is less bulky than the 3-thread stitch. Change the serger for 2-thread serging using the needle and lower looper, checking your machine manual for adjustment. Slightly loosen the needle thread to interlock with the looper thread on the fabric edge, creating Vs on the underside.

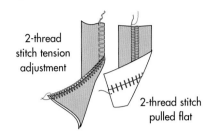

2-thread stitch tension adjustment

2-thread stitch pulled flat

The 3-thread flatlocking stitch uses one needle and both loopers; it requires tension adjustments from a balanced stitch on the needle and the lower looper. Loosen the needle thread almost completely to interlock with the upper looper thread exactly on the fabric edge with no loops showing. Tighten the looper thread to form a straight line on the fabric edge.

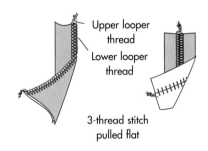

Upper looper thread
Lower looper thread

3-thread stitch pulled flat

## Flawless Flatlocking Tips

A perfect flatlocked stitch is always pulled flat; an imperfect stitch won't flatten even when pressed. Serge with the stitches hanging over the fold or edges to allow the fabric to lie flat under the stitches; trim seams before flatlocking, if necessary. A sufficiently loosened needle thread, interlocked with the looper thread exactly on the fabric edge also will allow the fabric to be pulled flat.

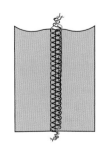

Guide the fabric edge or fold away from the knives and serge evenly from the edge to prevent irregular stitches. For easiest guiding, follow a presser foot marking or use a blind-hem foot. Adjust the foot guide so the stitches will hang over the edge.

If the stitch pulls apart too much, tighten the needle tension slightly or move fabric closer to the knives.

In a 3-thread flatlocked stitch, if the fabric puckers on the edge or if the stitch unravels, loosen the lower looper tension slightly.

Slightly loosen the tensions for clear or textured nylon threads.

## Flatlock Seaming Options

Flatlock seaming works well and is durable on nonraveling fabrics. It also can be used on many other fabrics when they're stabilized for durability.

Serge-finish edges with a narrow balanced stitch. Flatlock over the serged edges with a wider stitch.

*(Continued on next page)*

Stabilize edges by adhering fusible knit interfacing on the underside of both edges and flatlock.

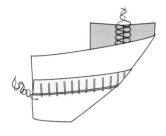

You can also flatlock and fuse the interfacing over the seam on the wrong side of the fabric. Topstitch on both sides of the stitch, if desired.

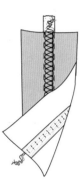

Serge-finish both edges and press the seam allowances to the wrong side. With folds and wrong sides together, flatlock the folded edges.

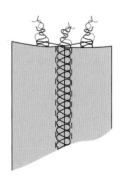

Serge-finish both edges and straight stitch the seam. Press seam open, fold the fabric wrong sides together on the seamline and flatlock over the seam.

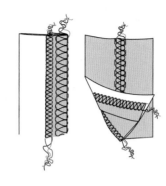

## Decorative Uses

When decoratively serging, remember one side of the stitch always will be visible, so flatlocking is an ideal stitch for using decorative thread. If the ladder stitch is visible from the right side, the decorative thread must be able to go through the needle eye. If the loop side shows on the right side, the decorative thread must go in the upper looper (lower looper of the 2-thread stitch).

### V-shaped Stitch

The 2-thread stitch adjusted to the widest and longest stitch, with buttonhole twist in the needle and serged from the underside, forms the blanket stitch that's popular on fleece fabric edges. The V-shaped needle stitch replicates that of ready-to-wear.

### Floating and Framed Flatlock Stitches

Use clear monofilament thread in the needle of the 2-thread stitch or the needle and lower looper of the 3-thread stitch and heavier decorative thread in the remaining looper. Wrong sides together, flatlock with a long, wide stitch for a floating flatlock stitch (stitches appear to "float" on the surface of the fabric).

Or use a contrasting color thread in the upper looper and matching threads in the needle and lower looper for a framed flatlock stitch.

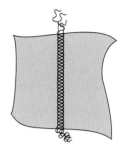

### Narrow Cording Look

For the look of narrow cording, flatlock with a narrow satin stitch. Slightly tighten the needle tension to raise the stitch. Try using the narrowest stitch (width of the rolled edge) but be sure to catch the needle into the fabric fold.

### Balanced Flatlock Stitch

Balance the flatlock stitch where the upper and lower looper threads overlock in the center of a 3-thread stitch. For this stitch, use contrasting threads in the loopers. Adjust for flatlocking, then tighten the upper looper tension and loosen the lower looper tension. The needle tension remains the same to allow the stitch to pull flat.

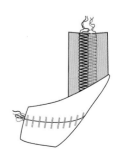

## Mock Hemstitch

Right sides together, straight stitch through a wide flatlocked stitch with matching thread in the needle and monofilament thread in the bobbin. The threads will automatically group together for a mock hemstitch. Test with different stitch lengths.

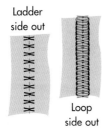

Ladder side out

Loop side out

## Fagoting

For a non-stress fagoted seam for heirloom sewing, use monofilament thread in the upper looper for inconspicuous loop stitches. Press seam allowances to the wrong side. Right sides together, flatlock the folds with a long medium-width stitch, just catching the needle into the folds. Thread narrow ribbon through the ladder stitches, if desired.

## Couching

Flatlock over trim, ribbon, or yarn that's narrow enough to fit between the needle and knives. Adjust the stitch width to just cover trim width. Use the left needle for wider trim and the right needle for narrower trim. The trim can just float on the fabric or it can be flatlocked to cover a seam.

To highlight the trim, use monofilament thread or lightweight matching thread in the upper looper (looper of 2-thread). Place the filler under the back and over the front of the presser foot and carefully serge over it for approximately ½". Insert the fold halfway under the ribbon. Be careful not to stitch through the trim or cut it with the knives. Pull the stitches flat.

Stitch over a wide satin flatlocked stitch from the looped side with decorative machine stitching.

## Follow this Thread

See page 206 for references to serger basics.
See pages 129–130 for fleece cutwork.
See pages 142–143 for embroidery on fleece.
See pages 211–212 for cover-stitching.
See pages 215–216 for flatlocking.
See pages 151–152 for fleece.

## Serger-embellished Fleece

### Naomi Baker

*Fleece fabric provides a wonderful canvas for serger stitched embellishments.*

When serging on fleece, decrease the presser foot pressure and lengthen the stitch to avoid distortion. Adjust the differential feed to a plus setting to prevent stretching while embellishing or constructing the garment.

Use a stabilizer when randomly serging or if serging on the fabric crossgrain. Serging in a straight line on the lengthwise grain does not require stabilizing.

Draw the design onto fusible or plain tear-away stabilizer. Lightly iron or pin the stabilizer to the wrong side of the fabric and stitch following the lines.

## The Stitches

### Chainstitch

When using the chainstitch for embellishing, the upper looper and knives are disengaged so the stitch may be used anywhere on the fabric without trimming as in regular serging.

Avoid distorted stitches at the beginning and end of a stitching line by first serging on a fabric scrap, then onto the fabric, and back onto the fabric scrap at the end, leaving the presser foot down.

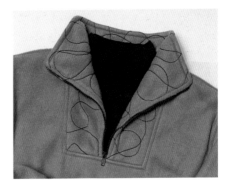

To prevent unraveling, at the end of a chain, pull the fabric carefully away from the serger and tie off with a knot or pull the needle thread through the last loop of the looper thread and knot.

### Coverstitch

Use a coverstitch with decorative thread in the coverstitch looper and matching thread in the needles. Serge from the wrong side of the fabric as with the chainstitch. Alternate rows of coverstitch with chainstitching.

### Lettuce

Take advantage of the fabric stretch and lettuce the fleece. Serge on the fabric bias, stitching lines at least 2" apart for less fabric distortion. Use decorative thread in the upper looper and adjust the machine for a short, rolled-edge stitch. Adjust the differential feed to a minus setting to stretch the fabric while serging, and serge on the fabric fold.

*(Continued on next page)*

### Scallop

Use a narrow- to medium-width, short flatlock stitch to scallop the fabric. Use contrasting thread in the needle and upper looper, and matching thread in the lower looper.

Texturized nylon or polyester threads work well for this stitch. Adjust for the flatlock stitch by loosening the needle tension and tightening the lower looper tension. Carefully serge along the fold and hold your finger against the upper looper thread above the tension discs rhythmically while serging to tighten the looper tension and form the scallops. Pull flat after serging.

### Flatlock

Sew a design with a narrow, raised flatlock stitch. With decorative thread in the upper looper and matching thread in the needle and lower looper, adjust the machine to a narrow, short- to medium-length flatlock and tighten the needle tension slightly. Serge along the fold and open flat. The tightened needle tension will give a raised, piping-like stitch.

### Wide Flatlock

Embellish with a medium-length, wide flatlock stitch using contrasting thread in the needle and upper looper and matching thread in the lower looper. Serge from the right side so the loops will be visible, or from the wrong side so the ladder stitches will show.

When serging, allow the stitches to hang off the folded edge to allow room for the stitches to lie flat when opened up. Alternate rows of loops and ladder stitches.

**Follow this Thread**

See page 206 for references to serger basics.
See pages 215–216 for more on flatlocking.
See pages 84–86 for stabilizers.

## Flatlocked Patchwork Embroidery

*Carola Russell*

*Use a serger flatlock stitch to create fast and fun patchwork blocks. The ladder stitches on the right side of the fabric provide the perfect framework for ribbon and lace embellishment.*

### Make Blocks

From a base fabric cut 2"- to 3"-wide strips from selvage to selvage.

Create your own embroidery blocks, use pre-made embroideries, or make quilt blocks of your choice.

Cut the embroideries into blocks, or use pieced quilt blocks.

With right sides together and edges even, place a fabric strip along one side of the block and flatlock together. Carefully pull open the seam, creating a ladder, press and cut the fabric strip even with the block.

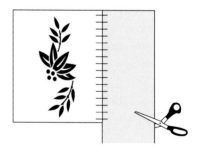

Use a bodkin to weave ribbon through the ladder stitches.

Turn the block counter-clockwise to the next edge, add a fabric strip, flatlock the seam, then weave ribbon through the ladder stitches.

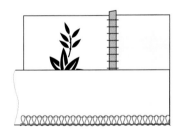

Continue clockwise around the block, flatlocking fabric strips and weaving ribbon, until you have completed all four sides.

## Add Lace to Patchwork

Use your own serger lace or use premade lace to dress up your patchwork. Insert ¾"-wide edging lace between the block and the fabric strips while flatlocking.

Tuck the lace between the block and fabric strip, just in from the edge (¹⁄₁₆" to ⅛"), to assure that the lace won't be trimmed by the serger's knife.

Don't be too concerned about catching enough lace in the serging, the needle only needs to catch the lace heading. When flatlocking, the fabric on top will always open flat, therefore you may wish to have the heavier fabric on top.

## Make Flatlocked Serger Lace

Determine how much lace is needed, then practice the technique before making the lace for your project.

Cut heat-soluble stabilizer 4" wider and longer than the desired finished lace size

With a chalk marker, draw gridlines ¾" to 1" apart on the stabilizer.

Fold and flatlock along one guideline, just catching the stabilizer (approximately ⅛"). The stitching will hang over the edge. Pull the fold open flat.

Continue flatlocking until every vertical guideline is covered. Turn the stabilizer and flatlock all the horizontal lines.

Reinforce the flatlocking with your sewing machine. Insert a topstitching needle into the sewing machine and thread it with 12-weight thread. Topstitch down the center of each flatlocked row, then again between each flatlocked row.

You can also make lace with a fabric backing by placing the flatlocked stabilizer on fabric before securing the stitches with topstitching. The fabric will crinkle during the topstitching. Press flat.

Follow the manufacturer's recommendations to remove the stabilizer with a hot, dry iron. Wash out any remaining residue.

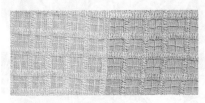

## Follow this Thread

See page 206 for references to serger basics.
See pages 185–186 pintucks.
See pages 235–237 for tucks.
See pages 241–242 for other techniques to create fabric textures.
See pages 244 for serging with decorative thread.

## Creating Serger Textures

**Naomi Baker**

*Create a unique, embellished fabric by serging with decorative threads.*

### Getting Started

Texturize fabric before cutting project pieces. Begin by practicing on fabric scraps.

If stitching in rows, use the presser foot as a spacing guide. Lightly press a fold in the fabric at the first stitch line or mark the fabric lightly with a water-soluble marker.

Select decorative threads that are care-compatible with the fabric.

Consider the stitches chosen for embellishment. Narrow stitches are less conspicuous and thus less likely to show stitching mishaps.

Contrasting thread colors are more conspicuous in decorative serging. Matching thread colors disguise any stitching problems more effectively.

Select easy-to-use threads such as buttonhole twist, texturized nylon, rayon, and heavyweight metallic.

When using heavyweight threads, begin with a 2mm stitch length and adjust if necessary. A too-short stitch length will stretch the fabric edge and create loopy stitches.

If the thread tends to slide off the cone, place it on the table behind a thread stand, use a thread net, or a specially designed thread stand. The decorative thread tension may need to be loosened if a net is used.

### Balanced-stitch Tuck

Use a balanced stitch on the right side of the fabric to make a tuck that can be left unpressed, pressed flat, or stitched flat to create a design. Fold, then serge the fold without cutting.

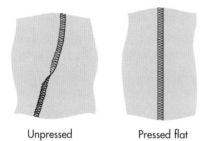

Unpressed        Pressed flat

For unpressed tucks, serge all the tucks in the same direction for more uniform stitch quality. If the tucks are pressed in opposite directions, serge them from opposite directions so the upper looper stitch will always be on the top. Press carefully, as texturized nylon threads may melt under high iron heat.

When serging tucks, use decorative thread in the upper and lower loopers, and a 3-thread balanced stitch. Test a swatch to be sure the decorative threads meet exactly on the fabric edge. Rayon threads work well, but tighten the looper tensions for the ideal stitch.

Test various stitch widths until the desired results are achieved.

For released tucks that don't run to the pattern or fabric edge, serge the desired tuck length, raise the presser foot and needle and carefully remove the fabric. Pull the thread ends to the wrong side of the fabric and knot. Dab the thread ends with seam sealant.

To create a wavy tuck design, use contrasting decorative thread colors in the upper and lower loopers. A short, wide stitch offers a bolder design. Press parallel folds into the fabric and serge without cutting. With the sewing machine, straight stitch vertical lines perpendicular to the tucks, pressing the tucks in opposite directions every other row.

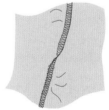

Use contrasting colors in upper and lower loopers.        Machine stitch in alternating directions.

## Roll-edge Pintucks

Create pintucks using a 2- or 3-thread rolled edge. This technique is widely used in heirloom designs and in ready-to-wear garments. For this narrow, delicate stitch, use 40-weight rayon thread in the upper looper when working on lightweight fabrics. Use matching all-purpose serger thread in the needle and lower looper.

Press folds in the fabric to mark the pintuck positions. Adjust the serger for a short rolled edge and serge the fold without cutting. Serge the tucks in opposite directions if tucks are to be pressed in opposite directions.

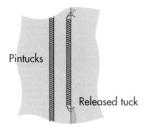

Pintucks

Released tuck

For released tucks, finish as with the balanced-released tucks.

Use texturized nylon thread in the upper looper for the best coverage. If the edge doesn't roll completely, also use texturized nylon in the lower looper.

## Roll-hem Lettucing

Use a roll-hem stitch for lettucing fabric edges. Lettucing requires a stretchy fabric or serging on the bias. To lettuce, adjust for a short rolled-hem edge with the differential feed on a minus setting.

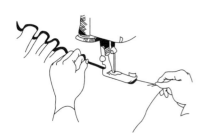

Serge the edge without cutting, pulling the fabric equally behind and in from of the presser foot.

Use texturized nylon thread in the upper looper for the best coverage. If the edge doesn't roll completely, also use texturized nylon in the lower looper.

## Roll-hem Shirring

Combining rolled hem serging with the differential feed on a plus setting (to gather) provides an easy ruffling embellishment on lightweight fabric. Use matching serger or all-purpose thread in both loopers and the needle.

Disengage the serger knives. Adjust for a roll-hem stitch, widen the stitch and set stitch length to 4mm. Adjust to the highest, plus differential feed setting.

To form a gathered, roll-hem stitch, fold the fabric wrong sides together and serge the folded edge. Keep the fabric folded edge next to the throat plate edge. Allow the fabric to feed easily for the most gathers.

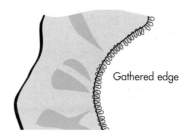

Gathered edge

Serge equidistant gathered rows 1" or more apart.

After serging, lightly pull the rows apart to distribute the gathers. Steam without touching the folds to set the gathers.

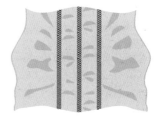

Pull and steam.

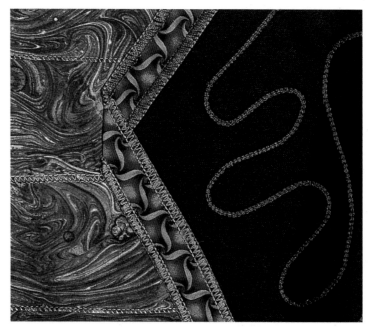

Detail of *Investments* by Cindy Cummins. See page 13 for vest.

**See page 206 for references to serger basics.**

## Yarn-serged Edges

**Naomi Baker**

*Yarn-serged edges have a heavy, dense look—perfect for using on fleece. Serging with yarn can be challenging, but by choosing the right yarn and stitch combination as well as making sure the yarn feeds evenly and smoothly, you can get uniform stitches with no glitches.*

### Yarn Selection

Yarn used for serger edging must be fine enough to go through the eye or tube of the looper when folded double. Three-ply baby yarn, or sock or sport yarn will work in the loopers. Heavier yarns can't be used in the needle.

Choose yarns with acrylic and wool content for their softness and flexibility. Nylon blended with wool also gives the yarn strength and washability.

Select yarn that has long fibers and is highly twisted. Loosely twisted yarn will be snagged by the needle when serging.

Pull a strand of the yarn to make sure it won't break easily; if you can easily break it, it's prone to break as it's serged. The yarn should be smooth with no texture or slubs for even feeding through the machine.

Many heavier yarns come on skeins, which require care for even feeding into the serger. Lighter weight yarns are available on cones—ready for the serger—but they don't furnish as dense an edge as heavier yarns.

Serging heavy yarn may require a lot of testing, so buy an adequate amount of yarn for experimentation.

### Serger Adjustments

Adjust to the widest, longest balanced stitch with one needle. Use a large, new needle to prevent snagging the yarn. Change to a new needle if skipped stitches are experienced.

Adjust the differential feed to a plus setting to avoid stretching the edge.

Heavier yarn works best in the upper looper. Test in the lower looper as well to see if your machine will accommodate it.

If the stitch will be visible from both sides, use yarn in both loopers. If unable to get a uniform stitch with yarn in both loopers, replace the yarn in the lower looper with a lighter weight matching yarn or heavyweight texturized nylon thread (like Woolly Nylon Extra).

Or wrap the edge, using either the lightweight yarn or Woolly Nylon Extra in the lower looper and tightening the tension so the upper looper wraps over the edge.

### Perfecting the Stitch

Loosen both looper tensions to allow the yarn to spread out to the edge of the fabric for a balanced stitch.

The yarn may need to be removed from one or more thread guides or removed completely from the tension discs, especially on sergers that automatically adjust the tensions.

Test to find the correct tension for the desired stitch. If a balanced stitch can't be achieved, experiment by varying the tension to find another unique stitch that can be used.

Begin serging by turning the hand-wheel manually to make sure a chain is forming and the yarn is feeding smoothly.

Serge slowly, holding the thread chain taut to prevent the beginning stitches from jamming.

## Tips

### Serging Tips

Thread the yarn using a thread cradle of all-purpose or serger thread, pulling gently through the looper eye or threading tube.

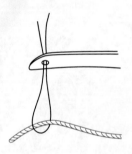

For the most uniform stitch, pull out several feet of yarn from the end of the skein. To prevent the yarn from tangling, reel it off to the side of the machine without crossing the threads.

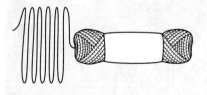

Allow the yarn to serge freely into the machine with no obstructions. The slightest tension on the yarn will form glitches in the edge, so watch the yarn as you serge, pulling out several more feet of yarn from the skein before the yarn is used up.

Remove tweezers, scissors, or anything else from the table that the yarn may catch on.

# SHISHA MIRRORS

### Follow this Thread

See pages 68–77 for threads.
See pages 84–86 for stabilizers.
See pages 147–148 for eyelets.

## Embellishing with Shisha

**Peggy Bendel**

*"Shisha" actually means mirror or glass. The dime- to nickel-size mirrors, an embellishment staple in India and Pakistan for more than 300 years, are becoming a trendy fashion detail adding visual excitement to today's popular, pared-down styles. The mirrors are traditionally circular, but squares, triangles, and irregular shapes also are available.*

## A Quick History of Shisha

Shisha were originally made of hand-blown glass, into which a metal solution was poured to create the mirror. Shisha labeled "antique" are still made this way; the term refers to the manufacturing process, not necessarily the mirror's age. These antique shisha have a smoky or iridescent look and may contain bubbles or other imperfections. They can be washed or dry-cleaned.

Contemporary shisha—often referred to as "perfect" because they're mass-produced and uniform—are slightly thicker, have a cleaner, more reflective surface, and can be dry-cleaned (but aren't washable).

Shisha add ethnic flair and dramatic glimmer to special wardrobe items. They also add weight. Although a single mirror seems light enough, adding multiple mirrors—and the embroidery that frames them—can dramatically influence fabric drape.

Add shisha to garment areas that have some inner construction for support. They are especially effective on accessories such as scarves, shawls, purses, totes, and pillows.

Look for shisha in sewing stores, bead shops, costume supply houses, and bead vendors at flea markets. In a pinch, imitate the look of shisha with large sequins, or fuse interfacing to the wrong side of metallic tissue lamé and cut to the desired shape.

*(Continued on next page)*

## Machine-stitched Frames

Position a shisha on the right side of the fabric, and trace around it. Mark an outline for the shisha opening about ⅛" inside this circle. Add enough tear-away or water-soluble stabilizer to the wrong side of the fabric for firm support, and staystitch around the inner circle twice, using a short straight stitch. If desired, insert the fabric and stabilizer in a hoop, drop or cover the feed dogs, and staystitch with free-motion stitching.

Cut out the shisha opening from the fabric layer only, leaving the stabilizer intact.

Thread the machine needle with a decorative embroidery thread, and cover the staystitching with wide, dense, satin stitches to make a solid frame for the mirror. It may be easier to drop the feed dogs for this step. Remove the stabilizer.

Use gem glue to attach the shisha to the embroidery, and tuck it behind the opening.

### Back the Mirror

Place a plain, lightweight fabric piece on the wrong side behind the mirror.

Thread the machine needle with fine monofilament thread, or use all-purpose sewing thread to match the satin stitching.

Attach a zipper foot and adjust the needle position so it penetrates the fabric close to the mirror's edge. Carefully straight stitch through the embroidered frame next to the edge of the mirror, using your fingertips to feel the raised outline of the mirror as you go.

Once the mirror is in its embroidered frame, add other decorative stitches around the opening, such as radiating spokes for a sunburst effect, or a border of small scallops for a flower treatment. Beads and sequins are popular accents to shisha embroidery.

## Appliquéd Frames

A shisha frame can be made as a separate appliqué, then topstitched to fabric to secure the mirror. The advantage to this method is that you don't have to cut the fabric.

Sandwich tulle or organdy between sheets of water-soluble stabilizer. Insert these layers in a machine embroidery hoop. Thread the machine needle with a decorative thread, and use free-motion embroidery to create a satin-stitch frame. Make the outline larger than the mirror and the center opening smaller than the mirror. Carefully cut out the frame.

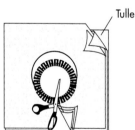
Tulle

Glue the mirror to the right side of the fabric, then position the frame over it. Topstitch through the frame close to the mirror edge as for the machine-stitched frame above. Remove the stabilizer.

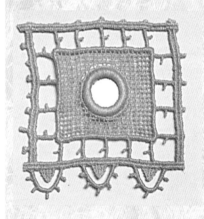

## A New Reflection on Shisha

### Pauline Richards

*Instead of throwing away those old CDs, use them as quick faux shisha. Make a quick purse, binder cover, or wall hanging in three easy steps.*

1. Select fabric and make any size or shape stitched or embroidered openings.

2. Create a pocket for the CD.

3. Slip the CD in pocket so that is shows through the embroidered openings!

See page 134 for references to embroidery basics.

## Embroidering with Shisha

### Barbara Weiland

*Attach shisha within embroidery designs created specifically for shisha, or incorporate them into other embroidered designs.*

Designs created specifically for shisha often include placement, anchoring, and decorative stitches. The first stitches, a circle of stitching, indicate the placement of the mirror. A smaller circle of stitches hold the rayon circlet around the mirror. The final stitches make up the embroidery design.

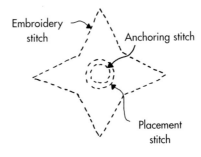

Embroidery stitch

Anchoring stitch

Placement stitch

Use a thread color that coordinates with the fabric for the placement stitches (if the mirror slips a little during the anchor stitching, the placement stitching will not be as obvious).

Each segment of the design has a color stop assigned to it. Choose the same thread colors as indicated, or use one thread color for positioning, and color-coordinating threads for the rest of the design.

## Shisha Designs

Some designs do not include an anchoring stitch or may not be digitized specially for shisha. In this case, stitch the design in its entirety, then use permanent fabric glue to attach the shisha to the fabric. Allow the glue to dry thoroughly before continuing with any additional decorative or garment construction stitching. Machine or hand-tack the outer edge of the rayon circlet in place: just a few stitches at the quarter points of each is adequate.

*Stitched at quarter points*

*Stitched all around*

*(Continued on next page)*

You can glue shisha in place even if the design includes anchoring stitches. Complete the embroidery, glue the shisha, then hand-tack the outer circlet onto the fabric. The finished appearance is slightly different.

*Shisha glued and anchored.*

*Embroidery stitched first and Shisha glued in place over embroidery.*

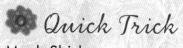

### Quick Trick
#### Mock Shisha
Use an embroidery design with fill stitches in the center to mimic the mirror effect. Use a metallic or glittery thread where the shisha would go.

*Embroidery designs: Sue Lord*

## SMOKING

### Follow this Thread

See pages 43–53 for a visual guide to decorative stitches.
See pages 68–77 for threads.
See pages 84–88 for stabilizers and toppers.

## Smocking by Machine

*Deborah Yedziniak*

*If you think smocking is too time-consuming, you'll love this easier and faster machine method. Use your sewing machine to pleat fabric, then use decorative machine stitches over the pleats. Use a pleating machine for even faster results.*

### Fabric
Cotton and polyester/cotton blend fabrics are the best choices for smocked projects because they make the neatest pleats. They're also easy to care for and comfortable to wear. Quilting cottons offer a great variety of colors and prints.

Because the smocking stitches are the decorative focus, select either a solid color or a small print without a lot of contrast. The featured dress incorporates a band of solid fabric for a smocked insert because the printed fabric in the body of the garment would overpower the smocking stitches. Prewash the fabric before cutting.

### Needle and Thread
A 90/14 embroidery needle works well with most machine embroidery threads and the thickness of the pleated fabric. Most machine embroidery threads come in a 40-weight. Try some of the heavier 30-weight threads, as well as

*See page 16 for dress.*

12-weight cotton threads. Experiment with other decorative threads to find the look you like best:

- Rayon threads give a lovely sheen.

- Polyester threads are colorfast and may be more durable with repeated washings.

- Cotton threads look more like hand-embroidery floss.

- Metallic threads add sparkle and a dressy look to the stitching.

### Presser Foot
Use a clear or an open-toe appliqué foot when stitching. These feet allow better visibility while sewing rows of decorative stitching.

### Pattern
When making smocked garments, use a pattern that's designed for hand or machine smocking.

### Pleating
Use one of the following methods to pleat the fabric for smocking. Use a contrasting quilting thread for the pleating—these threads are also the guidelines for the decorative machine stitching, and contrasting thread will be easier to follow.

The first and last rows of pleating threads are generally used to hold the pleats and keep them neatly in position at the seam allowance while attaching the pleated fabric to another garment piece. Decide how many rows of decorative stitching you want, then pleat an additional two rows.

There should be a guide (sometimes called a pleating guide) included in your garment pattern that will help you determine how much the pleated fabric needs to be pulled in to fit the pattern piece. When pleating the fabric, use long thread lengths (measure the pleating guide and add 10") to allow the pleated fabric to expand to fit the pleating guide.

### Pleater Machine

A smocking pleater quickly makes the neatest pleats. Follow the machine's directions to pleat the fabric.

### Hand Pleating

Commercial patterns usually come with an iron-on dot transfer to use when pleating by hand. Follow the pattern guidesheet to transfer the dots to the fabric and pleat by hand.

### Gathering

For smocking/heirloom patterns that don't have iron-on dot transfers included, hand-stitch even rows of running stitches. Place each row about ⅜" apart and try to line up the stitches as much as possible for even pleats. Pull up the threads to gather the fabric into pleats.

### Sewing Machine Pleating

"Pleat" the fabric by machine-sewing rows of long basting or gathering stitches. Stitch the rows ⅜" apart, then pull the bobbin threads to gather the fabric. At each end of the pleated fabric, gather all the thread ends and tie them into a knot at the thread ends.

## Stabilizing the Pleats

If there is a pleating guide with the pattern, carefully expand the pleated fabric to fit. Keep 1" of the fabric flat at both ends to eliminate bulk in the seam allowances. Try to keep the pleats straight and evenly spaced; run a comb or hair pick through the pleats to help position them neatly.

Cut a strip of fusible, lightweight woven interfacing the size of the pleating guide. Carefully fuse the interfacing to the underside of the pleated fabric to avoid distorting the pleats. This stabilizes the pleated fabric and keeps the pleats from shifting while sewing. The soft fusible interfacing will remain on the fabric after construction.

If you don't want the added interfacing layer, use a spray adhesive to apply water-soluble stabilizer to the wrong side of the pleated fabric. Wash away the stabilizer after the decorative stitching is done.

## Decorative Stitching

Practice different stitch combinations on plain fabric before sewing on the pleated fabric. Create a design by stitching down the center of the fabric strip, then working out to both sides.

The most effective stitches are tri-motion straight, zigzag, and decorative stitches, such as cross and feather stitches. These stitches are repetitive and show up better on the pleated fabric. Experiment with the stitches and adjust the stitch length and width to get the best result.

Some machines have built-in smocking stitches; other machines allow groups of stitches to be programmed into the memory to imitate the cable and wave stitches of hand smocking. When you're satisfied with your stitch combination and ready to sew, position the pleated fabric under the presser foot so the pleats run horizontally.

Sew the decorative stitching across the pleats from one end of the pleated fabric to the other, using the pleating threads as guidelines. Stitch along the threads or in between them.

The pleating threads will be removed once the decorative stitches are sewn, and they'll be easier to remove if the stitching isn't done directly on top of them. Sew each row of stitching in the same direction as the first.

(Continued on next page)

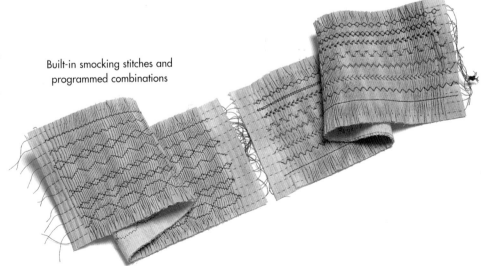

Built-in decorative stitching

Built-in smocking stitches and programmed combinations

## Embroidery Embellishment

With an embroidery machine you can add additional embellishment by embroidering a motif over the decorative or straight smocking stitches. Choose an embroidery motif that complements the print, or create a theme.

If possible, hoop the pleated fabric. If it's too bulky for the hoop, hoop a piece of stabilizer and use spray adhesive to secure the pleated fabric to the stabilizer. Use your machine's in-hoop basting option (if available) to secure the fabric to the stabilizer.

Select a relatively dense embroidery design so the stitches will cover the pleats well. Take care when selecting thread colors because the smocking stitches will shadow through if they're darker than the embroidery threads. To keep the embroidery stitches from sinking into the pleats, add water-soluble stabilizer as a topper over the pleats.

*Embroidery designs: Husqvarna Viking, Disk #44*

### Tip

## Smocking for Embroidery

An ordinary straight stitch doesn't show up well on pleated fabric. However, a straight stitch sewn in a thread color to match the fabric is an effective way to do a machine version of the "back smocking" done in hand smocking. Back smocking subtly holds the fabric pleats together.

### Follow this Thread

See page 44 for bartack stitches. See pages 161–162 another approach to smocking.

## Mock Smocking

### Elizabeth Tisinger

*Create a quick smocked look by using bartacks or a narrow zigzag on a sewing machine.*

Mark a grid on the backside of the fabric. The type of fabric and the size of the grid will determine the final look of the "smocking." A good starting point for a sample is to draw five horizontal lines ⅞" apart, and sixteen vertical lines ¾" apart. Mark a dot at each intersection.

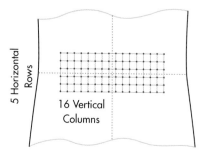

Set up the machine for either a narrow bartack, or a tight narrow zigzag stitch. Fold the fabric right sides together and pin aligning the dots in the first and second vertical rows. Stitch a bartack or zigzag on the second dot. Move to the fourth dot and stitch a bartack or zigzag. Clip the threads.

Open up the fabric and match the dots in the second and third vertical rows. This time stitch on the first, third, and fifth dots being careful not to catch the first fold in the stitching. Clip the threads.

Continue in this manner, opening and refolding the fabric, and alternately stitching the second and fourth dots and the first, third, and fifth dots.

The wrong side of the fabric will look like a basket weave, and the right side of the fabric will form pleated diamond shapes.

Experiment with the size and spacing of the grid to get the look you like. Be sure to plan ahead and allow extra fabric when using this technique.

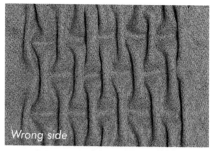

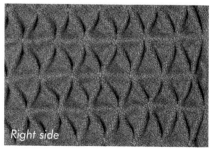

# SURFACE STITCHING

Follow this Thread

See pages 80–82 for needles.
See pages 68–77 for threads.

## Stitching on the Surface

### Wendy Hill

*With surface stitching, you can transform any piece of fabric into art, then use it to make part or all of a quilt, garment, or any other special project. Select your thread colors to coordinate or contrast, downplay differences or blend tones, or simply to unify a selection of fabrics.*

## Thread Colors

Selecting threads for surface stitching is every bit as important as the stitching itself. Look for the predominant colors in your selected fabrics, and pick spools of these colors. Also pick threads that match the accent colors in the fabric (no matter how small the areas), and add them to the collection. Sort the thread into piles of color families (reds, purples, blues, et cetera), then arrange each color group from light to dark.

Next look for thread colors that can form a link between color families, like a pile of teals or aquas that links blues and greens. If a large number of link threads form their own color family cluster them into their own pile.

For your final selection, take one spool of thread at a time from each pile until you have a good distribution of lights and darks that total the number of spools you need. For a small project you may have 10 different threads. For a large project with many different fabrics, don't be surprised if you have 40 different threads.

Use an assortment of texture and size as well as colors: Rayons, metallics, and variegated threads add variety and sparkle, as do different weights of threads. Threads that will easily go through the needle will range from a fine sewing thread (80-weight) to medium (30-weight) decorative thread. Use the appropriate needle for the type and size thread.

*(Continued on next page)*

## Thread Order

Surface stitching may appear to be random, but there is method behind all the stitching madness. Your primary goal is even density and distribution of color and texture, so it's important to have a plan to distribute the colors evenly across the surface. First, choose a method to determine the order in which you'll use the different threads:

- **Method 1.** Use an even mix of colors right from the start. Select one thread at a time from each color family, and add a layer of stitching with that thread. Alternating color families results in an even blend of colors with high texture.

- **Method 2.** Sort your threads by contrast, not color: those that contrast least with the fabrics, those that offer medium contrast with the fabrics, and those that create the most contrast. Begin stitching with the low contrast, then the medium-contrast, and finally the high-contrast threads. This gives you high texture and shows off the final few layers of threads.

- **Method 3.** Sort threads by contrast as above, but reverse the sewing order: Begin with the most contrast, and end with the lowest contrast. The difference is subtle, but the high texture shows more colors through the mix.

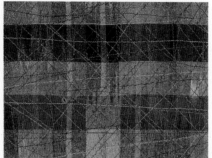
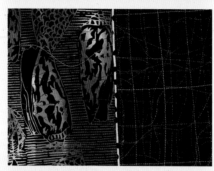
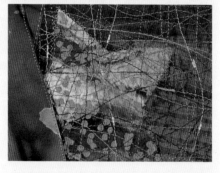

## Stitching Tips

- For uniformity, each color should be evenly spread over the entire piece of fabric. If, for example, you have only one small spool of pink, use a stitch style with widely separated lines so you evenly stitch the fabric.

  Keep stitched lines of the same color slightly apart—avoid "clumps" of similar colors too close together.

- It's actually possible to have so much stitching that the fabric is no longer visible, and the thread layers look cloudy. Even densely stitched fabric has spaces at least ⅜" square between lines of thread (and it's fine to have larger spaces as well).

- Areas with less stitching will shrink differently; for uniform shrinking, start with uniform stitching. If you're not sure, throw the piece into the washer and dryer. Sparse areas and bald spots show up as obvious areas of little or no crinkle. If necessary, press the piece flat, add more stitching where needed, and wash and dry again until you are satisfied with the result.

*(Continued on page 232)*

## Stitch Style

There are several different stitch styles to choose from, and you can use them alone or in any combination to fill your fabric. All are sewn with a straight stitch; use either a regular or walking foot, and keep your feed dogs up.

### Pivot

These rows of connected Vs use more thread and are more time consuming than other stitch styles. The results make up for that with density, texture, and visibility, especially when sewn with high-contrast color or heavyweight thread.

To pivot stitch, stitch forward, then in reverse, pivoting the fabric so you head at a slightly different angle. The stitching lines may be straight or wavy between pivot points.

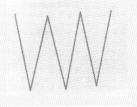

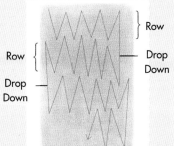

When you complete a row of pivots, drop down along the edge of the fabric and sew another row of pivot points underneath.

### Crosshatch

Sew parallel lines that intersect each other at approximately right angles—but don't measure. The stitched lines can be straight or wavy; they can go straight up and down or diagonally on the fabric surface. Crosshatching uses less thread than pivot stitching, and it's easier to control the stitching density.

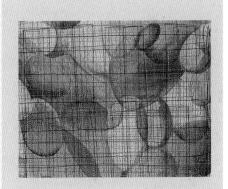

### Wavy

Place your hands at about ten o'clock and two o'clock on the fabric surface, almost as if you were holding the steering wheel of a car. While sewing slowly, guide the fabric in a slight back-and-forth motion.

Almost anything goes with wavy stitching lines: separate lines, lines that cross, tight curves, or loose, meandering curves.

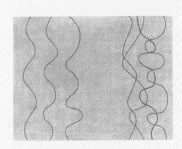

*(Continued on next page)*

## Circular

This "loop-de-loop" stitch is usually a free-motion technique, but it's actually possible to turn your fabric around with the feed dogs up and using a regular or walking presser foot. The circular lines, used alone or in combination with other stitching, add a fun, loopy texture. This works best when you're working on a relatively small piece; larger ones are difficult to squeeze through the space between the needle and the machine arm. Circular stitching takes some practice, so start sewing slowly.

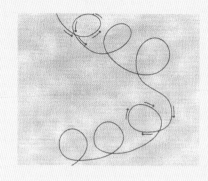 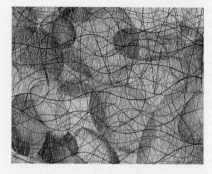

Circular stitching is easiest to use after the surface has already been textured with another stitch.

## Improvisational

Make it up as you go along. Use some or all of the above stitches, and throw in a little whimsy for good measure. A good time to become improvisational is after you've already done several layers of stitching. Zip around to fill in bare spots—sew any style, shape, or pattern that suits your fancy.

 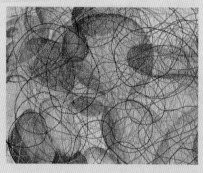

## Straight Stitch Variations

The straight stitch is anything but rigid—use the variety of features your machine offers to dress up surface stitching. Remember that basic straight stitches look every bit as good as a variety of straight stitches, so don't feel you have to get fancy.

- Stitch length. Adjust the length from very short to very long to change the look of your surface stitching.

- Thread thickness. Thicker thread makes a thicker line; thinner thread makes a thinner line. Or, run two contrasting threads through one needle.

- Thread color. Variegated thread changes color along the length of the thread, repeating the color pattern over and over, adding complexity and color with no extra effort.

- Specialty stitches. Avoid recognizable embroidery stitches; instead, play with your machine's "utility stitches." Some of these stitches sew forward and backward in some combination to make a thick, flexible, strong-looking straight stitch.

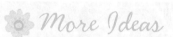
### More Ideas

- Use your surface-stitched fabric to make garments like vests and quilted jackets.

- Layer and baste a quilt top, batting, and backing, then surface-stitch it.

- Make reversible fabric by basting fabrics together, then surface stitching with different color threads in the top and bobbin.

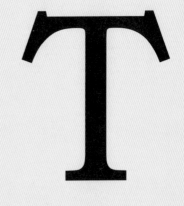

# TASSELS

 **Follow this Thread**

See pages 68–77 for threads.
See page 210 for serger chain tassels.

## Making Tassels

### *Carol Zentgraf*

*Making tassels is a great way to use thread and trim that are leftover or might not otherwise be usable.*

Tassels can be made from a wide variety of materials, including embroidery floss, perle cotton, decorative threads, cording, fringe, and ribbon. Tassels can be topped by decorative resin finials (sometimes referred to as toppers) especially made for tassels or by wood candle cups with a hole drilled in the base.

## Twisted Hanging Cord

Use 8" to 2 yards of purchased or twisted-floss cording, depending on the tassel style and whether it will have a hanging loop only, or a loop combined with a wrapped top. To make twisted-floss hanging cord, cut several embroidery floss (or other thread or cording) strands that are three to four times the desired finished cord length.

*Tassel with finial*   *Basic wrapped tassel*

Hold the strands together with the ends even, and tie them into an overhand knot close to one end. Hold the knot and twist the strands together tightly in a clockwise motion until they begin to kink. Bring the free end to the knotted end, allowing the two halves to twist together; knot the ends to secure. See page 210 for making twisted cord using a sewing machine.

## Wrapped-thread Tassel

Cut a piece of cardboard to the desired finished tassel length. Wrap embroidery floss, thread, or trim around the cardboard to the desired thickness. Insert a hanging cord under the wrapped floss at the cardboard upper edge.

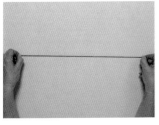  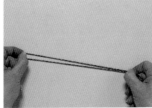  

*Making twisted cord*

*(Continued on next page)*

Slide the loops off the cardboard. Determine the desired tassel head size. Use floss, thread, or trim and wrap tightly around the tassel.

Use a blunt-tip needle or scissors to push the end up under the wrap. Cut the tassel ends or leave them looped.

## Tassel with Finial

Plan for a basic tassel with a longer hanging loop to allow for the finial height. If desired, glue additional trim such as pompom or tassel fringe around the tassel head edge before inserting it in the finial. Glue the tassel into the finial along the finial lower edge, pulling the cord through the hole in the top. Paint the finial with acrylic paints and varnish, or cover it by gluing on cording or fabric. If desired, glue trim to the finial lower edge.

### Mix and Match

For variety, mix different types and colors of thread, floss, or other materials when making tassels.

Box with tassel by Lynn Koolish.

# TRAPUNTO

### Follow this Thread

See pages 68–77 for threads.
See page 55 for darning feet.
See pages 152–158 for free-motion stitching and quilting.

## Trapunto by Machine

### Hari Walner

*Great for quilts, garments, and home décor, use trapunto as an accent or the main design element.*

For this technique thick polyester batting creates the raised designs, while thin cotton or cotton-blend batting is used for quilting. The key to this technique is the water-soluble thread used to define the trapunto designs.

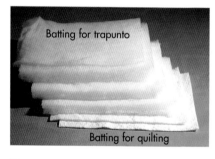

Batting for trapunto

Batting for quilting

## Trapunto Design

Place fabric on top of the trapunto design of your choice, and use a water-soluble marker to trace the design onto the right side of the fabric. Pin the thick polyester batting underneath the marked design, making sure it is at least as large as the design area. (You do not use a backing at this time.)

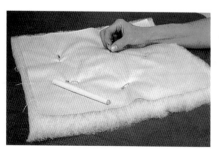

Thread the sewing machine needle with water-soluble thread, and fill the bobbin with regular white thread. Drop or cover the feed dogs. Attach a darning foot.

Free-motion stitch ⅟₁₆" inside the outline of the design. If the polyester batting is very thick, you might want to stitch further inside the outline. Stitching right inside the outline will result in very good definition of the finished design.

Turn the fabric over. With blunt scissors, trim away the batting that is outside the motif. Clip close to the stitched line, but don't be overly picky—stitching inside the outline of the design allows room to trim while keeping the batting inside the design.

## Quilting

Layer the completed trapunto with cotton batting and backing. Baste the layers together.

Rethread the machine with quilting thread instead of the water-soluble thread, and quilt by stitching directly on the design lines. Once the water-soluble stitches are gone, it will look fine.

Add background quilting in areas surrounding the motif to make the motif stand out even more.

## Finishing

Complete all your quilting, and bind (if making a quilt). Immerse the quilted fabric in clear, tepid water. Let it soak for 1 to 2 minutes, and swish it around by hand for a few seconds. All the water-soluble thread will dissolve and any water-soluble markings will disappear as well. Dry flat, and block into shape if necessary.

# TUCKS

 Follow this Thread

See pages 80–82 for needles.
See pages 181 and 185–186 for more on pintucks.

## Terrific Tucks

### Peggy Bendel

*There are an unlimited number of design possibilities when you work with the many different types of tucks.*

A basic tuck is made by folding fabric and straight stitching an even distance from the fold.

## Types of Tucks

### Engineered Tucks

Use the fabric design, such as stripes or the lines of a plaid, as a guide for the folds. This is an easy way to emphasize one of the fabric colors and add custom detail.

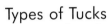

### Released Tucks

Add nice detail to a bodice front, skirt waistline, or sleeve cap. Instead of sewing from seam to seam or edge to edge, release the tuck for an effect similar to gathers, but with a more tailored look.

*Fantasy* (detail) by Lynn Koolish.
See page 22 for quilt.

### Lattice Tucks

Sew tucks on the lengthwise grain, then crisscross them with tucks sewn on the crosswise grain. This is especially effective with pintucks. Attach a quilting/edge guide bar to the presser foot shaft as a spacing guide to sew the tucks without measuring and marking the fabric. Sew the crosswise grain tucks at a slower speed to keep them uniform.

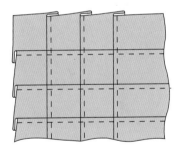

### Bias-effect Tucks

This is actually a kind of an optical illusion. Sew the tucks on the straight grain, then position the pattern section at a 45° angle to the tucks when you cut out your garment pieces.

*(Continued on next page)*

### Diamond Tucks

These tucks resemble smocking and are made from rows of small tucks ⅛" to ¼" deep, spaced ¾" to 1" apart, depending upon the fabric thickness. To form the diamond design, pinch two tucks together and sew across them, staggering the pinches in alternate rows. Use tweezers to pinch together the tucks as you stitch across them.

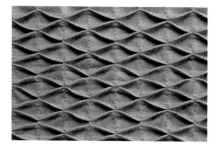

### Twisted Tucks

Fold a series of tucks first one way, then the opposite way, as you stitch across them.

### Bias Tucks

*Lois Ericson*

For a different take on tucks, try sewing them on the bias. Tucks ½" to ¾" deep work well for most fabric weights; deeper tucks work well on heavier fabrics. Test on fabric scraps to find a tuck depth that adds interest, but not bulk.

Working with a vertical or horizontal patterned fabric makes it easy to keep the tucks on the true 45° bias; otherwise, measure and mark the fabric carefully.

To create the tucks shown below: Before fabric is cut out for a project, create yardage by folding it right sides together, pinning, and stitching an even distance from the fold line.

Randomly leave part of the tucks unstitched, backstitching at each end to secure the openings. Spacing between the tucks, tuck depth, and the number and size of the openings is your choice and should be determined in the testing process.

When the yardage is tucked, press all the tucks down, so the openings are up, creating mini-pockets. Use yardage for garments, home décor, or quilt projects.

*Bias tucks with random openings*

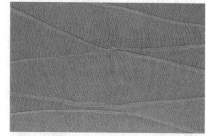

*Stitch narrow, curvy tucks from either the right or wrong side of the fabric.*

*Stitch symmetrical tucks in two directions.*

*Stitch random tucks in varying directions and widths.*

*Use decorative stitches to make tucks.*

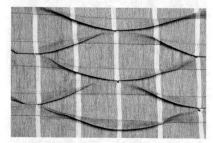

*Press tucks toward each other and stitch together.*

Flower embroidery is a built-in design from the Singer Quantum XL-1000.

Daisy embroidery design: Husqvarna Viking #36.

See pages 84–88 for stabilizers and toppers.
See page 134 for references to embroidery basics.

## Embroidered Tucks

### Elizabeth Tisinger

*What better way to showcase both embroidery and decorative tucks?*

1. Stitch tucks as desired.

2. Mark the position of the embroidery designs along the tucks.

3. Stabilize and hoop the fabric.

To prevent the tucks from being caught by the needle or embroidery foot, place a water-soluble topper over the hooped fabric. Secure it in place with basting stitches or a temporary spray adhesive (sprayed onto the topper, not the fabric).

4. Stitch the design, re-hoop as needed until all the desired embroideries are complete.

5. Remove the stabilizer and topper. Lay the embroidered fabric wrong side up over a towel and press the embroideries to set the stitches.

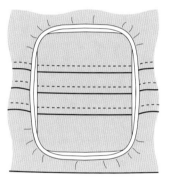

Stabilize and hoop the fabric.

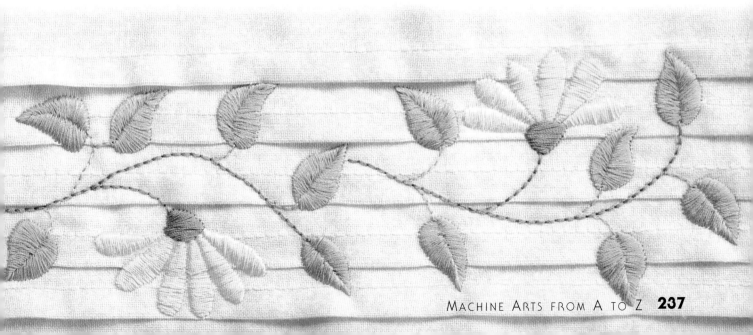

# U

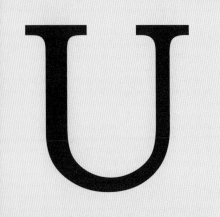

## UNDERLAY STITCHING

Follow this Thread

See page 134 for references to embroidery basics.

## Understanding Underlay Stitches

**Christy Burcham**

*Underlay stitches beneath a design are one of the most essential yet least understood aspects of embroidery. Underlay stitches form the foundation of a design and are stitched before the fill, satin, or other stitches.*

Underlay stitches can ensure successful embroidery results by providing cleaner satin stitches, more precise outlines, and less fabric puckering. Proper underlay stitches included in a design indicate the mark of truly professional digitizing. Whether digitizing your own designs or using designs digitized from another source, it is important to understand the concept of using underlay stitches in a design.

## Why Underlay Stitches?

Underlay stitches will help to improve your embroidery quality in many ways. First, the stitches secure the fabric to the stabilizer, which prevents the layers from shifting and reduces fabric puckering around a design. (This is particularly important when embroidering on knit fabrics, which distort easily.) Second, underlay stitches keep the fabric in its original hooped position and prevent design outlines from "drifting." In addition, underlay stitches produce a layer of stitches to help keep fill stitches from sinking into the nap or pile of the fabric.

## Zigzag

Used mostly on lettering, satin stitching, and appliqué, the zigzag can be single or three step, depending on the width of the area, and can be included with a running stitch on both sides encasing the zigzag stitches.

## Edge Runs

A single stitch just inside the edge of the design, used mainly in lettering and satin stitching. It gives the edges of the satin stitching a consistent edge. Used alone, it may not support the design; it is used in combination with a step underlay to give the fill a smooth edge.

## Step

This is the most common—and most useful—form of underlay. The stitches loosely fill the area to be embroidered. The actual stitch spacing will vary depending on the amount of fill stitching that will go on top of it, and the stitch angle is usually perpendicular to the fill stitches. This perpendicular stitching can reduce the pull of the fabric.

## Comparing Samples

Discover why designs look better with underlay stitches by comparing samples stitched with and without underlay stitches on a variety of fabrics.

### Cotton Fabric

While both designs use the same stabilizing technique, the one with no underlay stitching has puckering around it. Also notice the hoop tracings around the outside of the design. On both samples, the blue line was traced before the stitching was done, and the red line was traced after the stitching was done. The farther apart the lines, the more shifting occurred. Notice that with no underlay stitching, the fabric is pulled much more.

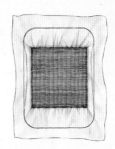

No underlay stitching was used.

Same design with underlay stitching.

### Knit Fabric

The fabric bunches and bubbles around the fill when there is no underlay stitching, as opposed to the smooth fabric around the design with underlay stitching.

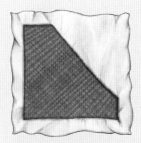

Knit design with no underlay stitching.

Knit design with underlay stitching.

### Pile Fabric

Underlay stitching is particularly important on fabrics with a pile (or nap), such as terry cloth. The underlay stitching "holds down" the pile of the fabric, and that keeps the fill stitching from sinking into the pile. On fabrics with a very high pile, even underlay stitching will not completely hold down the nap. Use a water-soluble topper (see pages 87–88) for best results.

Pile fabric without underlay stitching.

Pile fabric with underlay stitching.

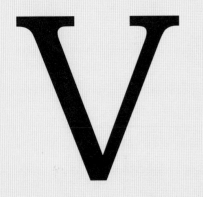

# V

*Vintage stitching, also known as heirloom stitching, uses a variety of stitches and techniques to capture the look of the detailed and delicate hand-stitched items that were meant to be used lightly and handed down from generation to generation.*

*Many of the old techniques can be reproduced using a sewing machine, or even a serger.*

Many built-in machine stitches are perfect for vintage stitching. (See pages 43–53.)

Embroidered or satin stitched, decorative edges provide a fine finish to your vintage project. (See pages 131–133.)

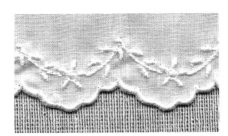

Entredeux is the perfect way to join lace to lace, or lace to fabric. (See page 145.)

Fagoting (or bridge stitching) is another way to join laces, trims, and fabrics, adding another dimension and texture. (See pages 115–116.)

In vintage stitching, gathering is used in many ways: to create ruffles, puffed insets, shirring, and other surface effects. (See page 159.)

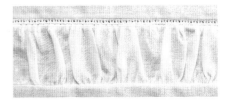

Hemstitching using a wing needle, can be used to create texture, make lacy appliqués, topstitch, or attach lace. (See page 160.)

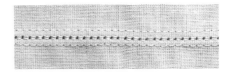

Nothing says vintage like lace. Make your own using embroidery designs (see pages 167–169), free-motion stitching (see pages 169–171), or using a serger (see page 219).

Choose your spacing, and let pintucks add another dimension. Corded pintucks, make an even more pronounced statement. (See pages 185–186).

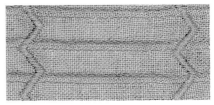

Scallops add a gentle curve and soft look to vintage stitching. (See pages 203–204.)

# WASTE NOT

Follow this Thread

See pages 233–234 for using thread to make tassels.
See page 172 for using thread to make thread and ribbon scarves.
See pages 169–171 for using thread to make thread lace.
See pages 149–150 and 220–221 for more ways to create textured fabric.
See page 206 for references to serger basics.

## Don't Throw That Fabric Away

**Stephanie Corina Goddard**

*Is the color just too "last year?" Perhaps it was a gift, or your taste has changed. Before disposing of a deplorable fabric that's been doing nothing but taking up space, consider masking its shortcomings or finding the right use for it.*

## Color Calamities

Eliminate the most offending colors or motifs in a fabric:

- Cut out the undesirable parts of the fabric, then sew the remainder back together.

- Decoratively serge the outside seams, emphasizing a color in the print that you like.

- Appliqué something over the offending areas. (See pages 106–110 for appliqué basics.) Or use it as a base for reverse appliqué.

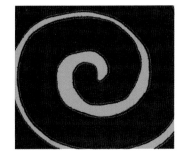

- Use quilting techniques to combine it with other fabrics. Scrap quilters know that when many fabrics are used in a project, it's not necessary to be in love with all of them.

- Try crazy-patch foundation piecing or strip-pieced bargello, surrounding the offending fabric with plenty of eye-pleasing companions.

- A wild print may be less offensive in small quantities. Seminole-style piecing where only narrow slivers of each fabric show, is particularly well-suited to creative garments.

- Use it in chenille. If the fabric has any polyester in the weave it won't "bloom," but it can be used as the base for other chenille-able fabrics. 100% natural fibers such as cotton, rayon, silk, and linen are suitable for layering and slashing. For best results, choose fabrics that have good color saturation through to the wrong side. (See page 122–124 for chenille.)

*(Continued on next page)*

- Use it to line a garment. Seldom seen, a fabric that's hard on the eyes enjoys a hidden life—peeking out from an open jacket or pocket.

- Turn it over. Does the wrong side look better? Only you will ever know there was an alternative.

## Cheap Tricks

The color's nice, but it looks cheap. Camouflage the "bargain bin" look with one of these techniques.

- Use matching or decorative threads for tucking or scrunching the fabric.

- Stitch multiple tuck rows, then anchor them down with perpendicular straight stitching in alternating directions across the tucks. (See pages 235–237 for tucks.)

- Machine-baste across the fabric width, or scrunch the fabric by hand, drawing up the fabric into slight gathers. Press lightweight fusible interfacing to the fabric wrong side, or pin it to a muslin base, then stitch over it to flatten.

- Embellish the surface—heavily. If you have a lot of yardage to cover, choose a utility stitch or decorative machine stitch that sews out fast. Use matching or contrasting thread. (See pages 116–119 for decorative stitches.)

- Use it as a base for surface stitching. (See pages 229–232 for surface stitching.)

- For more impact, couch down heavy decorative threads, yarns, or ribbons. Use invisible monofilament thread in the needle and matching thread in the bobbin. Use a basic zigzag or blindhem stitch and a presser foot designed to hold stranded fibers in place. Depending on the fabric and the desired

effect, it may be neces-sary to use a stabilizer under the fabric. (See page 126 for couching.)

- Weave it. Thread the serger loopers with decorative threads, and adjust for a compact stitch length. Cut the fabric into narrow strips and serge-finish the cut edges. On a cardboard or padded surface, lay fusible interfacing with the adhesive side up. Pin the serged strips vertically, side by side, over the interfacing, covering the desired area. Weave strips horizontally and pin securely. Press to fuse the strips to the interfacing. (See page 206 for references to serger basics.)

- Re-weave it. If the fabric has a loose weave, draw out some of the threads and replace them with ⅛"-wide ribbon, decorative thread, or yarn.

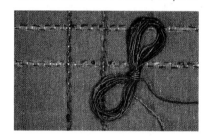

- Texturize it. Let the sewing machine do the work: use matching or contrasting threads with twin needles. Make sure the throat plate opening can accommodate the twin needle's extra width, and experiment with shallow zigzag or serpentine stitches. (See pages 180–181 for twin needle techniques.)

- Hand-wind elastic thread onto a bobbin, and use thread that matches the fabric in the needle. A simple straight stitch is all that's needed to "smock" the fabric. (See pages 161–162 and 226–228 for smocking.)

- Overlay it with a sheer fabric. Use that less-than-desirable piece as a separate underlayer for a sheer garment.

- Prior to garment construction, place sheer fabric over the offending fabric, and stitch through both layers in a grid pattern to create a new two-layer fabric.

- For maximum impact, consider adding batting and lining to the sandwich to make a unique quilted fabric.

## Flash Factor

Use beautiful fabrics that are too dressy for your lifestyle (or your personality) in one of these ways:

- Use it in small amounts: Make appliqués for a jean jacket, cover buttons, or make a shell to wear under a conservative suit. Use it for the collar and cuffs of a winter coat.

- Turn it into an accessory, like a scarf or purse.

- Cheer up a friend (or yourself) with a gift tote bag sewn from an outrageously glitzy fabric.

- Make decorations for holidays or special occasions. Lamé, velvet, brocade, and satin are right at home in Valentine-theme appliqués, Christmas stockings, ornaments, wedding banners (for indoor use), wall hangings, or gift bags.

- Incorporate it into your décor. If the fabric is washable, topstitch narrow serged strips onto bath towels, placemats, or table runners. If it's not washable, integrate it into throw pillows or window treatments, like valances or tie-backs.

# XTRA TIPS FOR SERGING

Follow this Thread

See pages 206–223 for serging.

## Making Uniform Stitches

*Gail Brown*

Remember that serging on the lengthwise or crosswise fabric grain usually allows for the most uniform stitches. When serging off-grain, the stitches aren't as consistent, threads react differently, and fibers may show through the stitches. To prevent this, recut the edge or stabilize the underside with a lightweight fusible interfacing or another layer of lightweight fabric. You could also serge over a strip of water-soluble stabilizer placed on top of the fabric. Tear away excess stabilizer after serging.

## Knife Safety

*Gail Brown*

Because the knives cut the fabric ⅝" before the needles touch the fabric, watch the knives instead of the needles, especially when serging curves or inner corners.

## Correct Tensions

*April Dunn*

Leave the knives engaged when adjusting the tension for a decorative stitch, such as a flatlock. After the correct stitches are formed, disengage the cutter if needed for your technique. The stitches are based on where the stitches lock or roll on the fabric edge so it's important to have a true fabric edge to judge correct tensions.

## Multiple Bobbins

*Cindy Kacynski*

Keep dozens of bobbins on hand. Then, when you purchase thread, buy two spools. Use one to thread the sewing machine and the other to wind bobbins, including three to five bobbins for the serger. Bobbins hold just the right amount of thread for serging most single-item projects and you'll waste no time finding a good color match.

## Secure Thread Tails

*Cindy Kacynski*

To quickly and easily secure serged thread tails, simply fold the tail back on to the serged seam allowance. Using matching thread, zigzag it in place for 1". Clip the excess.

## Rip Out Serged Edge

*Gail Brown*

To easily rip out a serged edge, simply pull out the thread chain. Find the shortest thread(s) in the chain (needle[s] in a balanced stitch and lower looper in a 3-thread flatlock) and pull that thread from the chain. The other threads will simply fall away. For a rolled edge, just trim the serged edge.

## Prevent Thread Breakage

*Cindy Kacynski*

Always glance at your thread paths before beginning to serge (even if you've stepped away from your serger for a moment). Make sure the threads are engaged in the tensions and placed properly through all guides. This step can prevent threads from breaking or jamming and save lots of re-threading time.

*(Continued on next page)*

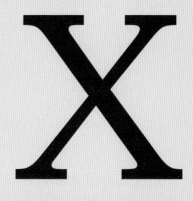

## Threads Hanging Off Edge

**Gail Brown**

If looper threads hang off the edge when serging knits or bias-cut fabric and tightening the looper tensions doesn't solve the problem, the cause is fabric stretching within the stitch. Adjust the differential feed to a slightly positive setting. This prevents the fabric from stretching and fills the stitch.

## Serger Appliqué

**Mary Mulari**

To use the serger for appliqué, fuse lightweight interfacing to the back of straight or gently curved fabric pieces. Using fusible thread in the lower looper and regular serger threads in the needles and upper looper, serge the edges. Serge pieces right side up, dab seam sealant on the thread ends, and cut or tuck the ends under the appliqué. Fuse the appliqués to the garment and sew through the serged edges to permanently attach them.

## Serging Points

**Cindy Cummins**

To serge points on lightweight, single layer fabrics and to prevent wrinkling at the corners, stabilize for stitching. Trim the seam allowances and press a square of tear-away fusible stabilizer to the wrong side of the fabric on each corner or point to be finished, with ¼" of the stabilizer extending beyond the raw edge. Serge all edges with a narrow, balanced stitch or roll edge. Gently tear away the stabilizer from the corners. This technique works for fine napkins or any project where perfect points or corners are needed.

## 5 Tips for Serging with Decorative Threads

**Alison Tucek**

1. Warm up first: Make sure your serger is functioning perfectly with a basic 3-thread overlock before threading with decorative threads. This insures the knives, needles, stitch fingers, and tension discs are in good shape.

2. Use the flow test: Pull each thread one-by-one through the threading passages. Have the tensions engaged and at the factory setting for this test. When adjusted properly, the looper threads will flow easily and the needle thread will hardly budge. Then you can adjust for special threads.

3. Two passes are better than one: Sometimes the fabric color or texture peeks through the stitches or the thread coverage looks wimpy. Serge as usual, then serge again on top. Disengage the knife for the second pass.

4. Blend color, texture, and sparkle: Have fun blending your own thread combinations. Thread multi-strands through the loopers. There are great cradles on the market; place on on the serger thread spindle and thread multiple strands at once.

5. Make extra: As long as you have your beautiful threads in the serger, why not chain off extra yards for later use as trims, tassels, and couching.

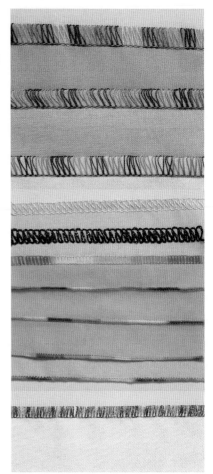

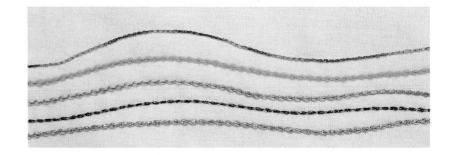

## YARN

🧵 Follow this Thread

See page 126 for couching.
See page 246 for bobbinwork using yarn.

## Couching with Yarn

*Linda Griepentrog*

*Couch yarn onto quilts, garments, and other projects for added texture and dimension.*

Drop the feed dogs for free-motion stitching and thread the machine with monofilament thread. Practice stitching on a scrap and adjust the tension as needed

### Stitching Techniques

If you couch the yarn too tightly it will lose its dimension and the stitching will show.

For the most inconspicuous look, follow the twist in the yarn as you couch.

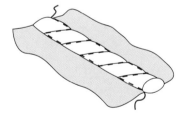

Depending on the yarn thickness, you may want to stitch along the side of the yarn strand and only catch it periodically to avoid flattening it.

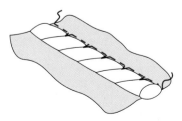

When you reach the end of the yarn strand, stitch in place several times to secure. Firmly anchor the yarn ends before clipping to avoid unraveling.

If you are using lightweight yarn, create a visually stronger line by twisting more than one yarn strand together—either the same or different yarns—before couching.

### Open Shapes

To create open shapes, loop a yarn strand into the correct shape, and lightly couch it down. For added dimension, tack only at the ends, leaving the sides free.

### Solid Shapes

To create solid shapes, coil the yarn into the shape, then stitch it in place.

*(Continued on next page)*

## Flowers

Cut a short piece of yarn, and stitch the end securely where the center of your flower will be. Twist the yarn into a petal-size loop, and stitch over the yarn at the flower center, leaving the petal freestanding. Repeat this procedure, rotating the fabric slightly each time, until you have the desired number of petals.

The number of petals depends on the yarn weight, twist, and desired flower size. For more dimension, continue to add layers of the same or coordinating yarn loops, always anchoring the flower center. To avoid needle breakage, change to a larger needle when making multi-layer flowers.

## Tip

### Fine Finishing

Thread your yarn ends into a needle, pull them to the back of the fabric, and knot them for an invisible finish.

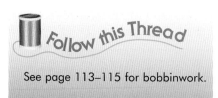
## Follow this Thread

See page 113–115 for bobbinwork.

## Bobbinwork with Yarn

### Helen Saunders

*In addition to couching, yarn can be used for bobbinwork. While yarns with large slubs won't feed through the machine, many, including chenille, will.*

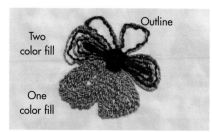

Hand-wind the yarn onto the bobbin. Place the bobbin into the bobbin case, bypassing the tension mechanism.

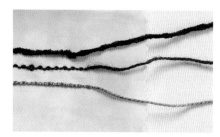

Thread the machine with clear or smoke monofilament thread or thread that matches the background fabric. Stabilize the fabric with fusible interfacing or stabilizer. If you like, you can draw the design you'll be stitching onto the interfacing.

For simple bobbinwork, set the machine to a straight or zigzag stitch, and use either a standard presser foot (for straight stitching) or a darning foot (for free-motion stitching). Sew with the project face down, so the decorative bobbin threads appear on the right side of the fabric. For a more intricate look, try using some of the machine's built-in stitches.

## Tip

### Leftover Yarn?

Odds and ends of leftover yarn are perfect for adding fill and body to thread and ribbon scarves. See page 172 for techniques.

*Bobbinwork examples stitched by Lynn Koolish.*

## ZIGZAG

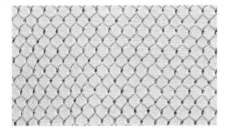

**Follow this Thread**

See pages 106–110 for satin
stitch appliqué.
See pages 201–202 for decorative
satin stitching.

## Sewing Zigzag Stitches

*Sallie J. Russell*

*Many functions once done by the zigzag
now are completed using specialty stitches
or the serger, but the zigzag probably is
still the second most widely used stitch,
surpassed only by the straight stitch.*

## Appliqué

Use the zigzag stitch for satin stitch
appliqué. The length and width of the
stitch depends on the fabric and the
look you want to achieve. Fabrics that
unsravel need a shorter stitch length
than those that don't. (See pages
106–110 for satin stitch appliqué.)

## Hemstitching

Try hemstitching with a wing needle
and a zigzag stitch. Or hemstitch an
entire fabric piece for textured
appliqué on garments or linens.

Using a wing needle and a medium-
width, medium-length zigzag, hemstitch a fabric section slightly larger
than the appliqué motif. Stitching on
the bias grain will result in more
defined holes.

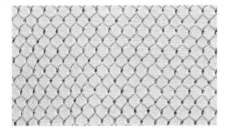

For hemstitched appliqué, place the
hemstitched fabric on the right side of
the garment and a stabilizer under the
area to be appliquéd. Use a marking
pencil to draw the appliqué shape on
the fabric. Straight stitch around the
shape, anchoring it to the garment.
Cut the excess appliqué fabric close to
the stitching.

Satin stitch over the raw edge and
straight stitching to finish the edges.
(See page 160 for more on hemstitching and hemstitch appliqué.)

## Twin and Triple Needles

Zigzag with twin and triple needles to
create interesting shadow effects; try
this with variegated thread.

*(Continued on next page)*

## Picot Edge Finish

Use the zigzag to picot edge finish a soft fabric folded edge. One stitch catches the fabric layers, and the next stitch goes off the fold edge. For a scalloped effect, try tightening the tension. Or, experiment with the stitch width and length for different fabrics.

## Applying Lace and Trim

Use the zigzag to apply lace to lingerie, taking advantage of the built-in stretch factor.

Apply trim or couch yarn or decorative thread to fabric with the zigzag and monofilament thread. For French machine sewing, use a narrow zigzag to apply lace to fabric and lace to lace.

**Quick Trick**

### Quick Shirring

Create shirring by zigzagging over rows of elastic thread.

## Gathering

Gather fabric easily with the aid of a zigzag stitch. Sew slightly inside the seam allowance, and zigzag over topstitching thread, cord, or lightweight string. Be careful not to catch the cord with the needle. Pull on the cord; stitch the gathering in place. Remove the cord.

*Zigzag examples stitched by Elizabeth Tisinger.*

# Suggested Reading

## Books

*250 Continuous Line Designs*, Laura Lee Fritz

*250 More Continuous Line Designs*, Laura Lee Fritz

*3-in-1 Color Tool*, Joen Wolfrom

*All About Quilting,* Quilter's Newsletter Magazine, *Quiltmaker* Magazine, and C&T Publishing

*Art of Fabric Collage, The*, Rosemary Eichorn

*Beautifully Quilted*, Alex Anderson

*Claire Shaeffer's Fabric Sewing Guide*, Claire Shaeffer

*Color Play*, Joen Wolfrom

*Cotton Candy Quilts*, Mary Mashuta

*Creative Serging: the Complete Handbook for Devorative Overlock Sewing*, Pati Palmer

*Decorative Machine Stitching*, Singer Sewing Reference Library

*Dream Sewing Spaces*, Lynette Black

*Embellishments A to Z*, Stephanie Valley

*Embroidery Machine Essentials*, Jeanine Twigg

*Embroidery Machine Essentials Fleece Techniques*, Nancy Cornwell

*Embroidery Machine Essentials: Quilting Techniques*, Linda Turner Griepentrog

*Exploring Machine Trapunto*, Hari Walner

*Fabric Savvy, The Essential Guide for Every Sewer*, Sandra Betzina

*Fast, Fun & Easy Fabric Bowls*, Linda Johansen

*Fine Machine Sewing*, Carol Laflin Ahles

*Free-Stuff for Quilters on the Internet*, Judy Heim & Gloria Hansen

For more information, write for a free catalog:
C&T Publishing, Inc.
P.O. Box 1456
Lafayette, CA 94549
(800) 284-1114
Email: ctinfo@ctpub.com
Website: www.ctpub.com

*Free-Stuff for Stitchers on the Internet*, Judy Heim & Gloria Hansen

*Free-Style Quilts*, Susan Carlson

*Ghost Layers and Color Washes*, Katie Pasquini Masopust

*Heirloom Machine Quilting*, Harriet Hargrave

*Laurel Burch Quilts*, Laurel Burch

*Luscious Landscapes*, Joyce Becker

*Machine Embroidery and More*, Kristen Dibbs

*Mastering Machine Applique*, Harriet Hargrave

*Quilted Garden, The*, Jane Sassaman

*Quilting Back to Front*, Larraine Scouler

*Rag Wool Applique*, Kathy MacMannis

*Ricky Tims' Convergence Quilts*, Ricky Tims

*Rx for Quilters*, Susan Delany Mech

*Secrets for Sucessful Sewing Techniques for Mastering Your Sewing Machine and Serger*, Barbara Weiland

*Serger Secrets*, Mary Griffin

*Sew Much Fun*, Oklahoma Embroidery Supply & Design

*Sewing with Sergers*, Gail Brown and Pati Palmer

*Show Me How to Machine Quilt*, Kathy Sandbach

*Sulky Secrets to Successful Applique*, Joyce Drexler

*Sulky Secrets to Successful Quilting*, Joyce Drexler

*Sulky Secrets to Successful Stabilizing*, Joyce Drexler

*Threadplay with Libby Lehman*, Libby Lehman

*Ultimate Guide to Longarm Machine Quilting, The*, Linda V. Tayor

*Ultimate Serger Answer Guide, The*, Naomi Baker

## Magazines

*Creative Machine Embroidery*

*McCall's Quilting*

*Quilter's Newsletter Magazine*

*Quiltmaker*

*Sew News*

# Resources

There are many excellent sources of materials and information for decorative machine arts. The following companies and individuals provided sample products and information for this book.

All of the websites listed below are excellent sources of information. Please be aware that some of the listed companies sell only to stores and distributors—be sure to check the websites for retail sources.

## THREAD, TOOLS, AND SUPPLIES

**Artfabrik**
www.artfabrik.com
Hand-dyed threads and fabric

**Aurifil Threads**
(Distributed by Tristan Embroidery Supplies, Inc.)
www.tristan.bc.ca
Threads, stabilizer

**American & Efird, Inc.**
www.amefird.com
Threads, YKK Zippers

**Coats & Clark**
www.coatsandclark.com
Threads, zippers, tapes & trims, yarn, crochet threads, hooks, sewing machine needles, embroidery floss

**Gütermann**
www.gutermann.com
Threads, beads, jewelry accessories

**Kreinik**
www.kreinik.com
Threads and thread collections, embroidery kits, embellishments, tools

**Madeira**
www.madeirausa.com
Threads, needles, stabilizers, scissors, accessories, spray adhesives, storage units

**Nancy's Notions**
www.nancysnotions.com

**Nordic Needle**
www.nordicneedle.com
RibbonFloss

**Oklahoma Embroidery Supply & Design, Inc.**
www.embroideryonline.com
Embroidery designs, threads, stabilizers, embroidery accessories, sewing machine needles

**Robison-Anton**
www.robison-anton.com
Threads, prewound bobbins

**Sally Houk**
www.picturetrail.com/sallyhoukexclusives
Ribbons and yarn

**Sulky**
www.sulky.com
Threads, stabilizers, books, Puffy Foam, transfer pens, adhesives, embroidery designs

**Sullivans**
www.sullivans.net
Clothing patterns, tassles, embroidery thread and floss, basting spray, notions, bobbins, crochet/knitting cotton, sewing machine accessories, sewing machine needles, scissors

**Superior Threads**
www.superiorthreads.com
Threads, thread stands, prewound bobbins

**ThreadPRO**
www.threadpro.com
Threads, thread stands, thread lubricant, stabilizers, embroidery designs, sewing machine needles, books

**YLI**
www.ylicorp.com
Threads, silk ribbon, Woolly Nylon

## SEWING MACHINES

**Baby Lock**
www.babylock.com

**Bernina of America**
www.berninausa.com

**Brother**
www.brothersews.com

**Elna**
www.elnausa.com

**Husqvarna Viking**
www.husqvarnaviking.com

**Janome**
www.janome.com

**Pfaff**
www.pfaffusa.com

**Singer**
www.singershop.com

# Embroidery Designs

**Amazing Designs**
www.amazindesigns.com

**Artistic Designs by Sue Box**
www.suebox.com

**Baby Lock**
www.babylock.com

**Bernina of America**
www.berninausa.com

**Brother**
www.brothersews.com

**Cactus Punch**
www.cactuspunch.com

*Creative Machine Embroidery* magazine
www.cmemag.com

**Criswell Embroidery and Designs**
www.k-lace.com

**Dakota Collectibles**
www.dakotacollectibles.com

**Elna**
www.elnausa.com

**Embroidery Resource**
www.embroideryresource.com

**Embroideryarts**
www.embroideryarts.com

**Husqvarna Viking**
www.husqvarnaviking.com

**Janome America**
www.janome.com

**Martha Pullen**
www.marthapullen.com

**Oklahoma Embroidery Supply & Desig.**
www.embroideryonline.com

**Pfaff**
www.pfaffusa.com

**Sew Man Design**
available from: www.embroidery.com

**Singer Sewing Company**
www.singershop.com

**Sue Lord**
www.suelord.com

**Tina's Cross Stitch**
www.tinascrossstitch.com

**Wimpole Street**
www.barrett-house.com

**Zundt Design Ltd**
www.zundtdesign.com

**For quilting supplies:**
Cotton Patch Mail Order
3405 Hall Lane, Dept.CTB
Lafayette, CA 94549
(800) 835-4418
(925) 283-7883
Email:quiltusa@yahoo.com
Website: www.quiltusa.com

# Contributors

# Photo Credits

Photography provided by *Sew News* magazine and *Creative Machine Embroidery* magazine except as noted:

**Joyce Becker**: 33

**Bernina of America**: 40, 42, 56, 59, 61, 63, 96

**Brian Birlauf**: 11, 23, 103

**Brother Industries, Ltd.**: 39, 41, 42, 60, 66

**John Bonath, Maddog Studio**: 14, 114 (bottom left); 155 (left)

**Steven Buckley, Photographic Reflections**: 8–9, 55 (top and bottom right), 105, 106 (top), 156 (bottom), 187, 201 (top), 229, 230 (top), 232

**Hollis Chatelaine**: 34 (top)

**Stephen Cridland**: 35 (bottom)

**Karen Dansby**: 36 (top)

**Travis Eck and John Flannigan**: 35 (top)

**Larry Flair**: 153 (top)

**Mark Frey**: 154 (right), 156 (top)

**Gregory Gantner**: 15 (bottom), 110 (top); 119 (bottom left and right), 189,

**D. L. Goddard**: 36 (bottom)

**Hawthorne Studio**: 157

**Chuck Humbert, Humbert Imaging**: 30, 32

**Husqvarna Viking**: 41, 49, 60

**Janome America Inc.**: 39, 41, 42, 60, 63

**Linda Johansen**: 27 (bottom), 202 (bottom left)

**Libby Lehman**: 18, 37, 106 (bottom), 201 (bottom)

**David Lovelace**: 174

**Dan Looper Photography**: 234–235 (trapunto)

**Mellisa Karlin Mahoney**: 94, 95, 97, 98

**Andy Payne and Oliver Ford**: 10, 13, 119 (top)

**Photographix—Andrew Payne, Oliver Ford, and Rachel Fish**: 126 (left), 191

**Pfaff**: 40, 41, 59

**Sharon Risedorph**: 28, 190, 230 (bottom)

**Lynn Ruck**: 19; 158

**Singer Sewing Company**: 40, 60

**Judy Smith-Kressley**: 119 (bottom middle)

**Sulky of America**: 27 (top), 116 Middle left), 124 (left); 137 (right), 166 (top left), 170 (left), 171, 178

**Daniel Tilton**: 152

**Laura Wasilowski**: 24 (top), 34 (bottom)

**White Sewing Machines**: 63

*Additional photography provided by C&T Publishing (Kirstie McCormick, Luke Mulks, and Diane Pedersen)*

# Index